Global Health Governance

For Robert D. Grey –
teacher, mentor, friend

Global Health Governance

JEREMY YOUDE

polity

First published in 2012 by Polity Press

Polity Press
65 Bridge Street
Cambridge CB2 1UR, UK

Polity Press
350 Main Street
Malden, MA 02148, USA

ISBN-13: 978-0-7456-5308-2
ISBN-13: 978-0-7456-5309-9(pb)

A catalogue record for this book is available from the British Library.

Typeset in 9.5 on 13 pt Swift Light
by Toppan Best-set Premedia Limited
Printed and bound in Great Britain by MPG Books Group Limited

The publisher has used its best endeavours to ensure that the URLs for external websites referred to in this book are correct and active at the time of going to press. However, the publisher has no responsibility for the websites and can make no guarantee that a site will remain live or that the content is or will remain appropriate.

Every effort has been made to trace all copyright holders, but if any have been inadvertently overlooked the publisher will be pleased to include any necessary credits in any subsequent reprint or edition.

For further information on Polity, visit our website: www.politybooks.com

Contents

Acronyms

ACHAP	African Comprehensive HIV/AIDS Partnership
AIDS	acquired immune deficiency syndrome
ANC	African National Congress
ARV/ARVs	antiretroviral drugs
CCM	Country Coordinating Mechanism
CCO	Committee of Cosponsoring Organizations
CHAI	Clinton HIV/AIDS Initiative
CSOs	civil society organizations
DALY	disability-adjusted life year
EBFs	extrabudgetary funds
ECOSOC	Economic and Social Council of the United Nations
FCA	Framework Convention Alliance
FCTC	Framework Convention on Tobacco Control
G8	Group of Eight
G20	Group of Twenty Finance Ministers and Central Bank Governors
GCGH	Grand Challenges in Global Health
GHG	global health governance
GOARN	Global Outbreak Alert and Response Network
GPA	Global Programme on AIDS
HIV	human immunodeficiency virus
HOLN	Health Organization of the League of Nations
IBRD	International Bank for Reconstruction and Development
ICCPR	International Covenant on Civil and Political Rights
IDA	International Development Association
IHD	International Health Division (of the Rockefeller Foundation)
IHR	International Health Regulations
ILO	International Labor Office
ISB	International Sanitary Bureau
ISC	International Sanitary Convention
ISR	International Sanitary Regulations
JOHAP	Joint Oxfam HIV/AIDS Project
MAP	Multi-Country HIV/AIDS Program
MDGs	Millennium Development Goals

MOU	Memorandum of Understanding
MSF	Médecins Sans Frontières/Doctors Without Borders
NCDs	noncommunicable diseases
NGOs	nongovernmental organizations
NIH	National Institutes of Health
OIHP	International Office of Public Hygiene/Office International d'Hygiène Publique
PCB	Programme Coordinating Board
PEPFAR	President's Emergency Plan for AIDS Relief
PHC	primary health care
RBFs	regular budgetary funds
RF	Rockefeller Foundation
SADOH	South African Department of Health
SAPs	Structural Adjustment Programs
SARS	severe acute respiratory syndrome
SPHC	selective primary health care
TAC	Treatment Action Campaign
TRP	Technical Review Panel
TTCs	transnational tobacco companies
TWG	Transitional Working Group
UN	United Nations
UNAIDS	Joint United Nations Programme on HIV/AIDS
UNDP	United Nations Development Programme
UNESCO	United Nations Educational, Scientific, and Cultural Organization
UNFPA	United Nations Population Fund
UNHCR	United Nations High Commissioner for Refugees
UNICEF	United Nations Children's Fund
UNODC	United Nations Office on Drugs and Crime
WB	World Bank
WFP	World Food Programme
WHA	World Health Assembly
WHO	World Health Organization
YLD	years lived with disability
YLL	years of life lost

Figures and Tables

Acknowledgements

This book would not exist without the assistance and support of so many other people. Garrett Wallace Brown, Josh Busby, Kim Yi Dionne, Sophie Harman, Yanzhong Huang, Adam Kamradt-Scott, Nathan Paxton, Drew Price-Smith, Simon Rushton, and Frank Smith have all contributed to my thinking about these issues of global health governance and helped me to refine my arguments – even if they did not recognize it at the time (and any errors, of course, remain entirely my responsibility). Jon Acuff, Jack Amoureux, Stephanie Carvin, Jon D. Carlson, Harry Gould, Eric Heinze, Tracy Hoffman Slagter, and Brent J. Steele have helped keep me sane. My colleagues at the University of Minnesota Duluth have proved a source of inspiration and provided me with a welcoming academic environment. The College of Liberal Arts at UMD provided me with a single-semester leave that proved invaluable in completing the manuscript. Sara Davies' book on global health politics proved inspirational, and I feel honored to consider her a friend. Not only was she an excellent sounding board as I worked through some ideas, but she arranged a one-month research fellowship for me at the Centre for Public Policy and Governance at Griffith University in Brisbane. That time was incredibly helpful in completing the manuscript, and I thank Pat Weller, Angela Mac-Donald, Paula Cowan, and everyone else at Griffith for making me feel so welcome. Louise Knight and David Winters at Polity have made the whole writing and publishing process painless, and Fiona Sewell cleaned up my manuscript masterfully. The two anonymous reviewers did an amazingly thorough job and have helped to make this book far more readable and useful. My parents, Jerry and Cynthia, continue to encourage me. Most importantly, my partner Ben makes everything possible.

Finally, I dedicate this book to Robert Grey. Bob served as my advisor throughout my undergraduate days at Grinnell College. I took my first "real" political science course from him – and many more after that. He always pushed me to refine my thinking, hone my analysis, and keep asking questions. More than what he did in the classroom, though, Bob inspired me as a teacher and as a researcher. He helped me to see that I might actually be able to take my interests and make a career out of them. He provided much-needed support and inspiration during the two years I taught at Grinnell, and he's remained an important advisor and friend to this day. After my very first meeting with Bob, when I was an awkward 18-year-old, I marveled to my roommates about how great Bob's office library was and how knowledge-able he was. I declared then that I wanted to be like him one day. That's still my goal.

Introduction

Scattered reports trickle in, telling the same general story. Some sort of illness is making people sick and has even started to kill people. It appears infectious and spread through person-to-person contact, but no one is entirely sure. Its origins are a mystery. Government sources seek to reassure people that they need not worry, but nongovernmental sources and rumors suggest the situation is far more dire. The disease appears in more and more countries. Doctors have no idea how to treat the sick. People are scared. Schools shut down. Businesses close. Travel advisories warn people against traveling to countries with this new disease, devastating local tourism industries. Contradictory theories about its origin and treatments emerge, and hucksters start selling "miracle cures." As more people get sick and die from the disease, international pressure mounts for a coordinated response to stop this illness in its tracks before it takes any more lives and causes any more disruption.

In this scenario, who should coordinate an international response to this public health emergency? Everyone sees a need for the international community to address the situation, and such a response could benefit everyone, but coordinating cross-border cooperation on health issues is tricky at best. Traditionally, the World Health Organization (WHO) would be the de facto leader of any such response, but it no longer possesses unquestioned leadership on international health issues. Are surveillance systems in place to track cases of the new disease? Should a new intergovernmental organization form? Who will provide the funding? Where do civil society groups fit into the equation? Is there a place for private actors? Should there be? What does international law say about the global response to such a health concern, and what obligations do states have regarding information sharing and maintaining public health surveillance systems?

As the international community has come to recognize the importance of cooperating on transborder health threats, the questions of who should respond and how these responses should best be organized become increasingly complicated. According to Article 2 of the Constitution of the World Health Organization, it possesses "directing and co-ordinating authority on international health work." Since WHO's creation in the aftermath of World War II, though, numerous additional organizations have emerged to tackle international health issues. The terrain of who gets involved in addressing global health concerns has vastly expanded. Some, like the Joint United Nations Programme on HIV/AIDS (UNAIDS), operate under the aegis of the United Nations (UN), but are distinct from WHO. Other intergovernmental organizations like the World Bank (WB) have increasingly adopted health concerns as central to their mission and operations. New organizations like the Global Fund to Fight AIDS, Tuberculosis, and Malaria (Global Fund) have emerged and exist independently of WHO. Others, like the Gates Foundation or the Treatment Action Campaign (TAC), exist wholly outside official governmental structures.

Funding has also dramatically changed. Overseas development aid for health has vastly increased since the early 1990s as donor states have conceptualized health as central to national security, economic development, and human rights. Multilateral initiatives, like the Global Fund, have emerged to play a significant role. State contributions to WHO are increasingly tied to specific projects chosen by the donors, giving WHO less budgetary flexibility. In addition, private actors – as large as the Gates Foundation and as small as neighborhood organizing committees – provide a significant, yet underappreciated, amount of financial resources to handle global health issues.

Finally, the range of health issues has also expanded in a major way. The first moves to create any sort of cross-border cooperation on health issues focused on cholera and yellow fever – infectious diseases that attracted attention because they disrupted international trade and commerce. Today, emerging and re-emergent infectious diseases – everything from HIV/AIDS (human immunodeficiency virus/acquired immune deficiency syndrome), tuberculosis, and malaria to SARS (severe acute respiratory syndrome), West Nile virus, and swine flu – receive the most attention and resources. Noncommunicable diseases (NCDs) and health care system strengthening are also part of the agenda, though they tend to receive less attention and fewer resources from the international community.

For these reasons, global health governance (GHG) structures have come under intense scrutiny. During the Cold War, health commanded little attention on the international agenda. It inhabited the realm of "low politics" – issues considered technocratic in nature and irrelevant to national and international security. Other than a few high-profile instances, like the smallpox eradication campaign and Health for All by 2000, health was not an area of major concern for global governance. The HIV/AIDS pandemic, the resurgence of infectious diseases, and the reconceptualization of health politics undermined some of the traditional structures designed to address crossborder health concerns. New organizations have emerged, new actors have taken prominent roles in addressing these concerns, and health occupies a prominent role on the international agenda. The fluidity of global health governance continues to this day.

What Is Global Health Governance?

David Fidler offers a succinct definition of GHG, describing it as:

> the use of formal and informal institutions, rules, and processes by states, intergovernmental organizations, and nonstate actors to deal with challenges to health that require cross-border collective action to address effectively. (Fidler 2010: 3)

This definition highlights two important and crucial differences that distinguish GHG from earlier modes of cross-border health cooperation. First, it explicitly recognizes that states are not the only relevant actors for addressing these health concerns. International organizations, civil society groups, and private philanthropic organizations can and do play significant roles in setting the global health agenda, mobilizing resources, and providing services. Appreciating the range of actors involved in dealing with cross-border health issues differentiates *global* health governance from *international* health governance. The latter focuses exclusively on cooperation among state governments and identifies states as having an exclusive responsibility to promote and protect health (Dodgson et al. 2002: 8).

Second, this definition implicitly acknowledges that there exists no single global health governance hierarchy and no single solution for global health concerns. By emphasizing the varying levels of formality among the institutions concerned with cross-border health issues, Fidler demonstrates that global health governance consists of a "collective of partially overlapping and nonhierarchical regimes" (Fidler 2010: 9). An effective intervention to stop HIV transmission will necessarily differ from strategies to prevent the spread of cholera or vaccinating children against polio, yet all three fall under the larger rubric of global health governance. Such diversity allows for an appreciation of the wide range of activities that this hodgepodge of actors undertake in the name of promoting and protecting health, but it also makes analyzing global health governance a more difficult enterprise.

For global health governance to be effective and useful, it must embody four key attributes. First, it must focus on factors that cross and ignore geographical boundaries. Globalization and its attendant deterritorialization drive much of the international concern about health and disease. The ease and speed with which people and goods can cross international borders vastly increase the range of people who could fall prey to infectious disease. This also highlights the need for public health systems and surveillance operations to be constantly at the ready to recognize problems and mobilize to stop the spread. This further means that the global health governance system must balance national, regional, international, and global needs when deploying resources, prioritizing issues, and mobilizing actors to create an effective response.

Second, it must employ multisectoral and multidisciplinary approaches to craft effective interventions. Addressing health concerns cannot solely be the province of public health systems. The spread of infectious diseases is intimately connected to politics, culture, social stratification, and economics. To effectively get a handle on any particular cross-border health issue, global health governance strategies will necessarily need to draw on the resources and expertise of a wide range of fields. Understanding health in its fullest, most holistic sense in a way that goes beyond the mere absence of disease necessarily entails incorporating more sectors and more actors to craft effective responses.

Third, effective global health governance requires giving voice to a wide range of actors. Government officials in national health ministries do not and cannot have all the answers necessary to identify problems, develop useful responses, and implement programs. They must rely on people working at all levels of government. This includes going beyond formal governmental structures to incorporate voices from a wide range of affected communities and knowledgeable information sources. Not only will such a strategy increase the likelihood of implementing an effective approach, but it will also encourage people to accept the programs and assist with their operation. If people feel that their concerns played a role in crafting the response, they are more likely to accept that response.

Finally, global health governance needs to rely on transparent and accountable systems. Popular oversight is important for building the authority and legitimacy of any global health governance systems. Opaque organizations or inscrutable practices give rise to suspicion and undermine the potential efficacy of health interventions. Transparency and accountability are particularly important when systems rely on people in many different countries and face different health issues (Dodgson et al. 2002: 17–21; Sridhar et al. 2008/9: 15–16).

Challenges for Global Health Governance

Global health governance and its implementation within the international community face a number of challenges, but three are most prominent and pressing. First and foremost, global health governance is, at best, a highly chaotic system – and getting more chaotic (Ruger 2004). So many actors and organizations are involved in global health that coordinating the bewildering array of initiatives and programs is impossible. Writing in 2008, McColl found "more than 40 bilateral donors, 26 UN agencies, 20 global and regional funds, and 19 global-health initiatives" (McColl 2008: 2072). Health is an explicit and central part of the mandates of some of these actors, but more and more organizations with minimal (or nonexistent) health mandates are implementing their own programs (Gostin and Mok 2009: 9). While it is useful for organizations to see how health connects to a wide range of issues, the proliferation of organizations getting involved in global health governance complicates coordination. Instead of reforming and strengthening existing organizations with explicit health mandates, greater energy has gone into creating new actors and expanding the mandates of others – a process which serves to further erode WHO's authority and leadership within the international community (Sridhar 2010a: 462).

While this diversity may constitute evidence that the international community takes global health seriously, it also means that there exists a serious lack of global health leadership. The World Health Organization once directed and coordinated international responses to health concerns on its own, but the diversity of actors demonstrates the inability of WHO (or any other organization) to coordinate action and ensure that resources are being used effectively, that programs do not significantly overlap, and that local needs are addressed (Gostin and Mok 2009: 9–10). The lack of singular leadership within global health governance also means that responses to health concerns may be rather ad hoc and fragmented, making it difficult create and sustain the long-term responses and commitments necessary to effectively address these problems. It becomes increasingly difficult to coordinate action as more actors get involved, and groups may not want to work together, in order to protect their turf or maintain some perceived competitive advantage.

Second, there exists a disjuncture within global health governance between the issues that donors and recipients prioritize. Not all health problems generate the same level of attention and interest, but those that rank highest among donors and on the global health agenda are not necessarily the ones that affect the most people or cause the highest number of deaths. Shiffman (2008) shows in convincing detail that, between 1998 and 2005, donor prioritization of HIV/AIDS displaced funds for other health issues and did so independently of the expressed or perceived need by recipients. AIDS is obviously an important issue, but it receives a higher percentage of resources than its morbidity and mortality rates would suggest. Furthermore, a significant portion of health aid goes toward programs targeting specific diseases, particularly those conceptualized as relevant for national and international security, instead of improving overall health systems (Gostin and Mok 2009: 14–15). This practice, known as "stovepiping," tends to reflect donor interests more than recipient needs. Garrett describes the situation starkly:

> A government may receive considerable funds to support, for example, an ARV-distribution [antiretroviral drug distribution] program for mothers and children living in the nation's capital. But the same government may have no financial capacity to support basic maternal and infant health programs . . . Diseases and health conditions that enjoy a temporary spotlight in rich countries garner the most attention and money. (Garrett 2007: 22–3)

By focusing on specific diseases rather than bolstering health systems as a whole, the global health governance system misses the opportunity to tackle root causes and improve a government's ability to react to new and novel problems. Furthermore, if disease-specific programs receive funding because of donor interests rather than recipient needs, resources miss the most pressing needs.

Third, funding shortfalls could imperil attempts to maintain current levels of support for global health governance – to say nothing of attempts to increase the available funding for global health. Beginning in the early 1990s, global health received significant year-over-year increases in the amount of foreign aid devoted to it. A World Bank study showed that development assistance for health increased from US$2.5 billion in 1990 to nearly US$14 billion in 2005, and private organizations accounted for nearly 25 percent of all development assistance for health in 2005 (McCoy et al. 2009: 407). While these figures fell short of estimated need, they demonstrated a consistent pattern of increased support by governments and organizations around the world (Kates et al. 2006: 187–8). With the emergence of the global economic recession in 2008 and the continued strains it has placed on national budgets, support for global health governance faces a significant threat. Sridhar notes that, during economic downturns, programs funding health and education tend to be among the first cut (Sridhar 2010a: 459). Fidler goes so far as to declare 2008 the year that global health governance officially ended. In the face of severe political and economic crises, he argues, the international community can no longer continue to provide the levels of financial and intellectual support that global health and global health governance previously received (Fidler 2008/9: 1–3).

The effects of the global recession on health assistance are becoming apparent. Statistics released by the Organisation for Economic Co-operation and Development in early 2010 showed that the amount of overseas development aid for health had increased in US dollar terms, but that it would fall short of what had been pledged in 2005 and would not keep pace with increased need. This has raised concerns within the international community that future aid levels, including those for health, could decline in the face of poor economic conditions and the adoption of austerity budgets by a number of governments (Organisation for Economic Co-operation and Development 2010). Further, disbursements for international AIDS assistance from donor governments declined from US$7.7 billion in 2008 to US$7.6 billion in 2009, while new commitments of assistance remained flat (Kates et al. 2010: 2). The concerns about decreasing support for health programs are not limited to government, though. A survey of commitment for HIV/AIDS programs by USA-based philanthropies in 2009 reported that disbursements declined 5 percent between 2008 and 2009. Perhaps more worryingly, pledges of support declined over the same time period by 12 percent. Analyzing the funding changes, the report's authors noted, "In the wake of the recent economic recession, flat or declining global and domestic government funding, and a growing need on the ground, any decrease is cause for concern" (Funders Concerned About AIDS 2010: 4). Given that the financial needs posed by global health governance are unlikely to decline in the short term, even small decreases in funding levels could have deleterious consequences. Further, given the lack of central authority within global health governance, concerns about the efficacy of funding and ensuring that it reaches the right targets become all the more imperative.

Plan for the Book

This book seeks to describe the evolution of global health governance, identify some key actors in its contemporary manifestation, and look at some of the pressing issues it will need to address in the coming years. Throughout the book, three themes will repeat themselves. First, global health governance lacks a singular motivating rationale. Initial efforts toward creating cross-border health cooperation structures found their rationales in economic concerns. Today, human rights and security have become particularly prominent in the discourses around global health governance. This transition has not necessarily been smooth or embraced by all, and economic concerns certainly continue to play a large role in how various actors view and respond to global health governance, but human rights and security perspectives have taken larger and larger roles in motivating global health governance efforts. Broadening the underlying logic for global health governance has allowed it to embrace a wider range of issues and promote a more holistic sense of health. At the same time, these logics can conflict with each other, undermining global health governance's efficacy.

Second, the range of actors involved in global health governance continues to expand. The World Health Organization dominated the post-World War II notion of international health governance, but a host of additional organizations have come to play important roles in global health governance. Existing intergovernmental organizations have expanded their mandates to incorporate global health issues. New organizations like UNAIDS have emerged within the UN framework to address new concerns. Outside the UN system, novel intergovernmental bodies like the Global Fund have emerged. Furthermore, civil society organizations (CSOs), private corporations, and philanthropic organizations have risen to prominence.

Third, global health's move from the realm of "low politics" to "high politics" has undoubtedly given it greater attention and a higher place on the international agenda. With increased attention have come more resources and greater resolve to address these issues. However, this move has also come with complications. As more actors pay attention to global health, the diversity of understandings of global health and its effects on the international community increases. More actors and more resources may, perversely, make it more difficult to create and sustain unified, coherent responses to global health challenges. Furthermore, a greater diversity of actors can make it difficult to prioritize particular issues or ensure that resources are going to appropriate places. More actors could theoretically mean more resources for the wide range of transborder health issues, but it can also make it more difficult to ensure that the most important issues are being appropriately prioritized if there is no division of labor.

While this volume aims to present a comprehensive overview of global health governance, it is important to acknowledge its limitations. First, this book focuses primarily on infectious and communicable diseases. Noncommunicable diseases like heart disease and cancer are significant causes of mortality and morbidity in developed and developing countries. Chronic and noncommunicable disease cause 60 percent of deaths worldwide, yet they receive less than 3 percent of all donor funding for health issues. The four largest health aid donors gave an average of US$3 per chronic disease death, but the figure soars to US$1,030 per AIDS death. This disparity may arise from the perceptions of the causes of these illnesses, with chronic diseases not seen as linked to poverty and development in the same way infectious diseases are (Sridhar 2010b). This disparity will certainly challenge global health governance structures in the coming years. That said, noncommunicable diseases receive relatively little attention in this book precisely because the international community has paid so little attention to them. Noncommunicable diseases have largely remained on the sidelines of global health governance (if they have achieved even that level of prominence), meaning that any discussion would be awfully brief and predominantly speculative. I do address the creation of the Framework Convention on Tobacco Control (FCTC) in chapter 2, but most of the discussion will focus on infectious diseases.

Second, no book can cover the full range of actors involved in global health governance. Many international organizations have embraced various elements of health as part of their agendas. For example, the United Nations Development Programme (UNDP) gave health issues a prominent place in its Millennium Development Goals (MDGs), and the International Labor Office (ILO) has taken a leading role in addressing workplace health and safety. Given the ever-expanding array of organizations involved in global health issues, it is simply impossible to catalog all of them in any single book. Instead of giving short snippets on all of the organizations doing health-related work in the international community, I focus sustained attention on some of the most prominent. For better or worse, the World Health Organization, UNAIDS, the Global Fund, and the World Bank are among the most visible and recognized actors working on global health. Focusing on them is not an attempt to denigrate or ignore the work done by other organizations; rather, it is a reflection of the current state of global health governance.

The book proceeds in three parts. The first emphasizes the evolution of global health governance, the second focuses on its leading actors, and the third looks at key issues facing it.

The first part describes the history of international health governance system over the past 150 years. Chapter 1 focuses on the origins of an international (as opposed to global) health governance system up through the creation of the World Health Organization. This system gave rise to the contemporary global health governance system, its leading actors, and the key issues facing it.

The second part focuses on the actions, mandates, histories, and controversies surrounding some of the dominant actors in global health governance in the contemporary era. Each chapter focuses on a specific actor or type of actor that plays a leading role in global health governance. Chapter 2 focuses on the World Health Organization. WHO is the most prominent global health organization today, but its history since 1948 demonstrates significant volatility in its ability to be a leading voice for health. Chapter 3 examines the World Bank and its role in global health. Primarily an organization dedicated to lending money to developing countries, the World Bank has become the leading funder for health programs internationally – a significant shift in the organization's mission. Chapter 4 looks at the emergence of new organizations like UNAIDS and the Global Fund to Fight AIDS, Tuberculosis, and Malaria. These organizations have sought to overcome the limitations of existing organizations to find innovative strategies and funding mechanisms to address pressing global health concerns. Chapter 5 steps outside the realm of state-based actors to look at two private philanthropic organizations addressing global health issues: the Bill and Melinda Gates Foundation and the William J. Clinton Foundation. Finally, chapter 6 examines the role of civil society organizations (CSOs) in addressing global health governance.

The chapters in the third part are forward-looking. Given the actors currently prominent in global health governance and the manner in which the system has evolved, what sorts of issues are looming on the horizon? What challenges may cause further changes to the global health governance architecture? These chapters highlight important issues within global health and discuss how the global health governance regime helps or hinders effective responses. Chapter 7 examines the current infectious disease surveillance regime as embodied by the International Health Regulations (IHR). Chapter 8 focuses on whether global health constitutes a security issue, while chapter 9 examines questions of ensuring access to pharmaceuticals.

PART 1

History

CHAPTER ONE

Early International Health Governance Efforts

Protecting trade, rather than improving health, drove early international health governance efforts. Diseases cross borders. They can disrupt trade, as states want to avoid importing new, exotic diseases from foreign countries. Such commercial worries inspired most of the impulses toward international cooperation on health issues from the mid-nineteenth century through World War II. Governments sought to work together because they did not want commerce interrupted, but they also wanted to ensure that disease prevention measures were not so stringent that they would impede international business.

This economic motivation significantly shaped the international health cooperation structures that developed before World War II. It oriented the system toward a dominant focus on a few commercially relevant diseases. Instead of taking steps to promote good health in a holistic sense, the system emphasized a more defensive stance against importation. It initially relied more on quarantines and bills of health instead of implementing health promotion programs or providing technical assistance to governments.

In the aftermath of World War I, shifts began to take place within health cooperation strategies. New actors, like the Health Organization of the League of Nations (HOLN) and the Rockefeller Foundation (RF), emerged with new outlooks. They encouraged cooperation among states on health issues, promoted the exchange of health information, and saw the relevance of implementing health promotion programs. These new actors challenged the existing thinking about health cooperation, but the conflict between paradigms led to much confusion.

This chapter examines the evolution of international cooperation on health matters from the mid-nineteenth century, when the first formal cooperative efforts began, through World War II. I start by discussing the International Sanitary Conferences and the eventual creation of the International Sanitary Regulations (ISR). At the start of the twentieth century, the first international organizations dedicated to health matters emerged – the International Sanitary Bureau (ISB, the forerunner of today's Pan American Health Organization) and the International Office of Public Hygiene (known by its French acronym, OIHP). The last section of this chapter examines the emergence of new forms of international health cooperation and the difficulties in fostering cooperation among its organizations during the interwar period.

The International Sanitary Conferences and Convention

Fear of cholera prompted the first serious coordinated efforts at creating a system of international public health governance. Not only did cholera kill quickly, but its spread tended to mirror trade routes. The illness spreads via a bacterium, *Vibrio cholerae*, through infected food, water, or bodily waste. Symptoms appear rapidly and include a bloated feeling in the abdomen, generally with no accompanying fever, that quickly gives way to very watery stool. The disease can cause severe dehydration and kidney failure, leading to death in as few as 18 hours. Without treatment, mortality rates range from 50 to 90 percent. Its lethality has made cholera one of the most feared diseases throughout history. In the early 1800s, before cholera itself reached Europe, reports from British colonial officials about cholera's effects in India terrified government officials and the general public alike. British Army officials reported losing 10,000 troops to cholera in India between 1817 and 1827, and McNeill estimates that upwards of one million Indians perished from cholera during this time (McNeill 1998: 269).

Cholera first reached Europe around 1829 during the second global cholera epidemic, spreading east to west along shipping traffic routes. It appeared in Poland in 1830 and 1831 before expanding to London and Paris in 1832. Over 6,000 Londoners died of cholera that first year, and Paris lost approximately 7,000 of its 650,000 residents (Rosenberg 1987). As the disease continued to spread throughout Europe between 1829 and 1847, tens of thousands of people lost their lives.

To prevent cholera's spread, governments initially relied on quarantines of goods and peoples from infected regions. Quarantine is perhaps the oldest form of trying to prevent the spread of infectious diseases, with evidence for its use going back to biblical times. Chapter 13 of Leviticus describes how certain skin ailments like leprosy make a person "unclean." When the priest finds someone with an infectious skin condition, he must cast that person out. Leviticus 13: 45–46 explains, "The person with such an infectious disease must wear torn clothes, let his hair be unkempt, cover the lower part of his face, and cry out, 'Unclean! Unclean!' As long as he has the infection, he remains unclean. He must live alone; he must live outside the camp." The authorities exile the infected to prevent the disease's spread.

Systemized quarantine began in the fourteenth century as a way to combat bubonic plague. In 1377, the Republic of Ragusa, a small republic centered on modern-day Dubrovnik along the Adriatic coast, introduced the first-ever organized quarantine procedures. By order of the Rector, ships coming from ports known to have or suspected of having bubonic plague were required to drop anchor away from the port for 30 days. If disease did not emerge during this time, then the ship could enter the port proper, and commerce could go forward as normal (Frati 2000). Land travelers were eventually added to the decree, and the isolation period was increased to 40 days, giving rise to the term quarantine (from *quarantena*, or "40-day period," in Italian).[1] Ragusan officials saw quarantine as vital for protecting the "quality and safety of the trade network" (Gensini et al. 2004: 258).

Over time, quarantine procedures expanded to include more diseases, including cholera. Despite their popularity, quarantine policies were of questionable benefit. Goodman calls successful applications of quarantine "largely fortuitous" and highlights the fact that "in any case, not only were these measures of quarantine generally useless, but they were exasperating, obstructive, oppressive, and often cruel to the point of barbarity" (Goodman 1971: 34). Police would arrest anyone who looked "suspicious" of carrying cholera, forcing them into squalid, isolated hospitals (Tesh 1987: 12). Aside from the human costs, quarantines undermined the growing commercial ties developing in Europe during the mid-1800s. They slowed down shipments, added costs, and were applied inconsistently. There existed little to no coordination among governments as to how and when to implement quarantine restrictions.

Peoples and governments feared cholera, but they also bemoaned the impediments to trade and travel that quarantines imposed. This combination prompted the first calls for international coordination for addressing a public health issue.

> What governments found most irksome were the often disastrous hindrances to international commerce, and it was this concern that finally prompted the European nations to meet to discuss to what extent these onerous restrictions could be lifted without undue risk to the health of their populations. If, in the old colonial days, it was true that "trade follows the flag," it was equally true that the first faltering steps towards international health cooperation followed trade. (Howard-Jones 1975: 9–11)

Calls for an international conference on cholera control emerged as early as 1834, but it was not until 1851 that 12 European governments agreed to meet in Paris. Conference participants initially endeavored to regulate the use of quarantines in a uniform manner and to discuss the feasibility of establishing an international sanitary board to oversee maritime activities (Goodman 1971: 42–3). This first conference eventually produced a convention with 11 Articles and 137 Regulations covering cholera, plague, yellow fever, and other diseases "reputed to be importable" (Goodman 1971: 46). In the end, though, only three governments eventually ratified the convention – and two of those states, Portugal and Sardinia, later withdrew their ratification in the face of logistical difficulties in implementing the regulations (McFadden 1995: 82). In essence, no one ended up agreeing to abide by the agreement.

What prevented agreement during these initial efforts toward international cooperation on a public health issue? All parties recognized the dangers of cholera and the usefulness of coordinating prevention measures, so it would seemingly have been in all parties' interest to come to agreement. This did not prevent the emergence and persistence of significant disagreements. Some of the disputes arose from commercial and geographic interests. Nations with significant trading interests showed strong resistance to any quarantine measures, since they impeded the free flow of goods. Countries bordering the Mediterranean Sea and the Ottoman Empire tended to favor quarantine, as they perceived cholera coming from the east or by sea and felt themselves in greater danger from its arrival (McFadden 1995: 80).

Disagreements also persisted over cholera's cause and spread. It is hard to agree how to contain a disease when the parties cannot even agree what they are trying to contain. Three theories dominated, each with its own policy recommendations. One camp subscribed to the miasma theory. Its adherents believed that weather, climate, and "pestilent air" gave rise to environmental conditions that caused cholera (Tesh 1987: 25–32). According to this theory, quarantine made little sense because cholera's origins were environmental. The miasmists instead called for improved sanitation and environmental conditions as the key to alleviating cholera. Since this theory saw no role for quarantine and other trade impediments, it appealed to the most trade-dependent states. British officials were particularly forceful advocates of this theory, recommending the abolition of quarantines and the "substitution of sanitary regulations" instead (Goodman 1971: 46).

The second theory, contagion theory, argued that cholera was transmitted from person to person via an infectious agent (Tesh 1987: 11–16). If cholera were communicable, then quarantines could potentially prevent the disease from entering a country by separating the infected from the healthy. In practice, government officials often used quarantine to justify discriminatory policies. They would round up and detain disfavored groups, particularly Jews and foreigners, in quarantine, but rationalize their actions by appealing to public health needs (Tesh 1987: 13). Spanish, Greek, Tuscan, and Russian delegates played a key role at the first conference in promoting this view and advocating for quarantine's positive benefits (McFadden 1995: 82).

The third theory about cholera's spread was supernatural. Illness was a sign of God's displeasure, and transgressing God's law provoked His wrath in the form of a highly fatal disease. Churches would hold special prayer services, encouraging worshippers to repent their sins and ask to be spared from the ravages of cholera (Tesh 1987: 17–21). This position gave little role for quarantine, as that would have little effect so long as God remained displeased. The head of the Austrian delegation went even further, arguing that cholera epidemics benefited society. Widespread illness and death would punish the "dregs of society" and encourage survivors to recommit themselves to a more pious life, he argued (Howard-Jones 1975: 13–15).

These competing theories about cholera's origin and spread prevented European governments from coming to agreement about the appropriate steps to take to prevent cholera – or whether they even should take such measures. Over the next 40 years, five more conferences were held – 1859 in Paris, 1866 in Constantinople, 1874 in Vienna, 1881 in Washington, and 1885 in Rome – but none produced any substantive agreement.

Successful efforts at crafting an international agreement on infectious disease control began at 1892's International Sanitary Conference in Venice. Robert Koch's work on cholera helped forge a scientific consensus on cholera's cause, spread, and treatment. The resultant agreement, the International Sanitary Convention (ISC), was extremely limited in scope. It allowed only for limited quarantine measures and medical inspections for ships passing through the Suez Canal going to and from Mecca for the annual *hajj* (Howard-Jones 1975: 45). Despite its narrow focus, the ISC helped launch efforts toward international coordination and cooperation on infectious disease control. As Howard-Jones acknowledges, "That such a declaration [on the cause of cholera] should have been generally accepted and that the conference resulted in the first International Sanitary Convention are landmarks in the history of international cooperation in matters of public health" (1975: 64). The following year, in 1893 at a conference in Paris, the assembled states expanded the limited 1892 agreement to cover movement by land and allowed greater use of medical inspections. A subsequent revision in 1897 added plague to the list of reportable diseases subject to the Convention (McCarthy 2002: 1111). Over time, the ISC was expanded to include diseases such as yellow fever, smallpox, typhus, and relapsing fever (Fidler 2005: 330).

The International Sanitary Convention of 1892, and its subsequent revisions over the next 58 years, focused its efforts on protecting states against the spread of infectious disease while minimizing interference with international trade and travel. Indeed, the Convention's Preamble stated that the signatory states had "decided to establish common measures for protecting public health during cholera epidemics *without uselessly obstructing commercial transactions and passenger traffic*" (Fidler 2005: 329; emphasis added). To achieve these goals, the ISC called on states to notify one another about outbreaks of specific diseases and to establish and maintain adequate public health capabilities at ports of entry and exit, such as seaports and airports. The ISC also limited the measures that states could impose to prevent the importation of infectious disease, establishing the ISC's rules as the most stringent regulations allowable under international law (Fidler 2005: 329). This clause sought to ensure that states would not impose overly burdensome regulations that could impede trade. States may not have wanted diseases within their borders, but they really did not want to stop the flow of goods across borders.

Early International Health Organizations

When initially adopted, the ISC lacked a formalized mechanism or organizational structure for coordinating the Convention's surveillance and reporting requirements. The absence of a central international health organization hampered communications and made surveillance difficult. During the first decade of the twentieth century, two organizations emerged to help fill a coordinating role. In 1902, the International Sanitary Bureau (ISB; later the Pan American Sanitary Bureau, and today known as the Pan American Health Organization) was established to implement the ISC in the Americas. Five years later, European states created the Office International d'Hygiène Publique (OIHP) to fulfill a similar role (Gostin 2004: 2623). While in many ways complementary, the two organizations did not specifically coordinate their activities or share their resources with each other. Their foci protected individual state sovereignty instead of focusing on the larger global efforts to implement infectious disease control (Gostin 2004: 2623–4).

International Sanitary Bureau (ISB)

The mishmash of quarantine regulations in the Americas impeded trade in the hemisphere and hampered the United States' business interests. Rules and inspection regimes varied widely throughout the region, limiting the easy movement of goods and frustrating economic expansion (Wegman 1977). To resolve these difficulties, the delegates to the Second International Conference of the American States in 1901 charged the Governing Board of the International Union of American Republics to call a convention to establish sanitary regulations that would harmonize and minimize quarantine restrictions throughout the region. The delegates also requested the creation of the International Sanitary Bureau to oversee and implement such regulations (Howard-Jones 1981: 7). The convention met in December 1902. It approved the ISB's creation, giving it a mandate to receive reports on the sanitary conditions of ports and territories throughout the Americas. While the convention created the ISB, it did not initially provide the bureau with any resources. The ISB had no staff, no facilities, and a minuscule budget. Instead, it relied upon the United States Public Health Service for its operations and even employed the US Surgeon-General as the ISB Chairman (Fee and Brown 2002: 1888).

The ISB's creation established an important milestone. For the first time, national governments came together to create an international organization with some measure of regulatory capability explicitly for health-related reasons. Health was not incidental to the ISB, nor was it a late addition to an existing organization's mandate. The ISB's creation also offered a significant innovation for international sanitary agreements. While some of the earlier International Sanitary Conferences resulted in agreements among the attendees, none of them had effective enforcement mechanisms. They relied primarily on moral suasion to ensure that members complied and interpreted the mandates of the agreements in the same way. By creating an organization, the International Sanitary Bureau demonstrated the practicability of enforcing and interpreting sanitary standards in a manner that would avoid impeding commerce unnecessarily.

International Office of Public Hygiene (Office International d'Hygiène Publique)

Like the ISB, the International Office of Public Hygiene (Office International d'Hygiène Publique, or OIHP) emerged out of an international agreement on sanitary regulations and sought to oversee quarantine regulations. While the OIHP lacked a specific regional mandate, it focused its attention on protecting European states.

At the 1903 International Sanitary Conference in Paris, the assembled delegates decided to combine the various agreements made at previous conferences into a single document. The resulting regulations, the International Sanitary Regulations (ISR), focused on cholera and plague; yellow fever received a fleeting mention. The ISR also mandated an international health office in Paris. Four years later, with the signing of the Rome Arrangements on December 9, 1907, the OIHP came into being with a small permanent staff and provisional headquarters – though it occupied those facilities until the organization's dissolution 40 years later (Howard-Jones 1978: 7). The OIHP's mandate was threefold: administering the International Sanitary Regulations; maintaining an epidemiological intelligence service; and collecting health data from member-states (World Health Organization n.d. b). Though the International Sanitary Regulations only applied to cholera and plague in 1903, the OIHP's epidemiological surveillance operations collected data on a wider range of infectious diseases including malaria, hookworm, and tuberculosis. It also kept an eye on the Middle East because member-states feared that Muslim pilgrims to Medina and Mecca could transmit disease outbreaks to Europe (Zacher and Keefe 2008: 34).

In its operation and outlook, the OIHP clung to a mission of protecting Europe from the importation of "foreign" diseases while ensuring minimal inconvenience for international trade. By one calculation, 71 percent of ISR rules focused primarily on Africa, Asia, and the Middle East (Fidler 1999: 19). This narrow focus undermined the organization's efficacy, instead of its being a robust presence. Howard-Jones described the OIHP's outlook in less-than-glowing terms:

> Fundamentally, it [the OIHP] was a club of senior public health administrators, mostly European, whose main preoccupation was to protect their countries from the importation of exotic disease without imposing too drastic restrictions on international commerce. (Howard-Jones 1978: 17)

The OIHP focused on limiting the spread of disease at borders, not by addressing the underlying causes of disease. Further limiting cooperation, states were slow to ratify the International Sanitary Regulations. By the time World War I broke out, nearly a decade after the treaty's creation, only 15 states had ratified the document and were bound by its provisions (Zacher and Keefe 2008: 34).

International Health Organizations after World War I

World War I had a profound effect on international governance in general, and the health sector was not immune from these changes. Existing organizations re-envisioned their operations and roles, and new organizations emerged. With more organizations, though, questions of coordination, cooperation, and strategy came to the forefront.

In the aftermath of World War I, the ISB expanded its mandate to create and enforce uniform sanitary regulations for the entire hemisphere. Dr Hugh S. Cumming, the US Surgeon-General and ISB Chairman, called a conference in 1920 to establish such standards and foster increased communication among member-states. These efforts culminated in 1924's Pan American Sanitary Code. The Code required signatories to prevent the international spread of diseases; promote cooperative measures to prevent the spread of diseases among member-states; standardize the collection of morbidity and mortality statistics; foster the mutual exchange of public health information among member-states; and standardize disease prevention measures at ports. By 1936, all states in the hemisphere had ratified the Code and implemented its measures (Acuna 1977: 579–80). During this time, the organization also began to establish its independence from the US Public Health Service and changed its name to the Pan American Sanitary Bureau (Howard-Jones 1981: 12–13).

After World War I, the OIHP also reinvigorated its mission and operations. With revisions to the ISR, its regulations applied to diseases like yellow fever, typhus, relapsing fever, and smallpox. To better address these changes, the OIHP altered its approach to epidemiological intelligence. Instead of simply receiving information, the organization introduced proactive measures to share these data with member-states. It began publishing the *Weekly Epidemiological Record* in 1926, providing one of the earliest accessible sources of information about infectious disease outbreaks and allowing for more timely responses to outbreaks (Zacher and Keefe 2008: 36).

Despite the positive moves on information sharing, the OIHP resisted efforts at collaborating with other organizations. For instance, at its first postwar meeting in 1919, the outgoing president of the Permanent Committee, Professor Rocco Santoliquido, called on the delegates to abandon its emphasis on quarantine and to focus more on attacking the sources of infectious disease. To this end, he recommended entering into a formal alliance with the League of Red Cross Societies to jointly develop medical projects. The incoming president, Oscar Velghe, rejected Santoliquido's plea. Velghe declared that the OIHP could not and would not enter into alliance with the League. He did allow, though, that the two could potentially work together on select, discrete projects solely at the OIHP's discretion (Howard-Jones 1978: 13–14).

Throughout the interwar period and during World War II, the OIHP remained focused on its mandate to implement and administer the International Sanitary Regulations. The emergence of two new international health actors – the International Health Division (IHD) of the Rockefeller Foundation (RF), and the Health Organization of the League of Nations (HOLN) – introduced significant changes within the international health organizational landscape.

The International Health Division of the Rockefeller Foundation

Founded in 1913, the International Health Division of the Rockefeller Foundation played a hugely significant role in mobilizing international support for public health programs. The IHD dedicated itself to "a search for a cause, an attempt to cure evils at their source" to improve physical conditions for humanity (Shaplen 1964: 1). Between 1913 and 1951, it operated in more than 80 countries on a wide variety of projects. Its health work was of such importance that Farley declared, "Before the founding of the WHO in 1948, it [the IHD] was arguably the world's most important agency of public health work" (Farley 2004: 2).

The RF's significance came in part from its wealth. In 1913, the American industrialist John D. Rockefeller, Jr, created his eponymous foundation with an initial contribution of US$35 million. He followed this the next year with an additional US$65 million. Over its first 14 years, Rockefeller gave the foundation US$182.9 million (Shaplen 1964: 8). This largesse allowed the IHD to spend, on average, US$18 million per year between 1913 and 1951. At its most active, between 1925 and 1935, the IHD averaged closer to US$25 million per year on international health programs (Farley 2004: 19–20).

The RF emphasized international health for two reasons. First, it saw a need for cross-border cooperation to address health challenges. Wickliffe Rose, the initial head of the IHD, wrote a letter to Frederick Russell, who would later hold Rose's job at the IHD, that laid out the justification for the IHD's work: "There are certain health functions that are international in character; national governments cannot undertake them; they are important for the health of the people of all lands" (cited in Weindling 1997: 269). Rose, Russell, and their compatriots recognized that the post-World War I world required new types of health organizations, and they saw philanthropies like the RF as uniquely well suited to addressing those tasks that crossed national borders.

Second, the RF believed that promoting public health internationally would lead to greater political and economic stability. Better hygiene and public health systems would create happier societies. Frederick T. Gates, philanthropic advisor to John D. Rockefeller, Sr, argued, "Disease is the supreme ill of human life, and it is the main source of almost all other human ills, poverty, crime, ignorance, vice, inefficiency, hereditary taint, and many other evils" (cited in Brown 1979: 128). Bringing disease under control would increase productivity, which would in turn promote economic development. RF trustees also connected supporting health programs with weakening support for radical labor and socialist movements (Brown 1979: 116–19). If people saw capitalist, democratic governments responding to their health needs, they would be less likely to want to overthrow those political systems – thus providing additional political stability in a world still recovering from the trauma and upheaval of World War I. It would usurp the attractiveness of communism, socialism, and the trade union movement.

Five principles guided the IHD's work. First, public health was, at its core, a government function, so there must be an emphasis on building local and national infrastructures. Second, it should work with government partners to develop successful, sustainable programs that could be replicated in other places. Third, there was a crucial need to develop training centers and support scholarships for training the next generations of local health workers. Fourth, the division should support basic scientific research and share the information gathered through that research broadly. Finally, health should be treated as a positive good, not just the absence of disease, and therefore required programs that addressed both hygiene and sanitation (Winslow 1951: 193). To these ends, the IHD declared it would only work through national governments and at the invitation of those governments. It would not establish programs in countries on its own, because "protecting a community against disease must be accepted by a government as its own primary responsibility" (*Lancet* 1927: 40).

After World War I, the IHD established programs in a number of European countries. Instead of providing direct war relief, the IHD's efforts concentrated on supporting scientific research to address health needs and encouraging social reforms that would both encourage democracy and improve health in general. Promoting public health was necessarily a long-term project, and it would require peace and democracy to sustain it (Weindling 1993: 253–4).

IHD officials soon realized that they needed partners to effectively carry out their mission. Since the IHD did not directly implement health programs itself, but rather supported the research that gave rise to new programs, working with organizations that could put their research into practice would enhance its efforts. It needed an organizational partner that could respond to new discoveries and disseminate information widely (Weindling 1993:

269–70). Thus, when the League of Nations formed and discussed creating a health organization, the IHD saw that it would be in its best interests to support that new organization and ensure its viability.

Health Organization of the League of Nations

Creating a health organization was one of the League of Nations' early objectives. At the first meeting of the Assembly of the League of Nations in late 1920, the delegates adopted a report that resolved to absorb the OIHP and create a new International Health Organization built upon the OIHP's foundation (Howard-Jones 1978: 22). As the delegates envisioned it, this new organization would be proactive. It would engage in direct technical cooperation with member-states, actively working with health ministries. It would establish international standards for health and health care. It would actively promote cooperation among public health officials around the world and collaborate with national, international, and nongovernmental organizations (NGOs) to promote the general health. This was a significant shift in existing practice.

By October 1921, the negotiations to merge the OIHP and the League's new health organization fell apart. Undaunted by this failure, the League of Nations opted to create its own organization, the Health Organization of the League of Nations (HOLN), in 1922. Some delegates questioned the wisdom of creating a new organization because they feared that a health organization would cost far more than the League could afford. To allay these fears, HOLN leaders announced that they were negotiating with the RF's IHD for financial support.

The RF agreed to support HOLN's request, thus beginning an almost symbiotic relationship between the IHD and HOLN. The IHD's first grant to HOLN came in 1922 and totaled US$492,000 over five years to create a "personnel interchange program." Over the next 15 years, IHD monies funded substantial portions of HOLN's budgetary outlays, though those funds were often not included as part of the regular budget. The IHD contributed US$1.3 million to HOLN between 1922 and 1930, and gave another US$723,000 between 1930 and 1934. These funds supported international exchanges for public health officials through 1929 and the epidemiological intelligence service until 1937 (Dubin 1995: 72).

IHD funding made it possible for HOLN to carry out much of its work. In 1934, for example, IHD support paid the salaries for 12 epidemiological staffers: a field epidemiologist, five physicians, three nonmedical professional staff, two junior assistants, and a clerk. By comparison, HOLN itself only employed 20 people (Howard-Jones 1978: 62). Even though HOLN designated all of the epidemiological staff as "temporary," the organization could not have functioned effectively without them. This became especially true when the League of Nations capped HOLN's budget at one million Swiss francs (excluding RF funds) in 1925, making the IHD's contributions all the more vital to the organization's continued existence. The League imposed the cap out of fear that HOLN's activities would overwhelm the overall organization's budget and crowd out other projects. When the League finally relaxed the cap in 1929, HOLN faced new monetary constraints. The Great Depression severely reduced the funds available to the League in general. All League programs, including HOLN, saw their budgets cut. With IHD resources, though, HOLN's budget decreased far more slowly and less severely than those of other League programs (Dubin 1995: 63). Dubin noted:

> These grants were a pittance in the [Rockefeller] Foundation's total public health budget, but they were a life-line for [HOLN director Ludwik] Rajchman. They permitted him to carry out important projects the League probably would not have financed, and, by conferring prestige on him and the HOLN, probably stimulated the League of Nations to appropriate more funds than it might otherwise have provided. (Dubin 1995: 72)

IHD grants allowed HOLN to maintain viable and visible programs at a time when the League of Nations as a whole came under increasing fire and scrutiny.

Given HOLN's reliance on IHD funding, both groups took pains to ensure that HOLN retained programmatic and political autonomy. In essence, the IHD gave funds to HOLN with a hands-off policy. Under this arrangement, the IHD agreed that it would not direct HOLN policy, and HOLN acknowledged that it needed to obtain funding from sources other than the IHD (Weindling 1997: 270).

Conclusion

World War II effectively ended this international public health governance arrangement. The OIHP lacked the resources or facilities to effectively carry out its mission to administer the International Sanitary Regulations, and it was nearly impossible for the organization to operate in Paris in the midst of the war. Delegates could not leave their home countries and travel for meetings during the war, so the OIHP largely stopped meeting after 1939. It strove to maintain its operations as far as possible, though, continuing to send out the *Weekly Epidemiological Review* to the best of its abilities and establishing a satellite office in Royat, France. However, restrictions on communications and movement hampered the OIHP's operation (Howard-Jones 1978: 76–9).

HOLN fell victim to the same maladies that undermined the rest of the League of Nations. HOLN delegates assembled as a complete group for the last time in 1939, and many of the staff fled Geneva for their home countries. After that time, the organization effectively ceased to function. Some staffers dispersed to other countries and tried to maintain operations, but any actions largely depended upon the resources and initiatives of those staffers

(Howard-Jones 1978: 74–6). The Rockefeller Foundation continued to operate during the war, but its health operations largely fell by the wayside.

In 1945 and 1946, discussions began about the creation of a single international health organization – much like those that happened after World War I. The next chapter will go into more detail about those discussions and the resulting international health governance structures. It is a testament to HOLN and the OIHP that government officials saw value in creating and supporting international health organizations. Dubin identifies seven major contributions HOLN made to international health and international governance: creating a worldwide clearing house of information to elevate public health practices and encourage discovery; creating an effective worldwide epidemiological surveillance system; establishing standardized international epidemiological databases; encouraging networking and exchanges among public health officials in different countries; encouraging international studies for biological agents; promoting the study of the effects of social and natural environments on human health; and providing technical assistance to governments (Dubin 1995: 59–60).

Pre-World War II international health governance ushered in a new paradigm to guide international cooperation on public health issues. It witnessed the move away from an entirely defensive posture, with an emphasis on a few commerce-related diseases, and toward one that encouraged greater emphases on technical cooperation and addressing a wider range of diseases. It demonstrated that there existed interest in genuine international cooperation, but also clearly showed that significant disagreements over tactics and strategies remained.

PART II

Actors

CHAPTER TWO

The World Health Organization

Writing in 1950, four years after the World Health Organization's founding, Charles Allen described the organization ebulliently. He described its creation as "an extraordinary advance in the evolution of international health institutions . . . whose responsibilities and powers far exceed those of its predecessors." He went on to call it "the broadest and most liberal concept of international responsibility for health ever officially promulgated" (Allen 1950: 30). He described an institution at the forefront of international cooperation on a whole range of health matters and a recognized leader for its expertise and willingness to tackle seemingly insurmountable problems.

Forty-four years later, public perception of WHO had significantly declined. "People know that it exists," Fiona Godlee lamented in 1994, "but few have a clear idea of what it does . . . Its slogan 'Health for All by the Year 2000' has entered the international vocabulary, but few people, aside from diehard enthusiasts in the organization, believe the target can be realized or understand how WHO intends to achieve it" (Godlee 1994a: 1424). Instead of WHO's being a leader and an exemplar of cooperation, its public image was one of bureaucratic bloat, irrelevance, and ineffective programs. When Hiroshi Nakajima's term as WHO Director-General ended in 1997, the *Washington Post* celebrated his departure by exclaiming, "Good riddance" (*Washington Post* 1997). This came two years after African delegates to the World Health Assembly (WHA) submitted a resolution demanding Nakajima's resignation (*Economist* 1995: 80). The resolution was withdrawn before a vote occurred, but it epitomized the low repute into which WHO had fallen.

By the beginning of the twenty-first century, WHO's reputation had improved, but remained contested. Under the leadership of Gro Harlem Brundtland, WHO resumed its prominent place in international and global health governance efforts. Morrison and Summers (2003) lauded her for rebuilding much of the organization's capacity for addressing HIV/AIDS, rehabilitating its reputation, and setting it on a path for continued success. At the same time, critics continue to chastise WHO for straying too far from its original mission, undermining its efficacy, and being too beholden to politics. Levine, for example, decries WHO for failing to live up to the mission laid out for it in its Constitution and calls on it to undertake a "major rethink" (2006: 1015). She argues that WHO is stretched too thin and falls victim to political debates that have nothing to do with health itself. Ruger and Yach find that WHO has shifted away from health promotion and toward disease treatment, which limits the organization's overall efficacy and influence (2005: 1100).

The rise, fall, and current ambiguous place of the putative leader of international health efforts illustrates the changing nature of global health governance since the end of World War II, the emergence of new health problems and challenges, and the conflicts over the most appropriate venues for addressing cross-border health concerns. The World Health Organization does not lead the global health governance regime, and it is not the totality of global health governance. It is also not the only United Nations agency focusing its energies on international health concerns. Despite these caveats, the fact remains that WHO is the most prominent intergovernmental organization addressing cross-border health concerns. Examining the operations and fortunes of WHO offers insights into how the international community has conceptualized responses to global health governance needs and how that conceptualization has changed over time.

This chapter traces the development of WHO in the aftermath of World War II, analyzes its structure and budget, and examines its successes and failures within global health governance. It pays particular attention to the Health for All by 2000 initiative and the Framework Convention on Tobacco Control (FCTC). Health for All by 2000 was ambitious, but it had the effect of diminishing WHO's international standing. The FCTC, on the other hand, was the first international treaty developed and ratified entirely under the auspices of WHO and an important element in rehabilitating WHO's international reputation.

Creating the WHO

Health received a good deal of attention when the United Nations came into being. Thanks to the advocacy of the Brazilian delegation to the United Nations Conference on International Organization in San Francisco in April 1945, the word "health" found its way into relevant sections of the United Nations Charter. At this same conference, the Brazilian and Chinese delegations put forward a resolution calling for an international conference specifically devoted to creating a new international health organization (Shimkin 1946: 281). The resolution received unanimous approval.

To create the new organization, the United Nations announced the International Health Conference in June 1946 in New York. Prior to the conference, the UN's Economic and Social Council (ECOSOC) nominated 16 public health experts to the Technical Preparatory Committee on Health. The committee met for three weeks, starting in March 1946, in Paris to lay the groundwork for creating the new organization. Chief among its missions, the committee crafted a draft constitution based on proposals from the

United States, the United Kingdom, France, and Yugoslavia (Shimkin 1946: 281–2).

On July 19, 1946, the International Health Conference began its meeting in New York. All 51 members of the UN took part in the deliberations, as did 16 non-member states and a variety of intergovernmental and private organizations, such as the Pan American Sanitary Bureau and the Rockefeller Foundation (Shimkin 1946: 282). Also in attendance were representatives from the OIHP and HOLN (Sharp 1947: 510). Their presence was particularly of note, since the International Health Conference's outcomes would effectively determine the future of those two organizations. The delegates decided to absorb the OIHP, taking over its responsibilities for monitoring and implementing the International Sanitary Regulations. The new organization would also take over HOLN, and a number of WHO's early leaders began their international health careers with HOLN (Howard-Jones 1978: 79). Absorbing HOLN was relatively uncontroversial, as its patron organization no longer existed. Absorbing the OIHP, though, provoked some resistance from the latter's delegates, who thought that their organization could coexist with WHO. Once states declared that they would not participate in both organizations and gave their support to WHO, the OIHP agreed to its own dissolution (Howard-Jones 1978: 81).

Over the course of the conference, a significant debate emerged over who should be eligible for membership in the new organization. Could states that were not members of the United Nations join? What status was available to territories? Since the new organization was to be part of the United Nations system, there were debates over whether states could join one part of that system without accepting or joining others. Furthermore, since the International Health Conference was the UN's first on creating specialized agencies, the decisions made in New York in June 1946 would set precedents for future organizations. After all the deliberations, the assembled delegates unanimously decided in favor of universality. Any member of the United Nations could join the new organization unless they specifically opted out. Non-UN-member states and territories could also join as associate members (Lee 2009: 21).

The other significant debate at the conference centered on the role of regional organizations. Regionally based health organizations like the Pan American Sanitary Bureau predated WHO and had their own staffs, resources, and missions. However, the existence of competing international health organizations could have undermined the new organization and led to confusion over responsibilities. The conference ultimately decided that regional organizations should be integrated into WHO through "common action based on mutual consent" (Shimkin 1946: 282), although the six regional organizations would retain a high degree of autonomy and decisionmaking power. They would run their own programs in accordance with their perceptions of need. This arrangement allowed WHO to both incorporate existing regional organizations and establish stronger ties with member-states (Lee 2009: 30–4). It sought to strike a balance between retaining a sense of autonomy for the regional organizations and simultaneously promoting cooperation.

Before adjourning on July 22, 1946, the International Health Conference opened the Constitution of the World Health Organization for signing. China and the United Kingdom both signed the document without reservation, while the other 49 UN member-states and 10 non-member states signed with minor reservations or clarifications (Shimkin 1946: 282). In order for the document to go into effect, 26 signatory nations had to ratify it. Despite the enthusiasm for WHO and the unanimity with which the International Health Conference delegates made most of their decisions, it took nearly two years for this to happen. The all-important twenty-sixth ratification did not occur until April 7, 1948. Lee argues that this delay arose because WHO got caught up in the politics of the day. Intense debates occurred in many countries over the relative merits of internationalism in the aftermath of a devastating war. Cold War tensions also gave rise to suspicions on both sides that the organization was a tool for the other side to advance its ideological objectives. In the United States, for example, WHO's broad mandate and its emphasis on social equity led to accusations that the group was a communist front organization (Lee 2009: 30–4). Once enough states ratified the WHO Constitution, Dr Brock Chisholm of Canada became WHO's first Director-General, and the Interim Commission that had conducted international health business since the end of the International Health Conference became the nucleus of WHO's nascent Geneva-based bureaucracy (Charles 1968: 294).

WHO Structure and Budget

WHO governance occurs through four different channels. The first, and the broadest in terms of inclusion, is the World Health Assembly (WHA). The WHA meets every May at WHO headquarters in Geneva. It serves as WHO's decisionmaking body, setting the organization's agenda and approving its biennial budget. In 2010, for example, the WHA focused on issues surrounding the implementation of the newest version of the International Health Regulations, monitoring health-related aspects of the Millennium Development Goals, determining useful strategies for reducing the harmful effects of alcohol, and combating counterfeit medical products (World Health Organization 2010c). The 2006 WHA agenda included issues like pandemic influenza preparations, the destruction of remaining smallpox stocks, tobacco control, and intellectual property rights (World Health Organization 2006a). It is also responsible for selecting the Director-General and electing members of the Executive Board.

All member-states send delegates to the WHA, and its deliberations and voting employ the same "one state, one vote" principle used by the UN

General Assembly. This theoretically gives all members an equal voice in determining WHO's direction. In practice, though, most WHA decisions come about through consensus rather than formal voting (Lee 2009: 25–6). While the WHA ostensibly directs the organization's agenda, its ability to do so has decreased since the 1970s. As a greater portion of WHO's budget comes from extrabudgetary funds (EBFs) given by donor states for specific programs (details of which are explained below), the WHA effectively controls an ever-smaller portion of WHO's activities (Davies 2010: 35).

The second element of WHO governance is the Executive Board. Its job is to implement the decisions of the WHA, figure out how to put its priorities into practice, and advise the WHA. The Executive Board meets at least twice a year; its main meeting occurs in January, and a smaller meeting takes place in May after the WHA's conclusion. Additional meetings may be called as needed. Chosen by the WHA, the Executive Board consists of 34 representatives (not including alternates and advisors) of member-states who are "technically qualified in the field of health" and chosen for three-year terms (World Health Organization n.d. c). The WHA selects which member-states will serve on the Executive Board, and that state then selects its delegate, alternate, and advisors.

The Secretariat is the third element of WHO governance. It serves as the main administrative and technical organ within WHO, carrying out most of the programmatic work and ensuring that the organization functions when the WHA or the Executive Board are not in session. The Director-General heads up the Secretariat and leads WHO as a whole from its headquarters in Geneva near the Palais des Nations grounds that previously housed the League of Nations (Lee 2009: 27–30). The Secretariat oversees the permanent bureaucratic structures.

The six regional offices comprise the fourth element of WHO governance. The regional offices carry out much of WHO's programmatic work, but they maintain a high degree of autonomy and can embark on programs of their own choosing. The six WHO regions and organizational headquarters are Africa (Brazzaville), the Americas (Washington), the Eastern Mediterranean (Cairo), Europe (Copenhagen), South-East Asia (New Delhi), and the Western Pacific (Manila). Each WHO member-state is also a member of one regional organization. While the assigning of member-states to regional offices largely occurs along geographic lines, some anomalies exist. Israel, for instance, is a member of the European group instead of the Eastern Mediterranean, its natural geographic home, due to political tensions with Arab states. The Korean Peninsula is also split, with North Korea belonging to the South-East Asia region and South Korea a member of the Western Pacific region along with regional neighbors like Japan and China.

The autonomy and independence of regional offices have created some problems. Each regional office, for instance, selects its own director, meaning that the Director-General of WHO does not have direct control over the leadership at the regional level. This arrangement was initially chosen to establish strong ties with member-state governments and incorporate existing regional health organizations, but it has also led to tensions between regional offices and the WHO Secretariat (Lee 2009: 30–4). Under Hiroshi Nakajima's tenure as Director-General, for instance, the regional organizations showed almost no willingness to work with WHO on implementing projects (*Washington Post* 1997).

In 1949, its first full year of operation, WHO's budget totaled approximately US$5 million. Sixty years later, WHO had a budget of US$4.227 billion (Johnson 2009). While the budgetary increase reflects the increasing scope of WHO programs and responsibilities, it also points to a radical shift in how the international community funds WHO and the sorts of programs the organization can support. WHO's budget consists of two different types of funds. The first is the core fund or regular budgetary funds (RBFs). Core funds support WHO's basic organizational costs, its annual health programs, and some research programs. Once these funds are collected, the WHA allocates them to various programs and controls their expenditure. Member-states have a voice in how WHO spends those funds through their participation in the WHA, but they cannot dictate specific uses for those funds.

Each and every member-state is expected to make an annual contribution to WHO's core funds in accordance with a formula that considers the size of a country's economy, similar to that used by other UN specialized agencies (Davies 2010: 34). According to this formula, no single state can contribute more than one-third of WHO's annual budget. The United States is the largest contributor of RBFs, originally responsible for 25 percent of these core funds, though this amount dropped to 22 percent after protests by the US government in 2001 (Lee 2009: 38). These funds have remained relatively constant in recent years, as member-states have resisted increases in their assessed contributions. In fact, when taking inflation into account, RBFs declined 20 percent in real terms during the 1990s (Bloom et al. 1999: 911). Furthermore, member-states have not always fulfilled their obligations to pay their assessed RBFs. In 2001, 61 percent of member-states paid their RBFs in full, while 25 percent had made no payments. This was actually a significant improvement; in 1992, a mere 49 percent of member-states paid their RBFs in full. As part of an effort to encourage states to pay their assessed contributions, WHO suspended voting rights for 20 countries whose accounts were in arrears in 2005 (Lee 2009: 42–3). For the 2008–9 biennium, RBFs totaled US$959 million of WHO's US$4.227 billion budget, or roughly 23 percent (World Health Organization n.d. f).

The vast majority of WHO's budget these days comes from extrabudgetary funds (EBFs). The growth, and now dominance, of EBFs in WHO funding represents the most significant change in the organization's financing. It has also had a major effect on WHO's operations. EBFs are voluntary contributions from member-states for specific projects. Instead of focusing on global health in general and going into the general fund like RBFs, EBFs are targeted by member-states on specific, particular interests. Because member-states choose how and whether to allocate EBFs, the WHA has next to no control over them (Davies 2010: 34–5).

EBFs have been a part of WHO's budget from the organization's earliest day, providing funds for specific disease control and eradication programs. In the 1950s, EBFs played an important role in financing WHO's malaria eradication campaign. This continued into the 1960s with the smallpox eradication program. By 1970, EBFs made up 20 percent of WHO's annual total expenditures, with the proportion steadily increasing over the following years. The 1990–1 biennial budget was the first where EBFs exceeded RBFs, and that imbalance has only increased since that time. The 2006–7 biennial budget saw 72 percent of its funds coming from EBFs (Lee 2009: 39–41), and EBFs increased to more than 77 percent in the following biennium (World Health Organization n.d. f).

When EBFs started increasing in the 1970s, many within WHO took this as a positive sign. EBFs, according to a report issued in 1975, could increase technical cooperation with a broader array of actors and bring attention to new areas, like tropical diseases and human reproduction. From this perspective, EBFs were a vote of confidence in WHO, helping the organization expand its programmatic portfolio (Lee 2009: 39). The situation started to change in the early 1980s, when the WHA introduced a policy of maintaining zero growth for the regular budget. This meant that if WHO wanted to introduce new programs, it either had to stretch existing funds ever more tightly or attract EBFs (Vaughan et al. 1996: 230–1). The zero-growth policy effectively represented a vote of *no* confidence in WHO and its operations, taking away more and more of its programmatic autonomy and budgetary decision-making powers (Lee 2009: 39). Leading member-states increasingly questioned the organization's efficacy and its political commitments. For example, a conference in 1978 in Alma-Ata, USSR (now Almaty, Kazakhstan), produced a declaration calling for the international community to ensure primary health care (PHC) for all by 2000. Critics called the declaration overly idealistic, too expensive, and perhaps even socialist. They instead wanted to reorient WHO programs toward vertical health interventions that focused on specific diseases and conditions (Magnussen et al. 2004). To achieve this, donors needed to maintain a higher degree of control over how their funds were used – something that was feasible with EBFs but not with RBFs, whose use was determined by the collective will of the WHA.

The rise of EBFs has raised concerns about their effects on WHO's overall organizational effectiveness. The governments of Australia, Norway, and the United Kingdom collaborated on a report about RBFs and EBFs in 1994. Their research concluded that donor preferences, as expressed via EBFs, unduly influenced WHO's policy agenda (Lee 2009: 102). In particular, they led to distorted and disproportionate funding of programs, undermined transparency and accountability, encouraged too much competition among programs, and made long-term planning increasingly difficult (Lee 2009: 40–1). Despite these warnings, EBFs have come to play an ever-increasing role in WHO's budget and appear unlikely to significantly decline. Indeed, the 2008–9 budget document describes the organization's efforts to "maintain a reasonable balance" between RBFs and EBFs and funnel EBFs toward strategically important programs (World Health Organization n.d. f: 110–11).

WHO in Practice

Since its emergence in 1948, the World Health Organization's stature within the international community has varied considerably. Throughout its history, WHO has had the image of a technocratic organization largely removed from political debates, a football in the Cold War's ideological battles, an irrelevant relic of previous eras, and an important leader in the battles against global public health threats. These changing assessments have had profound effects on WHO's ability to influence global health policy and lead global health governance efforts.

Davies identifies four distinct phases in WHO's authority over global health policy (table 2.1). The first, and longest, period runs from WHO's founding in 1948 through the mid-1970s. During this period, WHO focused its energies largely on technical matters and on providing programmatic assistance to member-states. It tended to favor vertical programs that focused on specific diseases as a strategy for reducing morbidity and mortality rates, as evidenced by its eradication programs for malaria and smallpox.

The second period started in 1973 with the election of Halfdan Mahler as Director-General and ran through the mid-1980s. During this time, WHO embraced a mission based on a wide-ranging notion of humanitarianism. Primary health care and health equity guided WHO programs, and the organization moved toward more holistic horizontal programs that sought

TABLE 2.1 Phases of WHO policy influence

Phase	Time period	Areas of focus and influence
First	1948 through mid-1970s	Largely technical; disease-specific interventions; optimism about disease eradication
Second	Mid-1970s through mid-1980s	Emphasis on humanitarianism; using WHO to promote health equity; more activist orientation
Third	Mid-1980s through mid-1990s	Neoliberal; collaboration with World Bank; WHO budget frozen; declining influence for WHO
Fourth	Mid-1990s to present day	Reassertion of WHO as leading international health actor; collaboration with diverse set of actors

to address the whole range of issues that affected human health. However, some member-states, particularly the United States, resisted this expanded mission and sought to restrain WHO's ambition. William Scranton, the US Ambassador to the United Nations, decried WHO's politicization in 1976 when the World Health Assembly debated issues like the plight of Arabs in the Palestinian territories, the morality of trade embargoes, and apartheid (Siddiqi 1995: 6–8).

WHO's third phase began in the mid-1980s and lasted until the mid-1990s. During this time, the organization returned to its earlier technical emphases, but tinged with neoliberalism. With its promotion of austerity and market-based principles, the neoliberal shift led WHO to freeze its budget, restrain the growth of programs, and encourage member-states to privatize their health care systems. Instead of its earlier promotion of primary health care interventions, this new model highlighted discrete interventions with the goal of reducing state involvement in health care as much as possible. It was during this time, too, that WHO saw the World Bank eclipse its leadership of global health governance efforts.

Finally, the fourth phase started in the mid-1990s with a renewed focus on institutional capacity building by WHO. It has taken proactive steps to draw attention to the interrelationships between health and economic development, political stability, and international security. Though WHO has sought to reclaim its leadership of global health governance efforts during this phase, it has also entered into collaborative arrangements with a variety of state-based, nongovernmental, and private actors (Davies 2010: 35–41).

Health for All by 2000

The debates over primary health care in WHO's second phase illustrate many of the battles over WHO's proper role and its contested status within the international community. In the 1970s and 1980s, policy entrepreneurs sought to inculcate the norm of universal primary health care. Despite strenuous efforts by some actors, the international community failed to embrace this idea.

Three thousand delegates from 134 countries and 67 international organizations met in Alma-Ata on September 6–12, 1978, at the International Conference on Primary Health Care. The conference, cosponsored by WHO and the United Nations Children's Fund (UNICEF), was the first international meeting devoted solely to primary health care (PHC). Unanimously adopted, the Alma-Ata Declaration listed eight crucial components of primary health care:

• providing education on health concerns and how to treat them;
• promoting proper nutrition;
• ensuring adequate supplies of clean drinking water and access to proper sanitation;

- providing maternal and child health care, including family planning;
- immunizing populations against major infectious diseases;
- preventing and controlling local endemic diseases;
- providing appropriate treatment for injuries and illnesses; and
- providing access to essential drugs. (World Health Organization 1978)

In order to achieve these goals, the Alma-Ata Declaration set specific targets for signatory states. These goals included:

- spending at least 5 percent of gross national product on health;
- having 90 percent of children at the appropriate weight for their age;
- providing clean water within a 15 minute walk of all homes and adequate sanitation either in the home or the immediate vicinity;
- making available trained personnel to attend to pregnancy and child-birth; and
- offering child care for children at least through 1 year of age. (World Health Organization 1978)

These programs sought to provide essential health care accessible to all at an affordable cost and in line with a country's sovereign right to self-determination. They afforded the majority of the country's population access to basic health care in line with locally determined needs. If states attained these goals and ensured the provision of primary health care, then it was hoped that the international community could meet its new goal – Health for All by 2000.

The impetus for promoting PHC evolved from changes in the international community. The 1960s and 1970s saw a great wave of decolonization and liberation throughout the Third World, and new governments often came to power promising better health care for all of their citizens. While many of these new governments did take steps to improve health care initially, often with the support and aid of Western states, services tended to be overly concentrated in urban areas, failing to reach into rural areas. This prevented the majority of the population in many newly independent states from accessing health care facilities (Hall and Taylor 2003). At the same time, an increasing number of studies criticized the idea that improved health in developing states was simply a matter of transferring Western technologies and health care systems to new places. These studies called for a more holistic approach to health care that emphasized integrating it into overall social development over technology transfers (Cueto 2004: 1864–5). Researchers and activists increasingly called for a "bottom-up" approach to health care that focused on local needs and ensuring equitable access without an emphasis on large hospitals or expensive technologies (Magnussen et al. 2004: 168). China, Tanzania, and Venezuela, among others, successfully instituted programs that offered basic, yet comprehensive, health care services to rural areas. They trained local personnel to provide essential basic health services. For example, China's "barefoot doctors" focused their energies on preventative care within the communities from which they were drawn and combined Western and traditional cures (Cueto 2004: 1865).

Inspired by their example and drawing upon his own experiences with health care policies in developing countries, WHO Director-General Halfdan Mahler of Denmark called upon the international community to learn the lessons from these cases and apply them throughout the world. He urged WHO and UNICEF to ensure "health for all" by changing both the provision of health care in developing countries and the role of developed states in ensuring this aim. The Alma-Ata meeting concentrated on spreading the message of Health for All by 2000 and devising strategies for putting this idea into practice.

The Alma-Ata Declaration and its Health for All by 2000 program were truly revolutionary. Up to this point, health care had generally been the sovereign domain of states. Previous cooperative efforts on international public health issues had been driven largely by specific disease outbreaks that threatened commercial interests. The delegates to the Alma-Ata conference sought to create a change in how states viewed their responsibilities to their own citizens and those in other countries. In the midst of the Cold War, they sought to bring together democratic and communist states, encouraging them to look beyond their economic and political self-interest to embrace a greater good for the international community as a whole. By promoting the Alma-Ata Declaration and Health for All by 2000, the assembled delegates sought to have states declare that public health was no longer simply a concern for national governments. They wanted national governments to set specific targets and adopt a framework that equated good governance with the provision of adequate health care standards. They encouraged states to move beyond reactive concerns with specific maladies and toward a more proactive, holistic understanding of health and health care.

Despite the efforts of the Alma-Ata delegates, the goals of Health for All by 2000 quickly encountered difficulties. It soon became obvious that advocates failed to attract a critical mass of supportive states that could further propel and promote the idea of universal primary health care within the international community. States did not alter their own behavior or their expectations of appropriate behavior by others. The very idea of primary health care itself came under attack as wildly unrealistic and inappropriate. Government officials in many developed countries refused to believe that developing states could or should implement the wide-ranging programs encompassed in Health for All by 2000 (Hall and Taylor 2003). Instead, they proposed a new solution, selective primary health care (SPHC), that would provide only those health care services that would have the greatest benefit to children under 5 (Walsh and Warren 1979: 968–70). Primary health care's supporters saw SPHC as a betrayal of Health for All by 2000's core vision.

In the end, WHO's vaunted drive for Health for All by 2000 failed to gain much traction in the international community. Its policy recommendations failed to make an appreciable difference in state actions. Improvements in health care happened largely on an ad hoc basis with little international coordination or overriding guiding principles. Even more damaging, WHO gained a reputation as overly idealistic and too political. Many of Health for All by 2000's supporters were bureaucrats within either their national health ministries or the World Health Organization. They may have had the technical expertise to understand the importance of universal primary health care and perhaps the experience to implement it, but they lacked the political sway within governments to effect genuine policy change. Health ministries unfortunately have a tendency to be political backwaters with little influence beyond technical matters (Vaughan et al. 1985). The World Health Organization also lacked the stature to significantly affect the international debates over universal primary health care. It lacked significant financial resources, and its political clout among member-states was negligible – despite a near-universal membership. The World Health Organization's low status was largely a reflection of the relatively low priority afforded to health within the international community at that point. Most states considered health to be a national responsibility and envisioned a limited role for the international community. The World Health Organization also sought, for much of its history, to consciously avoid political battles so as to avoid antagonizing its members (Godlee 1994a). When it did try to take a more assertive role with universal primary health care, it faced the very real threat of having states like the United States withdraw funding (Walt 1993).

After the Health for All by 2000 debacle, WHO lost much of its international stature. The huge growth in EBFs is significantly related to the diminished esteem many WHO member-states held the organization in at the time. Instead of WHO's being a leader in international health, many in the international community seemed uncertain what the organization's purpose was within the international community. Further compounding the problem, and described in greater detail in chapter 4, Mahler's successor as Director-General, Hiroshi Nakajima, had a reputation for unimaginative and uninspiring leadership. Nakajima unfortunately failed to rally international support or do much to rehabilitate the organization's image.

WHO and the Framework Convention on Tobacco Control

During the 1990s, WHO received a great deal of criticism for its failure to provide leadership or creative responses to the international community's emerging health problems. Fiona Godlee, editor of the *British Medical Journal*, lashed out at WHO and its leadership for "fail[ing] to come up with convincing new initiatives to confront major health threats such as population growth and tobacco" (Godlee 1994b: 1424). Ironically, as Godlee wrote these words, work began under WHO's auspices to draft the first international treaty devoted to tobacco control and the first wholly directed by WHO – the Framework Convention on Tobacco Control (FCTC). The FCTC's creation and promotion under WHO's auspices helped the organization regain its reputation for global health expertise, competence, and leadership.

Since its creation, WHO has possessed the authority to draft international treaties and agreements and submit them for ratification by member-states. Article 19 of the Constitution of WHO explicitly grants the World Health Assembly "authority to adopt conventions or agreements with respect to any matter within the competence of the Organization" (World Health Organization 1946). As of the 1990s, though, WHO had never exercised that authority, and there existed resistance within the organization to doing so. With the emergence of tobacco control as a significant health issue that required international cooperation and coordination to effectively address, voices inside and outside WHO began to call for the organization to take advantage of its statutory authority.

Worldwide tobacco consumption has reached staggering levels. The *World Health Report 2003* emphasized, "The consumption of cigarettes and other tobacco products and exposure to tobacco smoke are the world's leading preventable cause of death, responsible for about 5 million deaths a year, mostly in poor countries and poor populations" (cited in Dressler and Marks 2006: 604). Annual cigarette consumption totals 5.6 trillion per year – an average of 900 cigarettes per person worldwide. Current estimates put the number of smokers at 1.25 billion. By 2025, predictions suggest that number will jump to 1.7 billion, with most of the growth occurring in developing countries. On average, 35 percent of men in developed states smoke. In developing countries, 50 percent of men smoke (Warner 2008: S284). The growth in smoking, its negative health consequences, and the inability of state regulations to effectively curb tobacco use and production fomented support for governing tobacco control at the global level.

Transnational tobacco companies (TTCs) had repeatedly demonstrated their ability to skirt or prevent the adoption of meaningful regulation. They would create front groups to advance their arguments against government tobacco regulation. They presented their own research to counter the scientific consensus about smoking's harms, seeking to sow confusion. They gave politicians money. They introduced weak voluntary regulations to head off efforts to introduce stronger state-based regulations (Collin et al. 2002: 268–70). They sought to distract attention and generate public good will through various corporate social responsibility programs (Collin and Gilmore 2002). They infiltrated anti-smoking NGOs to sow discord. They hired academics to publish articles that supported their positions (Mamudu et al. 2008: 1696–7). They raised questions about WHO's budget, asking whether it was even appropriate to spend money on tobacco control and if that spending came at the expense of infectious disease control. They called tobacco control an imperialist First World project that would devastate the economies and livelihoods of farmers in developing countries (Yach and Bettcher 2000: 208–10). For a long time, these tactics worked, and the international community failed to introduce meaningful restrictions on TTCs.

By the 1990s, the tide began to turn against TTCs. Smoking rates were leveling off in developed states, but rapidly increasing in developing states. The health consequences of smoking were widely known and supported in the scientific literature. The high death rates for smoking-related illnesses encouraged policymakers and activists to reconceptualize tobacco control as a development issue requiring firm international action and cooperation (Collin et al. 2002: 274). More importantly, international organizations started to change their policies with regard to tobacco production and distribution. The World Bank announced in 1991 that it would no longer provide support for tobacco production due to its deleterious health effects. A few years later, the Bank publicly pledged to step up its tobacco control efforts and collaborate more closely with partner organizations like WHO to reduce tobacco usage (Mamudu et al. 2008: 1691–2).

Into this atmosphere of questioning the international community's role in promoting tobacco control emerged calls for WHO to exercise its treaty-writing powers. Roemer et al. describe the genesis of the FCTC matter-of-factly: "The idea of an international convention for tobacco control was born at a July 1993 meeting at the UCLA Faculty Center of Ruth Roemer . . . Milton I. Roemer . . . and Allyn L. Taylor" (2005: 936). As they tell the story, Allyn Taylor wrote an article advocating for WHO to use its power to develop and implement international health treaties, and Ruth Roemer suggested that tobacco control would be an ideal subject for such work. WHO had long-established policies and programs encouraging tobacco control, and the transnational nature of tobacco production and distribution necessitated an approach that went beyond individual states (Roemer et al. 2005: 936–7).

Once committed, Roemer, Taylor, and their allies began to develop an outline for an international legal instrument that would coordinate the international community's response to tobacco control. They opted to promote a framework convention specifically created and implemented under the aegis of WHO. A framework convention is a treaty that creates a set of principles and general duties within a broad subject area which state parties pledge to address. The specific requirements for implementing those principles and duties are developed in detailed protocols after states have ratified the convention itself (Warner 2008: S285–S286). Opponents argued that it would be better to craft an international code of conduct or to have the United Nations lead the treaty process. Roemer, Taylor, and their allies rejected both options. International codes of conduct lack any formal regulatory power or legal weight, and Roemer et al. thought it silly to have the United Nations take the lead on tobacco control treaty negotiations when this was an issue wholly within WHO's expertise (2005: 937).

Through the advocacy of a wide range of supporters in developed and developing countries, tobacco control firmly found a place on the international health agenda. In 1996, the forty-ninth World Health Assembly adopted a resolution specifically calling on the Director-General to start the process for developing a framework convention on tobacco control. The resolution passed despite opposition from the WHO Secretariat (Roemer et al. 2005: 938). The effort received a major boost in 1998 when Gro Harlem Brundtland assumed the position of Director-General. Upon her inauguration, she announced her two key leadership priorities: malaria and tobacco control. With Brundtland's enthusiastic support, informal working groups met throughout 1999 and 2000 to develop the processes and protocols for crafting a treaty. Formal negotiations over the FCTC's content occurred between 2000 and 2003, with twice-yearly negotiating sessions taking place in Geneva. Finally, in May 2003, the World Health Assembly approved the FCTC with 168 signatories. On February 27, 2005, the FCTC officially entered into force with 65 states having ratified the treaty (though it only required 40 ratifications to do so). The speed with which the FCTC was drafted, signed, and ratified makes it one of the most rapidly adopted treaties in United Nations history (Warner 2008: S286).

The FCTC's regulations focus on five main areas: advertising and promotion; labeling; taxation; smoke-free environments; and sales practices. In each of these areas, the treaty establishes minimal international standards (Holden and Lee 2009: 341), but the strength of those standards varies widely among the five issue areas. With regard to advertising and promotion of tobacco products, the FCTC calls on states to end all direct and indirect advertisements and sponsorships within five years of ratification. For labels, the treaty mandates rotating warning labels covering at least 30 percent of both the front and back of tobacco packaging. The FCTC is also fairly direct with its regulations on sales practices. It outlaws sales to minors, the sale of single cigarettes, and the distribution of free samples. In the other two areas, the FCTC's standards are relatively lax. Instead of calling for specific taxation rates or equalizing tax rates across countries, it merely encourages states to consider health objectives when setting tax rates for tobacco products. There are no specific requirements or suggestions for smoke-free environments beyond a call for measures that offer protection from second-hand smoke (Warner 2008: S288–S290).

The FCTC is a remarkable treaty on a number of different levels. First, since its creation and implementation derived explicitly from previously unused powers given to WHO in its constitution, the FCTC demonstrated that WHO could still exercise effective and meaningful leadership and creativity in dealing with pressing international health concerns. The FCTC was part of WHO's revitalization during the 1990s and 2000s. Second, the FCTC introduced significant restrictions on TTCs. Globalized industries like tobacco can escape effective regulation unless all states come together in a unified manner. TTCs cannot exit from the global economy to avoid regulation as they can from individual state economies, so creating an international treaty offered the only real ability to rein in their excesses and check their power (Holden and Lee 2009: 329).

More significantly, the FCTC's negotiation process represented a major shift in how WHO operated and the voices to which it listened. TTCs managed in the past to have significant influence in any debates and discussions about placing limits on tobacco production and distribution. Further, WHO deliberations had been entirely state-centric, with little opportunity for NGOs to have an influence or a voice. With the FCTC, both of these previous practices ended. TTCs found themselves largely excluded from the deliberations, despite their efforts to sway negotiators. NGOs made significant strides in engaging with delegates and played important roles in countering TTCs' propaganda.

From its initial proposal, NGOs and actors outside WHO led the push for the FCTC. Their active involvement presaged a distinct change in WHO deliberations. In October 2000, as informal meetings crafted the protocols for the FCTC's deliberations, WHO held public hearings. This was the first time the organization ever employed a formalized process that would allow a wide variety of non-state voices to affect its deliberations. Over the course of the hearings, 144 organizations gave public testimony, and an additional 500 groups submitted written comments (Collin 2004: 93). Tobacco-control NGOs did not limit their involvement to public testimony at the earliest stage. During the negotiations, they adopted a large-scale educative function. They organized informational seminars for delegates, prepared briefings on technical aspects of tobacco control, led policy discussions, organized letter-writing campaigns and press conferences, and published reports to counter TTCs' arguments (Collin et al. 2002: 277). NGOs also organized the Framework Convention Alliance (FCA), bringing together more than 200 tobacco-control NGOs in more than 100 countries. This move bolstered their influence and allowed them to pool resources to provide greater assistance to state delegations (Warner 2008: S287). The FCA also built bridges among NGOs in different parts of the world and facilitated broader public participation. When NGOs began lobbying FCTC delegations, most of the groups came from wealthy states. Developing country NGOs lacked the resources and connections to engage in similar lobbying activities, which allowed TTCs to claim that tobacco control was a First World priority that would hurt developing states. The FCA provided the outreach and resources necessary to allow for broader participation by NGOs from around the world (Collin et al. 2002: 277–8).

Tobacco-control NGOs played a significant role in the FCTC negotiations. Instead of restricting deliberation to member-states or only inviting select "approved" NGOs, WHO opened the process to allow for a more public discourse. Throughout the actual deliberations on the FCTC, they had semi-official status – while TTCs had a far more limited role (Studlar 2006: 390–1). However, the actual negotiations largely excluded NGOs; their lobbying efforts did not extend into the negotiating chambers themselves. Collin notes that many of the final negotiations took place during "informal" sessions, which allowed delegates to exclude NGOs (Collin 2004: 93). This does not diminish the contributions of NGOs, but it highlights the fact that limits exist within WHO on how far it is willing to incorporate non-state actors into the deliberative processes of global health governance.

Conclusion

Despite the optimism that greeted its founding, the World Health Organization has fallen prey to budgetary dispute, geopolitical battles, and allegations of uncreative leadership. Its role as leader and coordinator of international health activities is enshrined within its constitution, but it found itself unable or unwilling to carry out those duties through much of its history. Its budget came under attack, and donor states directly controlled more than half of it with their targeted contributions. This gave the organization more money, but it also tied WHO's hands, preventing it from using those funds in the most appropriate manner. Divides over the most appropriate techniques and interventions also undermined WHO's ability to exercise leadership. By the 1980s, the organization was held in low regard. However, through its skillful handling of the negotiations over the Framework Convention on Tobacco Control, WHO regained a measure of esteem and showed that it still had a significant role to play in global health governance.

Though WHO has regained a measure of public esteem within the international community, its previous position as the unquestioned leader of international health efforts is no longer tenable. Thanks to the organization's weakening during the 1970s and 1980s and the emergence of a host of new organizations, the architecture of global health governance is significantly more crowded. Instead of being hierarchical with WHO at the top, the system of global health governance has come to embrace a variety of intergovernmental and nongovernmental organizations. In addition, it has spurred the creation of new forms of global governance and allowed private actors to play significant roles. This change has not only complicated the lines of responsibility when it comes to global health issues, but also represents a significant shift in global governance writ large.

CHAPTER THREE

The World Bank

The most important intergovernmental organization working on global health issues is not a health organization at all. Since the 1980s, the World Bank has served as the largest funder of global health issues. It has integrated them into its mandate, and its health funding has proven of vital importance to many states. By conceptualizing health as a development issue, the World Bank has also helped to remake how the international community interprets health. It has persuasively argued that alleviating global poverty and achieving broad-based development requires healthy people. Ill health puts a drain on a state's resources, and unhealthy people cannot contribute to a country's economic development.

The emergence of the World Bank as a major player in the global health governance architecture has not occurred without controversy. The Bank's interpretations of health and its relationship to development have provoked outcries in some quarters that its commitment to improving health is transitory. Further, critics have charged that, by emphasizing the economic development elements of improved health, the World Bank has introduced skewed priorities that do not align with the needs identified by national governments.

This chapter examines the emergence of the World Bank as a prominent actor in the global health governance architecture. The chapter begins by briefly describing the creation of the World Bank and its initial mission before discussing how the Bank came to embrace health as a key element of its mission. The 1993 World Development Report receives sustained attention, as do the Bank's current health operations.

Early Forays into International Health

Toward the end of World War II, delegates from 44 Allied nations convened at the Mount Washington Hotel in Bretton Woods, New Hampshire, for the United Nations Monetary and Financial Conference in July, 1944. Its explicit purpose was to create a system of regulation and financial order for the postwar world. Establishing the World Bank was a key element of creating the postwar international financial architecture by creating a family of five interrelated organizations that would provide stability and jointly exist under the umbrella of the World Bank: the International Bank for Reconstruction and Development (IBRD); the International Development Association (IDA); the International Finance Corporation; the Multilateral Investment Guarantee Agency; and the International Centre for Settlement of Investment Disputes. The World Bank officially came into being on December 27, 1945, when 21 states signed the Articles of Agreement, and its Board of Governors met for the first time in March 1946.

Initially, the World Bank focused on servicing sovereign debt and providing leveraged loans for European nations devastated by World War II. It made its first reconstruction loan to France on May 9, 1947, for US$250 million – half the amount for which the government had applied. The funds came with strict oversight to ensure timely repayment. Later that year, the World Bank also made reconstruction loans to the Netherlands (US$195 million), Denmark (US$40 million), and Luxembourg (US$12 million) (World Bank n.d. a). With the creation of the Marshall Plan in 1947, though, the World Bank's focus shifted away from reconstruction in Europe and toward infrastructure projects like highways, ports, and power plants in developing countries. Chile received the first non-European loan for US$16 million in March 1948 to develop power and irrigation schemes.

During the 1950s and 1960s, infrastructural and industrial projects dominated the World Bank's loan portfolio. Little funding went toward social policy sectors (Davies 2010: 43). This emphasis was in keeping with the dominant development paradigms at the time. Development meant economic growth, and the way to promote economic growth was to fund loans geared toward power generation, transportation, and the industrial sector that would spur manufacturing and trade. Ruger remarks, "During this time, the World Bank shunned public investments in sanitation, education, and health," as they failed to produce tangible, measurable, direct returns (Ruger 2005: 62).

Health did not appear on the World Bank's agenda to any degree until Robert McNamara assumed the institution's presidency in 1968. McNamara encouraged the World Bank to reconceptualize what development meant and the factors that would promote poverty alleviation. He saw the "health of man" as central to the model of socioeconomic development promoted by the Bank (Harman 2010: 31). As part of this process, the World Bank came to see that social factors played an important role in development; a country could not hope to develop unless it also addressed its citizenry's education, sanitation, and health needs (Ruger 2005: 63). The Bank also understood that a lack of progress on social factors like nutrition undermined a country's efforts to boost productivity and economic growth (Sridhar 2007: 501).

The World Bank's initial conceptualization of health concentrated on family planning. In a speech in Buenos Aires before the Inter American Press Association, McNamara called on governments around the world to develop comprehensive family planning strategies to control population growth and pledged World Bank resources to support such efforts (World Bank n.d. b). Jamaica received the first World Bank funding for family planning when the Bank approved a US$2 million loan in June 1970 (World Bank n.d. c).

Over time, the World Bank adopted a more holistic understanding of health. It entered into partnership with the World Health Organization in 1971 to jointly finance sanitation projects in developing countries. Two years later, the Bank announced that it would take an active and leading role in an international effort to combat onchocerciasis, or river blindness. Onchocerciasis is a parasitic disease transmitted by blackflies, and 90 percent of cases occur in Africa. While the disease itself is rarely fatal, it does cause severe disability and imposes a heavy burden on families and communities. Working with the United Nations Development Programme, the Food and Agricultural Organization, and the World Health Organization, the World Bank released its onchocerciasis control strategy in September 1973. The program would concentrate on seven West African states in the Volta River Basin – Benin, Burkina Faso, Côte d'Ivoire, Ghana, Mali, Niger, and Togo; it later expanded to include Guinea, Guinea Bissau, Senegal, and Sierra Leone (Liese et al. 1991: 3). The first funds came available for onchocerciasis control projects in 1974, with most projects focused on controlling or eliminating blackfly breeding grounds (Akande 2003: 6). The program managed to control onchocerciasis in 90 percent of the program area, preventing more than 100,000 cases of blindness and keeping more than 9 million children from contracting the disease (Liese et al. 1991: 3). It was also the World Bank's first major foray into funding health-related programs in developing countries, setting the stage for additional operations in the future (Ruger 2005: 64–5). In 1979, the Bank established its health department and shifted its policies to consider loans for standalone health programs not directly linked to other sectoral reforms.

The following year, the *World Development Report* identified malnutrition and ill health as the two worst symptoms of poverty that could be addressed by World Bank funding (Ruger 2005: 65). That finding marked the beginning of the World Bank's active involvement in health activities, as it started to finance health sector reform programs (Harman 2009b: 228). In 1980, the World Bank spent approximately 5 percent of its funds on social services like health. By 2003, that proportion had increased to 22 percent (Ruger 2005: 61).

The nature of the World Bank's involvement in health shifted dramatically in the 1980s and 1990s. Shunning its previous focus on controlling specific diseases, the Bank instead concentrated on altering health care systems in accordance with the conditionalities associated with Structural Adjustment Programs (SAPs). Lending for health became directly linked to reforms in the health care system (Davies 2010: 44). Thanks to a combination of high rates of borrowing and the crippling economic consequences of the oil embargoes of the 1970s, many developing countries found themselves unable to meet their debt repayment obligations and without sufficient funds to cover their budgetary obligations. The World Bank introduced SAPs as a way to ameliorate these problems. Under a SAP, the World Bank would loan money to a government on the condition that the government agree to undertake fundamental and far-reaching economic restructuring. Reflecting the dominant neoliberal ideas in the United States and other leading World Bank funders, SAPs required states to reduce the size and scope of government, reduce government services, and privatize state-owned industries (Benatar and Fox 2005: 352). For health systems, this meant introducing user fees, cutting government budgets for health programs, and encouraging competition and privatization within the health system (World Health Organization n.d. g). The idea was that these cuts would introduce greater efficiency into the system, encourage proper utilization of the health care system, and foster innovation. The inadequate delivery of healthcare services was conceptualized as a problem of poor governance rather than one of inadequate resources or structural inequalities (Harman 2010: 32).

The reality of the effects of SAPs did not match the theory. The imposition of user fees reduced access to the health care system among the poor, and the removal of pharmaceutical subsidies made drugs less available. Instead of generating enough funds to sustain themselves, health care systems in many developing countries contracted and clinics closed in poor and rural areas. The health gains that many countries made during the 1960s and 1970s were reversed during the 1980s. A 1993 World Bank study posited that governments in developing countries needed to spend a minimum of US$13 per person to provide an "essential health services package." With the cuts mandated by SAPs, though, average public health spending in affected countries fell by 20 percent – at a time when those countries were already unable to meet the target of US$13 per person. Instead of increasing access, SAPs further reduced access to health care services (Hammonds and Ooms 2004: 35–6). The cuts also made people vulnerable to infectious disease epidemics and had a disproportionately negative effect on the health of women and children (Muiu 2002: 89–92).

Why was the World Bank able to have such a dramatic effect on health, an area in which it had no official mandate? Three reasons are of primary importance. First, the World Bank leveraged its image as technocratic and nonpolitical to gain influence. The World Health Organization had acquired an image of being overtly political and sympathetic to socialism during the 1970s as it promoted comprehensive primary health care through its Health for All by 2000 initiative. A number of policymakers in the United States and other leading states distrusted the World Health Organization's motivations. The World Bank, on the other hand, presented policymakers with equations and research that offered a technocratic sheen to its programs. Since voting in the World Bank was based on financial contributions (as opposed to the one-state, one-vote principle in the World Health Assembly and United Nations General Assembly), the wealthier states had a disproportionate influence and could use that influence to further their aims (Harman 2009b: 229).

Second, the World Health Organization's budget was frozen in real terms in 1980. This meant that it could not take on new projects without cutting other projects, and an international organization without financial resources tends to lose influence (Davies 2010: 44). While the World Health Organization was running out of money and had to turn states away, the World Bank had plenty of funds to lend. Governments may not have liked the conditionalities associated with World Bank lending, but they had few other options.

Finally, even without its financial limitations, the World Health Organization was in a state of disarray. The organization was slow to respond and adapt to new health challenges, and it seemingly lacked direction and cohesion. Hiroshi Nakajima, who became Director-General in 1988, received widespread criticism for unimaginative leadership and an inability to make WHO relevant and prominent. By contrast, the World Bank appeared robust, in charge, and focused on its mission of poverty alleviation (Abbasi 1999a: 868). Furthermore, the Bank leveraged its "nonpolitical status" and lending expertise to gain prominence and prestige within the international community on health issues (Harman 2010: 40). The Bank's positive image and financial resources allowed it to fill the void left by WHO's weakness and relative poverty.

The *1993 World Development Report*

Though the World Bank grew more influential in international health matters throughout the 1980s, the publication of the *1993 World Development Report: Investing in Health* firmly placed the institution at the center of the global health governance architecture. It identified key problems in health care systems around the world, laid out a new vision for the World Bank's involvement in health matters, and introduced new forms of analysis for the efficacy of health interventions.

The *1993 World Development Report* opened by noting that the world had made remarkable advances in health since 1960, such as cutting the mortality rate for children under 5 by more than half. Despite such progress, though, developing countries and the poor had shouldered an unacceptably high proportion of the global disease burden. Furthermore, the report argued that increasing health costs placed too great a burden on the national budgets of developing countries. To deal with these concerns, the World Bank recommended three solutions. First, states should undertake policies that "foster an economic environment that enables households to improve their own health." Second, governments should redirect their health care expenditures to "more cost-effective programs" that reach more people instead of more specialized care. Finally, the Bank suggested that states "promote greater diversity and competition in the financing and delivery of health services." Governments should focus their energies on public health and essential clinical services, but even those areas should be restructured so as to encourage private actors to get involved (World Bank 1993: iii). Implementing these changes, which the World Bank admitted were quite far-reaching, would lead to lower health costs for governments, greater access to health services for people, and higher efficiency levels in delivering services (Ruger 2005: 66).

The *1993 World Development Report* strongly emphasized the need for greater efficiencies; government health care spending should go toward those areas in which it could do the greatest good. To figure out which policies would lead to the greatest efficiencies, the World Bank introduced the DALY (disability-adjusted life year). DALYs quantify the effects of ill health by combining mortality and morbidity into a single measure. In its crudest form, DALY is the sum of years of life lost (YLL) and years lived with disability (YLD), or DALY = YLL + YLD. The measure's underlying theory posits that the effects of ill health are manifest not just in premature death, but also in the time lost due to an inability to contribute positively to society (World Bank 1993: 1). Each DALY is therefore the equivalent of one healthy year of life lost. The WHO describes the sum of DALYs across the entire population as a measure of the gap between a country's current health status and an "ideal health situation where the entire population lives to an advanced age, free of disease and disability" (World Health Organization 2011a).

Efficient health policies, by this argument, are those that reduce the most DALYs across the greatest number of people. Cancer surgeries or heart transplants, for example, are fairly inefficient by this measure because their benefits accrue to only a small number of people and they cost governments a lot of money. Treating tuberculosis and sexually transmitted infections, on the other hand, costs little and benefits broad swaths of society. By favoring the latter interventions, governments can allocate their resources in an efficient manner to reduce poverty in an effective, socially acceptable manner (World Bank 1993: 3–5).

The reliance on DALYs is not without its critics. First, Davies argues that the measure focuses solely on the absence of illness rather than a more holistic measure of health (Davies 2010: 45–6). In so doing, DALYs fundamentally contradict the ideals set forth in the World Health Organization's Constitution. In its first clause, the Constitution's signatory states aver, "Health is a state of complete physical, mental, and social well-being and not merely the absence of disease or infirmity" (World Health Organization 1946). Through its emphasis on years of life lost and years lived with disability, DALYs essentially equate health solely with the lack of illness. They pay no attention to the underlying causes of poor health or the socioeconomic conditions that give rise to illness. They focus solely on the disease itself, not why the disease emerged in the first place. This myopic focus means that DALYs fail to address the root causes and therefore do not really treat poor health.

Second, critics of DALYs charge that the measure values certain groups within society more than others. Years of life saved for the able-bodied, middle-aged, and currently ill are valued more than those for the disabled, the young and the old, and those who will become ill tomorrow (Ruger 2005: 68). DALYs emphasize and celebrate the most economically productive members of society, giving them greater weight in the short term without considering either how health interventions could allow other groups to become economically productive or how policies implemented in the imme- diate term could have consequences for economic productivity in the long term (Anand and Hanson 1998: 307–10). Neither the young, nor the old, are viewed as economically productive within most societies, so illnesses that primarily afflict them receive less attention. This inequitable valuing of citi- zens distorts policies.

Finally, critics allege that DALYs lack a sound theoretical framework. DALYs are calibrated from the assumption that men have a life expectancy at birth of 80 years and women have a life expectancy at birth of 82.5 years. From this starting point, DALYs are adjusted according to age, sex, disability status, and time of illness (Abbasi 1999b: 1005). This approach ignores other crucial factors, such as socioeconomic circumstance, that may play a vital role in understanding the effects of illness on a person's (and a society's) health. "An equitable approach to resource allocation," write Anand and Hanson, "will use a criterion which attaches a greater weight to the illness of more disadvantaged people" (Anand and Hanson 1998: 310). Along those same lines, the relationship between the theoretical expectations and real- world outcomes is questionable. The policy recommendations that emerge from the use of DALYs to assess health care efficiencies often have relatively weak evidence to support them or rely on data not collected in a systematic manner (Abbasi 1999b: 1005).

The World Bank's 1993 report focused on three goals and offered a range of policy options to achieve them. The first goal was to advance policies that promote economic growth. Fostering economic expansion, according to the World Bank, can improve the health outcomes of the poor in developing countries aside from any specific health care interventions. Child mortality rates fell throughout developing countries in the 1980s, but they declined by more than twice as much in countries that saw average income increase by more than 1 percent annually (World Bank 1993: 7). Indeed, the World Bank argued that improving average household income was the single most useful economic policy to better societal health. With additional income, the poor can spend that money on goods and services that promote good health, such as improved diet, better sanitation systems, and consistent access to clean water. They can also spend that additional money on schooling, and

higher rates of schooling correlate with greater interest in health information and ability to implement the received recommendations (World Bank
1993: 7–8). The report argued that the macroeconomic reforms implemented
as a part of SAPs were necessary for ensuring long-term growth in developing
countries. While the cuts in social services that accompanied SAPs slowed
advances in health, the World Bank asserted that the slowing did not reverse
these gains and were far less severe than critics alleged. Therefore, implementing SAPs and other macroeconomic reforms was an important element
of improving health.

To reorient policies to better invest in public health and essential services,
the *1993 World Development Report* urged governments to put their dollars
toward programs with low costs per DALY reduced, like childhood immuni-
zations, school-based health clinics, family planning programs, improved
nutrition, reducing drug and alcohol addiction, fostering healthier environments, and implementing AIDS prevention programs. Each of these interventions can reduce DALYs for far less money than building a new hospital in
an urban center or paying for cancer surgeries (World Bank 1993: 8). These
programs require relatively few resources, certainly fewer than those needed
for more specialized care. They also tend to be more preventative. A small
outlay up front can help governments avoid far more expensive interventions later.

For its second goal, expanding access to clinical services, the report again
focused on those that could reach the largest number of people for the small-
est amount of money. These clinic-based services include safe motherhood
initiatives and childbirth services, basic emergency and trauma care, family
planning services, tuberculosis control, treating sexually transmitted diseases, and caring for common causes of childhood mortality like diarrheal
diseases, malaria, and measles (World Bank 1993: 10).

Taken together, the report claimed that the public health and essential
health care policies could reduce the disease burden by nearly a third in the
poorest countries and 15 percent in middle-income countries. "This reduction in disease," trumpeted the World Bank, "is equivalent, in terms of
DALYs gained, to saving the lives of more than 9 million infants each year"
(World Bank 1993: 10–11). This would be an impressive achievement, but the
Bank acknowledged that it would require greater health expenditures. To
avoid increasing government budgets while still obtaining the higher level
of resources necessary for such comprehensive interventions, the report
discouraged universal subsidization. Instead, it preferred targeting the
poor with subsidies (through either proactive identification of the poor
by the government or attrition by the wealthy opting out of the state-run
health care system and into private services) and relying on community
financing programs. In these, users pay fees at health care clinics and phar-
macies for services. The collected fees are then retained and managed locally
instead of being sent to the central government. Such a strategy emphasizes

decentralization and local control, which the World Bank saw as being crucial for long-term sustainability and increased efficiency (World Bank 1993: 11).

Lastly, the report set a goal of promoting competition and diversity of service provision in the health sector in developing countries. One way to do this would be to get the wealthy to pay for their own health services through private insurance schemes. Taking the wealthy out of the government-financed system would free up more funds to be aimed at those who most needed them. Another strategy would be to emphasize decentralization and focusing resources on local clinics instead of major urban hospitals. Local providers were likely to have a better sense of the health needs of their populations, and these clinics also reached most people. Successful decentralization would require sufficient oversight and accountability, but these were not inimical to developing countries. Finally, governments should allow, and even encourage, private actors to provide health services. Competition could lead to greater efficiencies within the entire system and reduce the burden on state-operated services. The Bank's emphases on privatization, competition, and decentralization did not mean that the state had no role to play; rather, the World Bank argued that the state should focus its energies on regulation instead of direct service provision (World Bank 1993: 12–13).

By the World Bank's argument, the strategies and policies spelled out in the *1993 World Development Report* would lead to the progressive realization of greater access to health care for all, particularly the poor in developing countries. They would allow for the realization of the goal of health for all – a goal first declared in 1978 at an international conference sponsored by the World Health Organization in Alma-Ata – while limiting the role of the government (World Bank 1993: 13).

The World Bank and AIDS

Part of the reason that the World Bank became such a prominent player in global health was that it implemented a number of programs specifically aimed at HIV/AIDS. The World Bank traces its involvement on AIDS back to 1986. That year, as part of a larger loan to support the health sector, the Bank loaned Niger US$150,000 for equipment to screen blood for HIV. This was the first time that the World Bank made a loan specifically for HIV/AIDS (Lisk 2010: 102–3).

After this initial loan, though, the World Bank and the international community entered into a profoundly ambiguous relationship between the disease and lending. The World Bank's involvement with HIV/AIDS issues progressed in fits and starts. Instead of embracing the issue as a key development challenge, some departments treated AIDS as a severe threat while others underplayed its importance. The Bank initially resisted getting involved with UNAIDS and was reluctant to become a cosponsor. A legal opinion written during UNAIDS' creation by a Bank employee stated that, if the Bank joined UNAIDS, it should "assume no liability" for the new organization and seek "as little involvement as possible" (Mallaby 2004: 319). Personal advocacy by World Bank staffers played a large role in convincing various levels of the organization's hierarchy to recognize the potential consequences of leaving HIV/AIDS unchecked. Even when these personal appeals convinced the Bank to focus on the disease, efforts to expands AIDS lending faced another significant barrier. Mallaby describes the problem:

> The original obstacle to AIDS programs persisted: borrowing governments did not regard them as a priority. The consequent difficulties in the Bank's projects showed how crucial poor countries' attitudes can be – even in a case where the Bank has resolved to go all out for progress. (Mallaby 2004: 329)

Some countries were reluctant to address HIV/AIDS because of the taboos surrounding the disease. Others saw it as distracting from other development goals.

World Bank funding related to HIV/AIDS came in fits and starts during the 1990s. The Bank initially exhibited an ambiguous commitment, and few countries approached the Bank for HIV/AIDS-related loans. In 1994, the World Bank made US$67 million in loans on HIV/AIDS in sub-Saharan Africa. That figure dropped to US$48 million in 1995, US$2.3 million in 1996, and a mere US$1.7 million in 1997. Dr Debrework Zewdie, the World Bank's HIV/AIDS coordinator, lamented, "The funding has been going down . . . because there are no new projects in the pipeline . . . To my knowledge, no country that has requested funding for HIV/AIDS has been turned down" (Behrman 2004: 197). In 1997, the World Bank repositioned its HIV/AIDS programs as central to its larger mission of promoting and developing economic development in poor countries. That year, it issued a report that described the bidirectional links between AIDS and development. The disease has a negative effect on development, threatening to wipe out years' worth of gains. At the same time, development can improve a state's ability to respond to HIV/AIDS effectively. Separating AIDS and development ignored the intertwined connections between the two. AIDS prevents development, but development provides a state with the necessary tools to prevent AIDS. Because of this almost symbiotic relationship, the Bank called on governments in developing countries to take an active role in stopping the spread of the disease – not as a health issue per se, but as an issue of economic development (Lisk 2010: 77). It became a "non-health-specific development issue" (Harman 2010: 2). This same report suggested that energies and resources should focus on prevention efforts instead of treatments. Given the high cost of AIDS treatment, it was not considered a "cost-effective" strategy for developing states (Rowden 2009: 15).

After the World Bank published a report in 1997 that explicitly linked HIV/AIDS and development, there existed some interest in and momentum for promoting a more active lending program. That interest lacked an obvious outlet. Lending programs for AIDS remained rather scattershot and tended to focus exclusively on responses from the health sector instead of encouraging broad-based interventions that drew on all sectors within a state. Government officials in some recipient states lacked the political will to effectively implement such multisectoral programs, and it was not entirely clear what such programs would look like. To overcome these problems, the World Bank launched its Multi-Country HIV/AIDS Program (MAP) in 2000, making US$1 billion in loans available. Initially, the program focused solely on sub-Saharan African states; it subsequently broadened its mandate to include most developing states (Lisk 2010: 77–8). MAP offered a central, prominent lending program that mandated wide participation by all sectors of society. It drew on a similar program in Brazil during the late 1990s that raised awareness and strengthened responses to the disease by public and private institutions (Harman 2010: 42).

In many ways, MAP presented a new model of funding infectious disease interventions and demonstrated the feasibility of expanding programs beyond state structures. This new program featured three prominent innovations. First, it simplified the procedures for approving and disbursing loans. Its streamlined procedures allowed states to receive their money more quickly and put those funds to work instead of getting caught up in the Bank's bureaucracy. Second, it made funds available to projects not directly run by the state. Instead of simply funding programs created and implemented by the government, MAP drew on the expertise and resources of all segments of state and society. Nongovernmental and civil society organizations could receive funds for instituting and operating their own programs. The MAP funds would go to the state, which would in turn disburse them to NGOs and CSOs. Third, instead of restricting funds to a single state, MAP loans could also support cross-border and regional programs (Lisk 2010: 103). This approach recognized the reality that effectively addressing the effects of HIV and implementing meaningful prevention strategies required working across national borders.

To receive funds through MAP, countries had to satisfy three criteria. First, the government had to create a single national strategic plan to fight HIV/AIDS. This program would guide the country's response at all different levels and bring a sense of coherence to its proposed interventions. Second, the government needed to establish a national coordinating body to oversee the implementation of its HIV/AIDS programs. Crucially, this coordinating body had to be located outside the health ministry and draw on the resources and expertise of both state and non-state actors. Finally, the recipient country must pledge to direct between 40 and 60 percent of the funds it received to civil society organizations, national nongovernmental organizations, and community groups to implement the programs outlined in its strategic plan. This would allow for a wide variety of groups to take an active role in preventing the disease's spread and encourage a higher degree of commitment from all relevant parties. The government could not simply funnel money to one or two select and favored groups; it had to promise a broad-based program (Harman 2010: 11–12). On these criteria, the World Bank took on the role of liaison officer. Its job was to facilitate government involvement, ensure the existence of a proper system of checks and balances, provide technical assistance, and supervise the implementation of the projects (Harman 2010: 56). It was not directly implementing a program itself, but it was there to ensure that national governments took on a sense of ownership for their programs and had the tools necessary to put those programs in place. The World Bank managed to further its good governance agenda and encouragement of government reform by channeling it through MAP.

MAP vastly increased the resources available for fighting HIV/AIDS in sub-Saharan Africa, and its successes led the program to expand beyond its original geographic mandate. The program got off to a slow start; by April 2003, it had distributed less than US$90 million of its original US$1 billion (Mallaby 2004: 330). By 2010, though, MAP loans provided US$1.5 billion for 170 projects in more than 40 developing countries. In so doing, it encouraged a client-driven dimension with greater levels of national ownership to the World Bank's approach to funding AIDS interventions (Lisk 2010: 77–8). This led to the creation of innovative structures that could broaden involvement in and commitment to fighting AIDS.

That said, MAP was not immune to criticism. Three main critiques emerged, calling into question how well MAP's practices matched its ambition. First, Lisk alleges that MAP funds were not going to the countries that most needed them. Instead, he notes that the majority of funds went to countries in "good standing" with the World Bank already (Lisk 2010: 104). This approach would seemingly contradict the initial motivation behind creating MAP – funneling more resources to countries that needed funds to implement effective AIDS interventions.

Second, Harman points to a contradiction in the World Bank's approach to country ownership. While MAP's rhetoric focused on broad-based participation and creating innovative structures that would resonate with a country's on-the-ground realities, the actual program itself required states to fit into preordained structures, ideologies, and purposes (Harman 2010: 49). Each state had to follow the same basic template – establishing a unified national strategic plan, creating a national coordinating body outside of its health ministry, and pledging a significant chunk of its funds to groups outside government control – while simultaneously being told that it should innovate. By mandating specific structures, MAP ended up narrowing the options available to states and thus constraining their abilities to create programs that would genuinely resonate with the needs and contexts of local populations.

Third, Mallaby charges that the required state structures were no better than the ones they replaced. The national coordinating bodies, he argues, replicated existing structures instead of innovating and creating new structures that would function better, leading to even higher levels of redundancy. Furthermore, states showed a marked resistance to funneling MAP funds to a broad-based array of civil society organizations or legitimate groups. Instead of widely distributing the wealth, MAP introduced new opportunities for corruption and creating sham organizations (Mallaby 2004: 330).

Changing Health Lending Tactics

Of the five organizations that make up the World Bank, two are particularly relevant for health: the International Development Association (IDA) and the International Bank for Reconstruction and Development (IBRD; commonly referred to as the World Bank). IDA focuses on providing "soft loans" (loans at below-market interest rates) to the poorest countries in the world, while the IBRD offers low- to no-interest loans to developing countries for economic development projects (Lee and Collin 2005: 69). Between 1970 and 2006, the World Bank committed more than US$32 billion to health, nutrition, and population projects in 131 countries. Spending remained relatively low until 1990, when the figure first crossed the US$1 billion threshold. It peaked in 1996, when the World Bank committed approximately US$3 billion to such projects (Independent Evaluation Group of the World Bank 2007: 2).

By 2007, the World Bank's Health, Nutrition, and Population Strategy was facing some serious questions. World Bank funding in these areas had declined by 30 percent between 2001 and 2006. What's more, the projects the Bank was funding were being implemented poorly, according to its evaluations (World Bank 2007: 13). At the same time, the new and persistent health problems faced by developing countries continued to mount. Novel disease pandemics and epidemics emerged, while some existing ones spread into new areas. Chronic diseases were causing an increasing proportion of deaths in developing countries. Malnutrition was on the rise, and population growth made it ever more difficult for countries to feed their citizens. From a funding standpoint, an ever-increasing array of actors was getting involved in international health activities, clouding some of the lines of accountability and efficiency.

As a result of these changes, the World Bank identified three key challenges to its health-related lending programs. First, while additional funding for health had the potential to be beneficial, the World Bank needed to ensure that any increased monies provided tangible benefits to the people on the ground, particularly poor and vulnerable populations. Second, the World Bank and other international health lenders needed to align their funding priorities with each other and with recipient countries to decrease overlap and ensure that programs were meeting needs. Third, the World Bank needed to move beyond focusing its funding on programs that treated specific diseases and instead do a better job integrating its programs so as to strengthen local health systems (World Bank 2007: 14).

Keeping these challenges in mind, the strategy rolled out by the World Bank in 2007 emphasized lending to client countries that would be a part of their overall poverty reduction strategies. Bank lending for health should contribute to a recipient country's fiscal sustainability, economic growth, good governance, and global competitiveness. To do this, health lending needed to be results-oriented, help create and strengthen well-organized and efficient health care systems, intervene in those health issues deemed a priority by the recipient, and foster greater collaboration and cooperation among the range of international lenders and donors on global health matters (World Bank 2007: 17).

By 2007, changes in the global health governance architecture compelled the World Bank to re-evaluate its roles and reconsider how it contributed to the betterment of international health. Between 1997 and 2006, the World Bank funded more than 500 health projects in more than 100 countries, providing US$15 billion in new lending pledges and disbursing US$12 billion (World Bank 2007: 11–13). During that time, though, the global health funding environment changed significantly. New groups had emerged on the health funding scene, raising concerns about coordination across organizations and encouraging the World Bank to focus its energies on those areas where it had a unique comparative advantage. Its 2007 Health, Nutrition, and Population Strategy highlighted the nature of the changes in the global health arena and sought to reposition the role the World Bank could play.

How did the global health environment change between 1997 and 2007? The World Bank's *Healthy Development* (2007) highlighted nine key issues. First, the world was paying more attention to international health issues in general. Greater interest led to more actors and more money getting involved. Second, because more groups were funding global health, the relative importance of the World Bank's health lending decreased. From 2001 on, it was funding a smaller and smaller proportion of international health activities. Third, funders paid too little attention to monitoring and evaluating the projects they were funding. Money was going to more programs, but it was unclear whether they were working. Fourth, states were taking a greater ownership stake in their health programs, but that meant that there was a growing demand for technical assistance from international organizations like the World Bank. Fifth, donors paid too little attention to the importance of strengthening health systems in general. They tended to focus on unique programs without addressing the overall strength and resilience of the public health system. Sixth, most international resources for health concentrated on vertical, disease-specific interventions. This led to some important issues getting overlooked and complicated attempts to coordinate action and prevent overlaps. Seventh, linkages between the public and private sectors received too little attention. Eighth, much effort had gone into developing new drugs and vaccines, but there had been comparatively little effort to ensure that poor and vulnerable communities could gain access to those medicines. Finally, different health issues were coming to dominate international health concerns – new pandemics, the role of noncommunicable diseases, and increases in obesity rates, for example (World Bank 2007: 35–7). All of these changes meant that the World Bank still had a role to play in global health, but that its role needed to change to keep pace with the rapid changes in the system.

To achieve this, the World Bank announced a shift in its health lending strategies. No longer would the World Bank focus most of its attention on disease-specific programs. Instead, its main focus would be to provide loans that would allow for the strengthening of health systems as a whole (World Bank 2007: 28). Underlying this shift was the belief that disease-specific programs could only be successful if they built upon firm foundations of existing health systems. If a country's health care system as a whole lacked facilities, personnel, and an ability to address basic needs, any disease-specific intervention would lack the resources necessary to reach those in need and sustain operations in any meaningful sense. Building stronger health care systems would also provide states with the tools necessary to achieve their other health-related goals. Stronger health systems, therefore, were not an end in and of themselves, but rather a means for achieving a wide variety of health ends.

Furthermore, the World Bank's health lending portfolio was its most poorly performing sector. Only two-thirds of its projects were rated as "satisfactory" or better – and the trend was not improving. To counteract this poor performance, the World Bank argued that it needed to implement better quality control measures (World Bank 2007: 40–1). Focusing on strengthening health systems would allow them to do this. It would help build good governance and accountability procedures, decreasing the chances of corruption and allowing other health interventions to succeed.

In this new global health funding environment, the World Bank saw itself as possessing unique comparative advantages that made its focus on strengthening health systems a natural outcome. First, the Bank emphasized the need to build partnerships between the public and private sectors in order to create resilient health systems. Since this was something it had done in other economic sectors, it had the experience and connections that would make this feasible in the health sector. Second, the World Bank had existing ties with finance ministries in most recipient countries. These ties, it argued, would allow it to work collaboratively to enact the sort of macroeconomic changes that would be necessary to strengthen health systems. Third, the Bank saw itself as uniquely placed to undertake and successfully oversee such large-scale overhauls. Nongovernmental organizations could not match its experience in effecting such transformative reforms. Finally, the World Bank already had an in-country presence in most developing countries. It would thus not be starting from scratch; it could build on its existing relationships and augment its existing structures (World Bank 2007: 43–4).

Criticisms of the World Bank's Involvement in Health

The World Bank's activities as a development organization have attracted criticism for as long as the Bank has operated. Many have questioned the appropriateness of the Bank's strategies and alleged that it is promoting a narrow agenda that benefits the wealthy. Such criticisms continued as the World Bank took an increasingly prominent role in financing global health and explicitly linking health with development. The 1993 *World Development Report* came under particular attack. Critics see the policies laid out in that report as emblematic of a fundamental shift in global conceptions of health. Nuruzzaman describes the World Bank's strategy as a change from understanding health as a fundamental human right to a conception of health as a private, market-based good (Nuruzzaman 2007: 59). Ugalde and Jackson describe the report as focusing on promoting the World Bank's ideology more than addressing international health needs. The report emphasizes minimizing the role of the government, focusing too heavily on the role of the individual in achieving health, ignoring the role of corporations in causing ill health, and encouraging profit-seeking over positive health outcomes (Ugalde and Jackson 1995: 530). Ugalde and Jackson also see the World Bank's strategy as ignoring the unique contexts in which health and illness emerge. Instead of assuming that the same interventions can work everywhere, they claim:

> Since health is a culturally- and socially-defined concept which varies from context to context, it is perhaps problematic for an institution with such a narrow view of development to be involved in determining what health is for the world at large. (Ugalde and Jackson 1995: 528–9)

The World Bank's approach is too homogenizing and cannot appreciate the diverse experiences of health and illness around the world.

These and other critics suggest that SAPs and the strategies outlined in the 1993 report had widespread negative consequences. In Costa Rica, for example, a 35 percent cut in the country's health budget is blamed for dramatically increased rates of infant mortality and infectious diseases. Further south, in Peru, SAP-mandated budget cuts and the introduction of user fees for health clinics are blamed for declines in average daily caloric intake and a serious cholera outbreak in 1994. KwaZulu-Natal, a province in South Africa, experienced a severe cholera outbreak in 2001, and health budgets cuts receive the blame for its origins (Lee and Collin 2005: 70). The introduction of user fees in China is implicated in the reason for 1.5 million people abandoning their tuberculosis treatment regimens. These untreated people are believed responsible for causing 10 million new cases of active tuberculosis in the country (Werner and Sanders 1997).

Conclusion

Though it was a relative latecomer to the global health governance infrastructure, the World Bank has come to play a hugely important role. Though it has no formal mandate to address health issues, it has gained an impressive foothold in this realm. It is the largest financer of international health programs, and its financial muscle allows it to have an effect even larger than that of international health organizations themselves. The World Bank's approach to health, though, has come under intense criticism at times. Structural Adjustment Programs have received opprobrium for prioritizing a neoliberal vision and promoting the interests of the Bank's funders over the needs of the countries receiving aid. Other projects have been criticized for taking an overly narrow approach to international health, emphasizing the absence of disease over the more holistic vision of health put forward in the WHO Constitution. Despite these criticisms, though, the World Bank's prominence within global health governance is unlikely to decline any time soon.

The World Bank is by no means the only new actor getting involved in global health governance in recent years, and it has collaborated with some of the novel groups that have emerged. Entirely new organizations have formed in response to perceived needs within the international system. Part of this need focuses on the financing structures that are available to states, while part comes from a desire to better coordinate the actions of multiple intergovernmental organizations all working on the same issue. UNAIDS and the Global Fund to Fight AIDS, Tuberculosis, and Malaria, the two new organizations examined in the next chapter, represent new sorts of intergovernmental organizations and have sought to create spaces for innovation within the global health governance structures.

CHAPTER FOUR

UNAIDS and the Global Fund

Global governance structures traditionally focus on states, and the global health governance architecture is no different. With the emergence of the AIDS epidemic, these state-centric structures appeared unable to respond to this new challenge in a timely and comprehensive manner. The sheer scope of the pandemic, the amount of money needed to combat it, and the stigma attached to the disease posed significant challenges. Existing organizations proved themselves unable to coordinate actions or unwilling to invest significant resources in addressing these new problems. Jealousy, competition, and serious disagreements about appropriate tactics undermined efforts. Disjunctures developed between what international organizations wanted to do and what national and local governments believed to be most appropriate. Nongovernmental organizations, which often took the lead in providing services to those shunned by their families and by unresponsive governments, had no official standing within global health governance. Finding the financial resources necessary became a significant struggle. These problems made crafting and implementing effective international responses to HIV/AIDS increasingly difficult.

All hope was not lost, though. Instead of trying to force existing organizations to awkwardly graft programs onto their existing mandates or ignoring the problems, HIV/AIDS encouraged some measure of innovation. The international community came together specifically to craft two new organizations – the Joint United Nations Programme on HIV/AIDS (UNAIDS) and the Global Fund to Fight AIDS, Tuberculosis, and Malaria (Global Fund) – to overcome the above-mentioned challenges. These were intended to give a place to nongovernmental organizations in deliberating and implementing policies, simplify funding mechanisms, and coordinate international actions. The organizations introduced substantial changes to the global health governance architecture – pregnant with possibility, but also fraught with danger by straying outside the traditionally accepted lines.

This chapter explores why new organizations were considered necessary, how UNAIDS and the Global Fund work, and where they have succeeded and failed in setting out a new model for global health governance. These new structures did not emerge simply out of a desire to try something new;

instead, they came about in response to specific and public failures by existing organizational arrangements.

Creating UNAIDS

Founded in 1996, the Joint United Nations Programme on HIV/AIDS (UNAIDS) introduced a wholly new type of organization to the United Nations system. When creating UNAIDS, donor states and the United Nations system were not simply looking to create a new office within WHO. Instead, they envisioned UNAIDS as a new type of organization. Instead of focusing its energies on directly funding or implementing programs, UNAIDS would act as a catalyst and coordinator. It would manage the various UN-related agencies to encourage cooperation and prevent overlap. Furthermore, it would have a strong advocacy role by bringing attention to the disease and keeping it at the top of the international agenda. To do this, UNAIDS would collect and disseminate data, formulate (though not directly implement) prevention and treatment strategies, and raise awareness among both donor and recipient states (Piot 2000: 2177). Indeed, Morrison and Summers credit UNAIDS' publication of comprehensive data on the magnitude and trajectory of HIV infection around the world with spurring international action and attention (Morrison and Summers 2003: 181).

UNAIDS' creation and unique structures are a direct result of the initial international response to AIDS. After AIDS' discovery in 1981, the international community took little action to mobilize a response to the disease. Few envisioned the need for a forceful international response, as most of the earliest known cases were in wealthy states that could afford to handle them on their own (Lisk 2010: 11–12). When WHO held its first meeting on AIDS in Denmark in October 1983, the overwhelming majority of known cases were in the United States; Zaire was the only African state reporting any cases of AIDS (AVERT 2010a). Given these statistics, WHO's priorities for addressing AIDS were to safeguard the blood supply and to alert homosexuals to this new disease. As late as 1985, WHO Director-General Halfdan Mahler told representatives from African states that they should not focus their energies on AIDS. Doing so, he warned, would distract attention from malaria and other tropical diseases (Lisk 2010: 13).

As the number of HIV cases increased worldwide, calls for some measure of coordinated global action increased. In early 1986, the WHO Executive Board instructed Mahler to create programs within the organization that could support member-states' AIDS control efforts. This directive resulted in the Control Programme on AIDS, housed within WHO's Division of Communicable Disease by year's end. The program was spun off from the Division of Communicable Disease and rechristened the Special Programme on AIDS in 1987. The following year, it again received a new name: the Global Programme on AIDS (GPA). The GPA quickly assumed leadership of international

AIDS control efforts. The UN designated it the lead agency for coordinating AIDS activities throughout the organization (Lisk 2010: 13–15).

Despite its relatively high profile, the GPA found itself in an awkward position. While it was wholly housed within WHO, it received no funds from WHO's regular budget. All of its funding came from extrabudgetary funds (EBFs). To sustain the program, Jonathan Mann, the GPA's Director, had to personally appeal to governments around the world to raise the funds necessary to support its efforts (Lisk 2010: 16–18). By 1988, the GPA was providing financial and technical assistance to more than 130 states, making Mann's international fundraising appeals all the more pressing (Knight 2008: 16–17). That the GPA could support programs in so many different countries was a testament to Mann's success and personal charisma.

Mann's fundraising success bolstered the GPA's capabilities and profile, but it also generated jealousy and friction within WHO. Critics bemoaned the fact that the GPA was not working within traditional WHO structures and requested that it be brought more directly under the control of the WHO bureaucracy. The GPA's fundraising achievements led to calls for the agency to share its largesse with other WHO programs whose budgets came from regular budgetary funds (RBFs). These clashes and disagreements reached boiling point in March 1990, when Mann resigned in protest. With his departure, contributions to the GPA declined (Lisk 2010: 20–1).

After Mann's very public resignation, WHO appointed an External Review Committee to evaluate the GPA's efficacy. When the report came out in 1992, it raised serious questions about the GPA's operations and structures. The evaluators faulted the GPA for failing to effectively collaborate with other organizations, especially those outside the medical community. The desired broad participation in GPA programs remained elusive. Knight writes, "GPA staff tried hard to take a multisectoral stance, but, as part of WHO, they invariably had to work with ministries of health that were wary that multisectoralism would take power and money away from them" (2008: 18). Furthermore, the evaluators highlighted the problems and inefficiencies that emerged from inter-agency rivalries. Instead of effectively collaborating, WHO's AIDS efforts too frequently fell victim to costly duplication of programs and activities in multiple offices and a weakened overall global response. Many of these problems, the evaluators argued, resulted from the GPA's awkward fit within the UN bureaucracy; it was *in* WHO, but not really *of* WHO, frustrating efforts at coordination and depriving the organization of the stature necessary to conduct its work (Knight 2008: 20–1).

To create a more effective international response, the External Review Committee recommended creating a new coordinating structure – a new body that would work across high-level UN agencies, but exist separately from WHO. Instead, a number of different cosponsoring UN agencies would have joint ownership of the program (Lisk 2010: 24–8). Such a structure would give these agencies a vital stake in the new organization, thus making them more accountable and reducing inefficiencies by better facilitating program coordination. It would also please the donor states. Susan Holck, a former GPA staffer, remarked on the creation of UNAIDS:

> The push for [UNAIDS] certainly did not come from the UN agencies. The push came from the donors, who were fed up with having to individually respond to requests for funding from each of these different agencies, fed up with the lack of coordination, and fed up with WHO's inability to really be operational at country level. (Knight 2008: 23)

While the various UN agencies deliberated over whether and how to adopt the External Review Committee's recommendations, international AIDS programs stagnated in the face of an uncertain organizational future.

The deliberations culminated on July 26, 1994, when the UN's Economic and Social Council (ECOSOC) adopted Resolution 1994/24 to create the Joint United Nations Programme on HIV/AIDS (UNAIDS). The resolution detailed the new organization's six programmatic objectives: providing global leadership on AIDS; promoting and disseminating policy and programming consensus; strengthening monitoring and surveillance capacities; strengthening the abilities of governments to develop national AIDS programs; promoting broad-based social and political mobilization; and advocating for greater national and international political commitments to addressing AIDS (Knight 2008: 29). It also called for the United Nations Development Programme (UNDP), the United Nations Educational, Scientific, and Cultural Organization (UNESCO), the United Nations Population Fund (UNFPA), the United Nations Children's Fund (UNICEF), the World Bank, and the World Health Organization to work together as cosponsors of this new organization (Lisk 2010: 28–9). Instead of being housed within any one of these organizations, UNAIDS would draw on all of them while existing as an independent entity.

While Resolution 1994/24 laid out the broad outlines of UNAIDS, the details of its funding, management, and organizational structures remained unsettled. It took another year before five of the six United Nations agencies signed a Memorandum of Understanding (MOU) that established their relationships with UNAIDS; the World Bank chose not to sign the MOU at that time. On January 1, 1996, UNAIDS formally began its operations with a mission to "coordinate, strengthen, and support an expanded UN response aimed at preventing HIV transmission, providing care, reducing the vulnerability of individuals, and alleviating the impact of the epidemic" (Poku 2002: 288). This expansive mission did not come with an expansive budget or staff, though. As a coordinating agency, UNAIDS was not supposed to implement or fund programs on its own. While its biennial funding still relied entirely on voluntary contributions, its budget was 15 percent less than the GPA's – even though UNAIDS had a more extensive mandate and explicitly incorporated more organizations. Its staff was less than half the size of the GPA, and the majority of UNAIDS staffers were in the field as opposed to working at UNAIDS headquarters in Geneva (Lisk 2010: 33–5; Poku 2002: 288). These changes led to a measure of confusion over UNAIDS' role and how it was similar to or different from the GPA. For instance, the GPA had directly funded national AIDS programs in some countries, while UNAIDS was not equipped to do so. The potential loss of funding led some countries to worry about the continued viability of their programs. They would have to find monies to replace the lost GPA funds, during which time their programs would suffer and drastically reduce services. In response, UNAIDS went against its mandate and funded some national AIDS programs in 1996 and 1997 (Knight 2008: 56). While this undoubtedly allowed AIDS prevention efforts in the recipient countries to continue, it inadvertently added more confusion as to what UNAIDS' role within the global health governance architecture would be.

Structure of UNAIDS

UNAIDS operates with a tripartite organizational structure: the Secretariat; the Programme Coordinating Board (PCB); and the Cosponsors (see figure 4.1 below). The Secretariat oversees UNAIDS' day-to-day operations from its headquarters in Geneva in a building shared with WHO. The UN Secretary-General

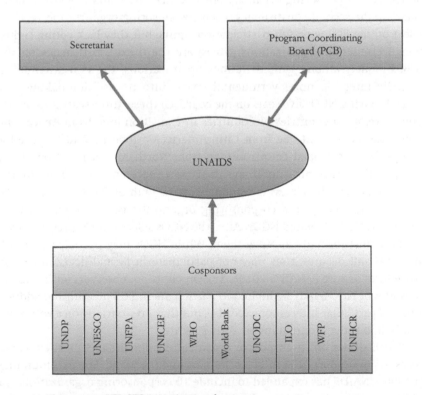

Figure 4.1 *UNAIDS organizational structure*

appoints the Executive Director, who is assisted by two Deputy Executive Directors and a number of Special Envoys appointed for their special expertise and experience in particular areas. The Secretariat employs approximately 900 people, with 65 percent of the staff working in the field and 35 percent in Geneva.

The Programme Coordinating Board (PCB) functions as a board of directors for UNAIDS. It oversees UNAIDS' operations and helps set the organization's direction and mission. It reviews and approves action plans and budgets, and engages in long-term strategic planning. It also evaluates UNAIDS' progress toward meeting its goals. By statute, the PCB meets twice a year. However, guidelines allow for canceling the second meeting in odd years if there are insufficient resources or no pressing reasons to meet (UNAIDS 2010b: 19).

The PCB's 37 members represent three distinct constituencies, and they have different rights on the board. Member-states of the cosponsoring organizations have the largest bloc of seats. Twenty-two member-states are elected on a regional basis – 7 from the Western European and Others group; 5 from Africa; 5 from Asia and the Pacific; 3 from Latin America and the Caribbean; and 2 from Eastern Europe and the Commonwealth of Independent States – to serve staggered three-year terms. The member-states have full rights to participate in PCB debates and deliberations, and they also have voting rights. The cosponsoring organizations like the UNDP and the World Bank make up the second constituency. Each cosponsoring organization receives a seat on the PCB with full participation rights, but they lack voting rights. Nongovernmental organizations (NGOs) are the third constituency on the PCB. Uniquely among United Nations organizations, the PCB attempts to formally integrate nongovernmental voices into its decisionmaking processes by giving NGOs five seats on the board. Of these, three seats go to NGOs from developing countries or countries in transition (one from Africa; one from Asia/Pacific; and one from Latin America/Caribbean), and two are for groups from developed countries (one from North America and one from Europe). The NGOs may nominate their own representatives from among groups that already possess consultative status with ECOSOC, are in a relationship with one of the cosponsoring organizations, or are on the UN's roster of HIV/AIDS-related NGOs. After the NGOs select their representatives, the PCB must formally approve them. While NGOs may participate in PCB meetings and debates, they may not participate in formal decisionmaking procedures or vote (UNAIDS 2010b: 18). On occasion, observers (either member-states or NGOs) may be invited to participate in PCB meetings to address topics of particular interest or expertise, but they do so strictly on a voluntary basis without decisionmaking or voting rights.

UNAIDS draws on its cosponsor organizations for the technical expertise necessary to support AIDS interventions around the world. Since its founding in 1996, UNAIDS has expanded to include 10 cosponsoring organizations. In addition to the initial organizations – the UNDP, UNESCO, the UNFPA,

UNICEF, WHO, and the World Bank – four more UN agencies have taken official roles in UNAIDS. The United Nations Office on Drugs and Crime (UNODC) became UNAIDS' seventh cosponsor in April 1999. The International Labor Office (ILO) followed in October 2001, and the World Food Programme (WFP) joined in October 2003. The Office of the United Nations High Commissioner for Refugees (UNHCR) officially joined UNAIDS as a cosponsoring organization in June 2004 (see figure 4.1). Together, these 10 agencies work together to collaborate and coordinate on the range of AIDS programmatic efforts sponsored by the United Nations. To prevent the duplication of efforts and provide the best technical assistance to UN member-states, the cosponsors have identified 17 broad areas of support. In each area, one cosponsoring agency is identified as the Lead Organization, and additional agencies with expertise and technical skill in that area serve as Main Partners. For example, UNICEF is the Lead Organization for providing care and support for persons living with HIV, orphans, vulnerable children, and affected households. Working with UNICEF in that area as Main Partners are the WFP, WHO, and the ILO (UNAIDS n.d.). Each cosponsor is the Lead Organization for at least one area of technical support.

The cosponsors meet twice yearly as the Committee of Cosponsoring Organizations (CCO), a standing subcommittee of the PCB. The CCO links the cosponsors and the UNAIDS Secretariat to review budgets and work plans, review each other's AIDS-related activities, and examine annual reports submitted by UNAIDS' Executive Director. The committee chair of the CCO changes annually, with the position rotating among the cosponsoring agencies.

UNAIDS' Successes and Failures

When it began operations in 1996, UNAIDS was supposed to represent a new sort of organization and a new approach to dealing with global health crises. Instead of directly implementing and funding programs, it would coordinate the activities of others. Its job was to raise awareness and facilitate information sharing. It would cross boundaries between different international organizations and bring governmental and nongovernmental organizations together to implement the most appropriate interventions possible. It would offer "the promise of what most people want – a thin layer at the top which can take innovative steps to reach the grassroots" (Awuonda 1995: 1563).

Evaluating UNAIDS' efforts, it is clear that the organization has succeeded in raising awareness and collecting and disseminating information about the epidemic. Having a focal organization has concentrated public and governmental attention. However, the organization struggles to coordinate activities among its 10 cosponsors and engage nongovernmental organizations in a substantive manner. Those areas in which UNAIDS was hoped to be the most transformative are precisely where it has found the most difficulty.

UNAIDS has taken its place as a lead international organization on AIDS. Through its activities, its visibility, and the tireless personal diplomacy of its Executive Directors, it has succeeded in raising awareness of the disease. More than just highlighting the disease, though, it has convinced states to see the importance of addressing its control and treatment through coordinated international programs. It has also helped broaden the international response beyond states, giving validity to the involvement of non-state actors. Jon Lidén, the Communications Director for the Global Fund, praised UNAIDS:

> UNAIDS has made AIDS cool . . . The fact that so many celebrities have been engaged with AIDS and [that] AIDS has been adopted by the culture industry has, I think, helped tremendously to destigmatize AIDS. (Knight 2008: 181)

Indeed, in a five-year evaluation of UNAIDS in 2001, the reviewers praised the organization, and particularly the Secretariat, for raising the disease's profile and mobilizing support for international AIDS programs (Knight 2008: 148). A subsequent independent evaluation reaffirmed the value of UNAIDS' activities in raising awareness of the disease within the international community (UNAIDS 2009).

Furthermore, UNAIDS has used its clout and its independent status to bring attention to issues and groups that often get overlooked. Cultural, social, and political stigma prevents many politically marginalized groups from getting the attention and services they need. These groups may include men who have sex with men, commercial sex workers, and intravenous drug users (Morrison and Summers 2003: 189). National governments may be reluctant to reach out to these groups or may deny services to them, which allows the epidemic to continue. Because UNAIDS does not face the same sort of domestic political and social pressures, it can collect information and make informed policy recommendations insulated from domestic political factors.

Stopping the spread of an epidemic takes more than awareness, though; it requires money. This was another area in which the five-year evaluation praised the organization. While cautioning that states need to go beyond simply giving money in order to effectively stop the disease, the evaluation highlighted the organization's success at encouraging states and private organizations to increase their pledges for international AIDS programs (Knight 2008: 148). Between 2000 and 2008, global financing for AIDS programs increased more than tenfold, reaching US$13.8 billion (McInnes and Rushton 2010: 243). Much of this explosive growth in funding for international AIDS programs is the result of UNAIDS' advocacy efforts, even though UNAIDS itself receives only a small fraction of this funding. Commenting on

UNAIDS' achievements in 2008, Elisabeth Pisani praised the organization and its first Executive Director, Peter Piot:

> UNAIDS dramatically raised the profile of the epidemic, and I think it can take most of the credit for dramatically raising the funding available for treatment and prevention. A lot of that is because of Peter. His commitment is unquestionable, and that commands respect. Politicians treat him as a peer, and he has I think been quite bold in demanding political leadership on HIV. (Das and Samarasekera 2008: 2100)

UNAIDS' prominence and visibility helped to firmly establish AIDS' place on the international political agenda.

While UNAIDS has received praise for calling attention to the HIV/AIDS pandemic and mobilizing government action, it has encountered greater difficulty actually coordinating the diverse array of UN agencies, national governments, and civil society organizations that work with and through it. After five years, the independent evaluation of UNAIDS noted that the organization had failed to get its cosponsors to provide extra funds or resources for combating the pandemic. It even went so far as to say that "the word Cosponsor is a complete misnomer" (Knight 2008: 148). This lack of coordination and cooperation weakened the capacity for translating data and findings into effective in-country policy outcomes (Knight 2008: 148-9). The follow-up independent evaluation, covering 2002 through 2008, called UNAIDS only partly successful at promoting and achieving policy and programmatic consensus among the wide range of interested actors. It did give the organization credit, though, for encouraging broad-based mobilization efforts and for being mostly successful at encouraging greater political commitment to address HIV/AIDS both globally and nationally (UNAIDS 2009).

Similarly, UNAIDS' relationship with CSOs and NGOs has not necessarily proceeded smoothly. While there exists a professed interest in collaborating with such groups and giving them a real voice, translating that into practice has happened in fits and starts. There remains a wariness or uncertainty about which groups to involve, the level of their involvement, and their ability to effect real policy decisions. Seckinelgin highlights the tension: "The acceptance of NGOs as part of the international policy environment is observable in many international policy documents. However, this acceptance appears to be highly managed by the system" (2009: 206). The fact that UNAIDS controls which organizations may cooperate with it and the nature of that cooperation leads to allegations that civil society groups merely serve as window dressing to make UNAIDS appear more inclusive than it really is. During PCB meetings, for example, NGOs could only address the attendees last. This gave them an opportunity to contribute to the dialogue and have access to the discussions, but it prevented them from having any substantive effect on power relations or altering the state-centric nature of the policy recommendations (Seckinelgin 2009: 220-1). The *Second Independent Evaluation of UNAIDS* in 2009 echoed these concerns, describing the PCB as innovative but falling short in building the relationships with other organizations necessary to make it a truly effective body (UNAIDS 2009).

UNAIDS is a new creature in the global health governance realm, and in global governance more general. It has succeeded in attracting attention and putting AIDS squarely on the international agenda, but it has had less success in providing space for nongovernmental entities to participate in international decisionmaking processes. While UNAIDS has focused on providing technical and informational support, it has largely avoided directly funding programs itself. For that, the international community created yet another innovative governance structure, one that focuses solely on providing funding: the Global Fund to Fight AIDS, Tuberculosis, and Malaria.

The Global Fund to Fight AIDS, Tuberculosis, and Malaria

When the Global Fund to Fight AIDS, Tuberculosis, and Malaria (commonly shortened to the Global Fund) came into being, it marked something new in the global health governance architecture. It was a wholly new international organization, deliberately created to stand apart from the United Nations or any other existent international bureaucracy. It had a relatively small staff. Its budget depended wholly on voluntary contributions from both state governments and private sources. Uniquely, the Global Fund explicitly refused to conduct programming and interventions on its own. Instead of directly implementing programs, it distinguished itself within the global health governance architecture by operating solely as a funding agency. It would provide grants, but not personnel or technical assistance. The Global Fund also set itself apart by explicitly recognizing the unique role of civil society organizations and mandating their inclusion in the applications made by national governments. Such innovations offer new opportunities for creating responsive global health structures, but the Global Fund's inability to live up to its promises and aspirations calls its ambition into question.

The movement toward creating an autonomous international funding organization for global health issues started when leaders of the G8 (Group of Eight) countries met in Okinawa in 2000. For the first time, the G8's agenda included health issues. The assembled states acknowledged that poor health threatened international prosperity and development. In their post-conference communiqué, the leaders proclaimed,

> Health is key to prosperity . . . Only through sustained action and coherent international cooperation to fully mobilize new and existing medical, technical, and financial resources can we strengthen health delivery systems and reach beyond the traditional sources to break the vicious cycle of disease and poverty. (Ministry of Foreign Affairs of Japan 2000)

The communiqué further expressed a commitment to reducing HIV/AIDS, tuberculosis, and malaria rates and involving civil society organizations,

industry, and academia in reaching their goals. Furthermore, the G8 countries pledged to hold another conference to agree "on a new strategy to
harness our commitments" (Ministry of Foreign Affairs of Japan 2000).

In calling for a new funding mechanism for global health, the G8 countries
implicitly acknowledged that existing institutional arrangements fell short
in tackling the challenges posed by HIV/AIDS, tuberculosis, and malaria.
Though a relatively new disease, HIV/AIDS threatened to overwhelm states
with high infection rates and imposed severe strains on national health
budgets. Tuberculosis, long thought to be under control, made a dramatic
resurgence as it co-infected HIV-positive persons and drug-resistant strains
emerged. Malaria rates also increased as drug-resistant strains came to cover
more and more territory. These new crises overwhelmed the World Health
Organization – an institution whose regular budget had remained stagnant
since the early 1980s and commanded relatively little power or attention in
international politics. With the 2000 G8 summit in Okinawa, the leaders of
the world's leading economies acknowledged that health was more significant to international politics than previously assumed. They also acknowledged that additional actors and resources were vital for effectively addressing
these crises. Instead of relying on outsiders telling countries how to implement programs, the attendees recognized that states needed to rely on local
expertise and take ownership of their health interventions if they were to
succeed (Brown 2010: 517–18). Crafting better interventions would require
states to create and implement their own programs, but they would need
resources to carry them out. That is where the G8 saw the potential for a new
international health organization.

Building on Okinawa's momentum, the Organization of African Unity held
a special session in Abuja, Nigeria, in April 2001, dedicated entirely to the
challenges its member-states faced from AIDS, tuberculosis, and malaria.
The resulting Abuja Declaration noted that these diseases were "decimating
the adult population, the most productive group, and leaving in its wake
millions of orphans, and disrupted family structures" (Organization of
African Unity 2001: 1). It further described halting the spread of HIV, tuberculosis, and malaria as its "top priority for the first quarter of the 21st
century" and declared a state of emergency across the continent due to AIDS,
and that the member-states needed to "secure adequate financial and human
resources at national and international levels" (Organization of African Unity
2001: 3, 4). While the assembled governments pledged to increase their
own health funding levels, they requested donor states to "complement our
resource mobilization efforts to fight the scourge of HIV/AIDS, tuberculosis,
and other related infectious diseases" (Organization of African Unity 2001:
5) by creating a global fund of US$5 billion to US$10 billion for creating and
implementing programs targeting these diseases.

With the promulgation of the Abuja Declaration, both donor states and
recipient countries acknowledged the need for new financial resource
streams, funneled through some sort of new institutional arrangement, to

effectively combat these diseases. Both groups also acknowledged the importance of giving recipient states a sense of ownership over their health intervention strategies.

The creation of the new organization came about at a rapid pace. At the United Nations General Assembly's Special Session on HIV/AIDS in June 2001, member-states pledged to create and support a new international funding mechanism for addressing HIV/AIDS. They affirmed their desire to create a fund with US$7 billion to US$10 billion available annually to low- and middle-income states and those with high HIV infection rates, and called on donor states to pledge 0.7 percent of their gross national products for overseas development assistance and to offer debt relief to the most heavily indebted states (United Nations General Assembly 2001: 38–40). This declaration both got the international community on board with creating the Global Fund and allowed the United Nations to give its official support for the Fund's creation.

Informal organizational meetings for the new Global Fund began in July 2001 in Geneva. Nearly 40 delegates attended these early planning meetings of the Transitional Working Group (TWG). Significantly, TWG members came from a wide range of concerned actors – donor states, recipient states, civil society organizations, the United Nations, and private industry. Drawing on this wide range of interested parties, the Global Fund presented itself as a positive-sum public–private partnership that could combine the group's collective strengths into a force for good. The meetings in Geneva set the general framework for the new organization, established its parameters, and put forward the Global Fund's mandate. In January 2002, the Global Fund's Executive Board met for the first time, and the Fund issued its first grants to 36 countries three months later (Bartsch 2007: 149–51). By 2010, the Global Fund had provided US$19.4 billion for 780 grants in 144 countries. Those funds have allowed 2.82 million people to access antiretroviral treatment to fight HIV, treated 7.11 million people for tuberculosis, and distributed 124 million insecticide-treated nets to stop the spread of malaria (Global Fund to Fight AIDS, Tuberculosis, and Malaria 2010b).

Structure of the Global Fund

Unlike most international organizations, the Global Fund extends beyond states to include non-state actors as active participants with a voice in the policymaking process. It provides explicit roles for donor countries, recipient states, and civil society organizations in an effort to achieve a high degree of deliberative governance and allow as many voices as possible to be heard. It functions as a hybrid, operating between public and private sources of authority and legitimacy. Bartsch describes it as "a new way of doing business in the field of development cooperation and health that goes beyond the state-centered intergovernmental approach of other actors in global health

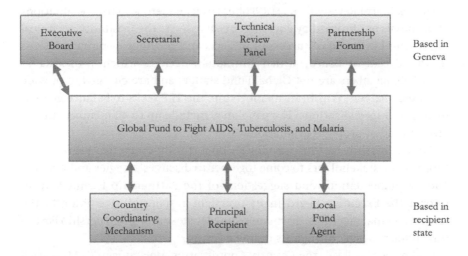

Figure 4.2 *Global Fund organizational structure*

governance" (2007: 147). With its unique structure, the Global Fund has the potential to transcend traditional boundaries, but it frequently finds itself unable to fully live up to its stated goals.

The Global Fund's operations are divided into seven key groupings: the Executive Board; the Secretariat; the Technical Review Panel (TRP); the Partnership Forum; the Country Coordinating Mechanisms (CCMs); the Principal Recipients; and the Local Fund Agents (see figure 4.2). Some parts work at the organization's headquarters in Geneva, while others work at the country level (Bartsch 2007: 151). Overseeing the whole organization is the Executive Board. It is this Board that ultimately makes all the decisions on strategy, policy, operational guidelines, and funding. During its twice-yearly meetings, the Board provides oversight and ensures that the organization is fulfilling its mandate, though it does not deal with day-to-day operations. Reflecting the diverse constituencies involved with the Global Fund, the Executive Board's membership includes donor countries, recipient states, and representatives from civil society organizations around the world.

The Secretariat handles the Global Fund's daily operations, working to ensure compliance with Fund directives, raising additional funds, and reporting on the Fund's activities to the Executive Board and the public. The Secretariat works out of the Global Fund's headquarters in Geneva. The Global Fund's Secretariat is small when compared with those of UN agencies; it has fewer than 300 staff at its headquarters in Geneva and does not have direct institutional representation in its recipient states. Instead, its local presence comes through contractual arrangements with local operators. Until 2009, the Global Fund relied on WHO to provide much of its administrative and financial support services. This arrangement allowed the Global Fund to begin operations soon after its establishment (Lisk 2010: 99).

The Technical Review Panel (TRP) offers independent scientific evaluations of proposals put forward by governments. It assesses the feasibility, technical merit, and likelihood of success of projects and provides recommendations to the Executive Board, which ultimately decides which proposals to fund. TRP members are not Global Fund staffers and are charged to provide unbiased analyses. Within its membership, the TRP seeks to balance gender, region, and specializations. The panel may include up to 40 members in any given round of proposal evaluations.

The Partnership Forum provides an opportunity every two years for all Global Fund stakeholders to come together to discuss strategies and policies. The recommendations and suggestions of the Partnership Forum help to inform the Executive Board in its oversight responsibilities. Prior to the formal biennial meetings, discussions and debates among Partnership Forum stakeholders occur through its online e-Forum.

At the country level, the Country Coordinating Mechanism (CCM) plays a vital role in crafting and putting forward proposals. It is through CCMs that the Global Fund seeks to fully realize its principles of country ownership and participatory decisionmaking. CCMs bring together local stakeholders to develop proposals for funding from the Global Fund, drawing on governmental and nongovernmental expertise. CCMs also serve as the vital link between the Global Fund and the recipient country, operating as an informational conduit. Once a country receives a grant, the CCM also oversees the implementation of the grant.

To provide that oversight, the CCM nominates a Principal Recipient. The Principal Recipient receives the actual grant from the Global Fund and implements the prevention, treatment, and care programs associated with the grant. Initially, the Principal Recipients tended to be government agencies (particularly ministries of health), but nongovernmental organizations, academic institutions, faith-based organizations, and local UNDP offices increasingly act as Principal Recipients. Countries may designate multiple organizations to serve jointly as Principal Recipients.

Finally, overseeing the Principal Recipient and providing accounting and auditing services is the Local Fund Agent. The Local Fund Agent oversees, verifies, and reports on grant performance to the Global Fund. It serves as an independent auditor, and is usually selected by the Global Fund through a competitive bidding process from in-country professionals where possible. As a matter of Global Fund policy, the Local Fund Agents may not be involved with any element of the project's implementation, nor may they be hired to audit the Principal Recipients.

Among these seven groups, the Executive Board receives the bulk of attention. Since it is the body that ultimately approves grants, it can obviously have an important effect on countries. More importantly, though, the Executive Board's composition makes it the key site for bringing together a wide variety of stakeholders and concerns about the relative weight of their influence. The board consists of 25 members (not including the Global Fund's Executive Director) coming from three different blocs; one bloc represents donors, one bloc represents recipients, and one bloc without voting rights represents international organizations and the Swiss government. Within these blocs, there exist careful formulas to maintain balance and provide for a higher degree of representation of different constituencies. Among the donors' bloc, eight of the representatives come from donor states themselves (generally selected from the most generous donors). The other two bloc members represent private interests in donor states, one from private indus- try and one from private foundations. Within the recipient bloc, seven members come from developing countries, one from a Northern-based civil society organization, one from a Southern-based civil society organization, and one from a civil society organization representing the interests of those affected by HIV/AIDS, tuberculosis, and/or malaria. The non-voting bloc rep- resents the World Health Organization, UNAIDS, the World Bank, global partner organizations that often work with Global Fund recipients, and the Swiss government.

Despite attempts at balance and providing opportunities for genuine delib- erative decisionmaking, the Executive Board has come under fire for not living up to its promises. The civil society organizations taking seats on the Executive Board have tended to deal with HIV/AIDS issues, leaving organiza- tions with more direct experience with tuberculosis and malaria without direct representation. Representatives from some developing states have also expressed dismay that they are losing influence relative to donor states. When the board decided to add a seat for an affected community civil society organization, it also added another seat for the donor states to keep the two blocs balanced by size. This raised concerns that the donor states would have an oversized influence on the board and dilute the ability of the recipient states to make their voices heard. Some recipient states also saw this move as an attempt to weaken the influence of national governments in develop- ing countries vis-à-vis civil society organizations, many of which relied on funds from donor states for their operations. They instead envisioned an organizational structure more akin to the World Health Assembly, where each member-state gets a vote and an opportunity to participate in debates regardless of funding (Bartsch 2007: 152–3).

At a more fundamental level, questions have emerged about whether it is even possible for recipient state interests to get a fair hearing within the structures of the Executive Board. The Global Fund's mandate explicitly rec- ognizes the importance and value of providing a wide range of consti- tuencies with the opportunity to have a genuine influence on policy. The board's structures and mechanisms greatly emphasize the need for delibera- tive, participatory decisionmaking (Brown 2010: 519). Despite such pledges, interviews with Executive Board members suggest that these deliberative efforts are undermined by the ability of donor states to effectively set the agenda and the terms of debate. Because they have the power of the purse, the donor states can remove or promote certain alternatives, be more or less generous with their pledges, and steer policies in certain directions that will benefit their interests (Brown 2010: 522–5). One study of the Executive Board's deliberative practices found that some recipient states felt that the interests of the donors, rather than the recipients, were paramount within the organization and that the local health experts consulted by the donor states often lacked local legitimacy or accountability (Brown 2009: 171). In other words, some recipients felt that the Global Fund talked a good game about wanting to be deliberative and inclusive, but that the donor states still ran the show.

The Global Fund's Successes and Failures

The Global Fund's creation presented the international community with a new type of international organization – one that focused solely on funding rather than program implementation, and sought to empower recipient states and to incorporate state and non-state actors into all levels of the decisionmaking process.[2] In these regards, it has achieved a number of successes and benefited the efforts to combat HIV, tuberculosis, and malaria.

First, by creating a primary multilateral source for channeling resources to states in need, the Global Fund has helped add greater efficiency to the foreign aid process. Bilateral funding, which still makes up the majority of development assistance for health, tends to favor recipients with long-standing or strategic ties to the donor state rather than the relative need of the recipient states. Bilateral aid flows also do little to promote widespread information sharing and can add additional administrative costs for recipient countries, meaning that a lower proportion of the aid actually goes to help people (Doyle 2006: 403). Furthermore, existing bilateral and multilateral funding sources proved themselves unable to mobilize enough resources to effectively combat HIV, tuberculosis, and malaria (Bartsch 2007: 147–8). Since its creation in 2002, the Global Fund has become an increasingly important source of development assistance for health. In its first year of operation, donations to the Global Fund made up less than 1 percent of all global funds for development assistance for health. By 2007, the Global Fund received 8.3 percent of the global total of development assistance for health (Ravishankar et al. 2009: 2117). By 2009, nearly one-quarter of all international assistance for HIV/AIDS went through the Global Fund (Kates et al. 2010: 8). With these funds, the Global Fund is responsible for providing approximately 25 percent of all HIV/AIDS funding internationally, 67 percent of the international funding for tuberculosis, and 75 percent of international funding for malaria (Global Fund to Fight AIDS, Tuberculosis, and Malaria 2010a). It distributes approximately 60 percent of its annual grants to HIV/AIDS programs, 24 percent to malaria programs, 14 percent to tuberculosis programs, and 2 percent to health systems development. Roughly half of the grant money goes toward paying for pharmaceuticals and treatment supplies (Lisk 2010: 100–1).

The funds available through the Global Fund have added to the overall international resource pool for these three diseases. The Fund's allocation decisions are guided by the "additionality principle" – grants provided by the Global Fund should not subtract from other donors or funding commitments. Instead, Global Fund grants increase the amount of money going to a particular country for work on reducing the effects of these three diseases. The grants do not replace other funding sources; they fill gaps (Lisk 2010: 102).

Second, the Global Fund's structure and grant application process require a high degree of country ownership that should increase efficiency and the likelihood of an intervention's success. Because the Global Fund operates solely to fund projects proposed by states, it is, in essence, an entirely reactive body. It employs a "country-defined" or "demand-driven" model. Since the Global Fund cannot implement its own programs, it places the burden on applicants to identify their problems, suggest a solution, and demonstrate the feasibility of their proposal (Kaiser Family Foundation 2009). With such a format, the Global Fund has sought to encourage higher levels of country ownership, bottom-up participation, and opportunities for countries from the Global South to take an active role in global health governance processes. It also empowers the recipient countries to make decisions about potentially sensitive issues, such as the role of generic pharmaceuticals in national treatment strategies and creating prevention strategies that will resonate with local populations (Bartsch 2007: 161–3). CCMs coordinate a state's application and offer opportunities for a wide variety of actors to take an active role in identifying proper prevention, treatment, and care strategies.

The major problems with the Global Fund tend to focus on the disjuncture between the organization's stated goals and its actual operation. It is one thing to proclaim a new approach to addressing global health needs; it is entirely another thing to put that proclamation into practice. The difficulties faced by the Global Fund implicitly raise questions about the ability to craft and effectively implement a new approach to international organizations given the existing state of the global health governance architecture.

Realizing the new structures and strategies envisioned by its founders continues to bedevil the Global Fund, and the promises of broad participation from a wide variety of stakeholders have largely failed to materialize. As noted above, deliberations within the Executive Board are largely seen as favoring the donor states and giving recipient states and civil society organizations a marginalized voice. The promises of accountability and broad participation run into problems when faced with the realities of the distribution of political and economic power in the international arena (Brown 2009, 2010). The problems with a lack of voice go beyond the Executive Board.

CCMs, designed to coordinate a country's Global Fund application and draw on a wide range of local expertise, frequently fail to involve nongovernmental sources. Government ministries tend to dominate CCMs, and NGOs have little or no input in many cases. Where NGOs have formal representation within CCMs, they often face significant obstacles to meaningful participation, such as a lack of funds to travel to meetings or information deficits that limit their ability to contribute to policymaking (Bartsch 2007: 155–6).

Complaints about the lack of representation for NGOs have not gone unheeded. Current CCM guidelines from the Global Fund recommend that nongovernmental organizations make up at least 40 percent of the membership of a given CCM (Global Fund to Fight AIDS, Tuberculosis, and Malaria 2008). Prior to the release of these guidelines, there had been a push to mandate 40 percent as the minimum level of NGO representation on CCMs. CCMs failing to meet this requirement, according to the proposal, would be ineligible to receive Global Fund grants. Ultimately, the Executive Board decided against requiring a minimum level of representation on the grounds that such a requirement would violate the spirit of country ownership (Bartsch 2007: 156–7). It is an odd position. The Executive Board wants to encourage widespread participation in CCMs so as to encourage a greater sense of country ownership in their projects, but rejects an attempt to require it because that would violate country ownership. In the place of a formal policy, the Executive Board strongly encourages countries to have their CCMs meet the 40 percent goal, and the Global Fund's studies suggest that countries are increasing the participation rates for NGOs on CCMs (Global Fund to Fight AIDS, Tuberculosis, and Malaria 2008).

More recently, some donors have raised significant questions about the level of oversight that exists for Global Fund grants. In early 2011, Germany announced that it would suspend its €200 million annual contribution to the Global Fund in light of reports of a high degree of corruption. (Germany restored half of its pledge in July 2011.) Germany is the Global Fund's third-largest donor, and its decision to withhold payments until satisfied that the Global Fund employs sufficient measures to prevent money from going missing could strike a significant blow at the Global Fund's financial viability (BBC 2011). Two months earlier, the Swedish government, which had contributed US$85 million per year for the previous three years, announced that it would not be making pledges to the Global Fund over its concerns about corrupt activities in four African grant recipient states. Sweden's AIDS ambassador, when making the announcement, stated that Global Fund officials failed to adequately investigate the allegations and punish the misdeeds (Usher 2010: 1631). Responding to the German and Swedish governments' charges, a spokesperson for the Global Fund stated that its investigations found that US$34 million – or 0.3 percent of all of its allocations to that point – had been misallocated. While deploring those instances, the Global Fund representatives argued that the low amount proved that corruption was not endemic among its grant recipients and that it was the Global Fund's own accounting requirements that brought the corruption to international attention (BBC 2011). While some have taken the evidence of misallocated AIDS funds as proof that the Global Fund's systems are inadequate, others have praised the Global Fund for its vigilance. Roger Bate, a fellow at the American Enterprise Institute, wrote in praise of the Global Fund's transparency, "If the Global Fund operated like every other multilateral aid agency, we wouldn't have the information about fraud and other bad behavior that is leading to these funding suspensions. The Fund is admirably open about its failings" (Bate 2011).

Conclusion

It would be hasty and inaccurate to call the new approaches embodied by UNAIDS and the Global Fund either unalloyed failures or successes. Both UNAIDS and the Global Fund demonstrate that there exists a willingness within the international community to create new types of global health governance organizations to address new problems and concerns. In both instances, traditional structures proved themselves unable to adjust to the unique contours of the AIDS epidemic. UNAIDS emerged to try to coordinate the activities of a disparate arrangement of UN agencies while not being a part of any particular agency itself. The Global Fund sought to provide a funding mechanism that could combine resources from many different sources as well as ensure that the recipient states had a strong sense of ownership and commitment to the proposed project. In both organizations, there exists a concerted and overt effort to explicitly incorporate nongovernmental organizations into deliberations and project management, thus acknowledging the necessity of broadening global health governance beyond the traditional realm of states.

Recognition of the need for innovation, though, does not make changes to governance structures necessarily any easier. Stepping outside the traditional governance architectures requires states to step outside their comfort zones. It introduces uncertainty and confusion, which can in turn undermine efficacy and lead to confused lines of accountability. Further, bringing non-state actors into systems which have always relied almost solely on sovereign state governments invariably leads to confusion over how and whether these new actors can get involved.

CHAPTER FIVE

Private Actors

Bill Gates and Bill Clinton have both played important roles on the international stage in a wide range of issues, but their contributions to global health may be among their most far-reaching. The Bill and Melinda Gates Foundation is the world's wealthiest philanthropy, and it has used its wealth to help set the global health governance agenda. The Clinton Foundation has used the former president's stature to negotiate agreements between governments and pharmaceutical companies that have eluded international trade negotiations for years.

Traditionally, governance within the anarchic international sphere has come from states. Individual governments provide leadership on a given issue, or states cooperate through formal international organizations or international regimes. International actions derive their legitimacy and authority through their connection to sovereign state governments. In recent years, though, non-state actors have played an increasingly important role. Nongovernmental organizations have produced authoritative reports on human rights abuses, multinational corporations have worked to create standards of conduct, and citizen movements have pressured repressive governments to step down. The presence of these non-state actors within the realm of international governance has complicated lines of authority, but has largely left the traditional system in place.

Gates and Clinton, on the other hand, have shown a willingness to blaze their own trails and participate in international governance without the explicit sanction of any national government. Indeed, some of the traditional organs of international governance have expressed alarm or discomfort with Clinton's and Gates' autonomous roles. To whom are Gates and Clinton accountable? On whose authority do they operate within the international arena? Are their agenda-setting actions benefiting global health or distorting priorities in accordance with their own selfish interests? The prominence of Gates and Clinton raises a host of issues about the role of private actors in international governance, policy accountability within the international community, and the ethical obligations for eliminating global health disparities.

This chapter proceeds in five sections. The first section examines the ethical issues surrounding global health inequities, while the second focuses explicitly on the operations of and details about the Bill and Melinda Gates Foundation and the Clinton Foundation. The third section examines the role of these foundations within global health governance. The fourth section takes up criticisms leveled against these two private actors, while the final section offers an appraisal of the two foundations and their larger implications for global health governance and ethical obligations in global health governance.

Ethics and Global Health Disparities

The current global health regime disproportionately benefits the wealthy and those in developed countries, reflecting international power disparities. The global health inequities starkly illustrate Rudolf Virchow's dictum, "Medicine is politics, and social medicine is politics writ large" (cited in Benatar et al. 2003: 126). Under the current regime, the vast majority of medical benefits and medical research go to the wealthiest 20 percent of the world's population – even though poor countries shoulder 80 percent of the global burden of disease. These disparities are widening, increasing calls for new ways of promoting global health equity. "In a world of relative economic abundance," Benatar et al. argue, "we need to focus more closely on the basic human needs that must be met if we wish to call our world one that is civilized" (2009: 348). By the early 2000s, worldwide annual expenditures on medical research totaled US$70 billion, yet 90 percent of this funding focused on diseases that constitute a mere 10 percent of the global burden of disease (Benatar et al. 2009: 249–367). Of the 1,223 new drugs developed between 1975 and 1997, only 13 – a mere 1.06 percent – were for treating tropical diseases (Benatar et al. 2003: 110). Pharmaceutical manufacturers focused their energies on developing products for illnesses in the developed world because that was where they could make a profit.

Righting these wrongs and increasing access for all to health and health care will require a substantial effort and a reconceptualization of how we provide health services in under-resourced areas. International public health programs have traditionally been the domain of state action, but the enormity of rectifying the global inequities in health requires a broader range of actors. O'Neill notes that international organizations, nongovernmental organizations, and multinational corporations "may be able to take an effective role in improving public health, and contribute thereby to just health policies" (O'Neill 2002: 44). Murphy extends this idea to people he terms "super-empowered individuals" – the vastly wealthy and/or globally notable whose philanthropic contributions could potentially have a major effect on international politics. Like John D. Rockefeller using his personal fortune and international standing in the early twentieth century to promote health, the current crop of super-empowered individuals such as Gates and Clinton have the ability to funnel their largesse and use their global stature toward bettering the lives of the dispossessed. These non-state actors can function as "agents of justice" whose work can augment the work of state authorities (Murphy 2001: 353–4).

The international community needs to find avenues for altering incentive structures that encourage investments in medical and pharmaceutical research that will benefit the poor, who disproportionately suffer from the global burden of disease. People in developing countries have limited access to medical services and drugs due to the high cost of pharmaceuticals and the failure of drug companies to produce medicines for the unique medical concerns of those regions ('t Hoen 2002: 29). In other words, it is a failure of incentives. Drug companies fail to see the payoff for investing in diseases that primarily afflict the poor. If the medical marketplace as currently constituted fails to offer sufficient incentives for drug manufacturers and medical researchers to invest their time and energies in programs that will explicitly benefit the health of the poor, then ethics demands some sort of correction. While there has been much discussion about the demand side of the equation and its current failures to satisfy global health needs, relatively little attention has focused on the supply side. Altering the incentives to encourage greater supply of necessary drugs – while simultaneously ensuring access for those that demand these drugs – could encourage greater interest in addressing the health needs of the global poor. While adjusting the supply-side incentives alone is unlikely to eradicate all global health inequities, and there exist serious limitations to what market-based incentives can do, it has the potential to contribute to these efforts.

The William J. Clinton Foundation

After leaving office in 2001, Bill Clinton created the William J. Clinton Foundation to "focus on the areas where he could make the most difference as a private citizen." Those areas are ones that "demand urgent action, solutions, and measurable results – global climate change, HIV/AIDS in the developing world, childhood obesity and economic opportunity in the United States, and economic development in Africa and Latin America" (William J. Clinton Foundation n.d. a). Since its founding, the Foundation has established offices in more than 40 countries, working with more than 1,100 employees and volunteers.

While Bill Clinton is one of the more prominent figures in international politics today, the Clinton Foundation is not among the wealthiest philanthropies. At the end of 2009, the Foundation reported net assets of US$181.9 million and revenues of US$252.7 million (William J. Clinton Foundation 2009). Although this is hardly a negligible amount, it is far below the asset holdings of some of the wealthiest prominent health-related philanthropies, like the Wellcome Trust (US$19 billion), the Ford Foundation (US$13.7 billion), and the Henry J. Kaiser Family Foundation (US$500+ million). The

Clinton Foundation, however, does have one key advantage to give it great prominence on the international stage: William Jefferson Clinton. Clinton has a "personal bully pulpit." He possesses "mind-boggling convening power" and an "ability to motivate people and move mountains" (McLean 2006).

Interestingly, the Clinton Foundation pointedly rejects the label of philanthropic organization. Instead, it sees itself more in the model of social entrepreneurship, whereby the foundation takes business-oriented approaches and applies them to providing social goods and addressing social problems (Dees 2007). It runs its own programs instead of providing grants to other organizations. Instead of asking for donations, the Clinton Foundation focuses on finding ways to appeal to private businesses' profit motives to encourage them to get involved in providing these goods and services in a sustainable, mutually beneficial manner. "The idea is," writes Jonathan Rauch in a profile of the Clinton Foundation, "to identify markets that aren't supplying enough socially beneficial goods or services to meet potential demand, and then lead them to a new equilibrium" (Rauch 2007: 67). The Clinton Foundation's approach focuses less on providing funds and more on providing leadership to bring stakeholders from the public and private sectors together to jointly arrive at mutually beneficial solutions to providing social goods and services.

The Bill and Melinda Gates Foundation

Bill Gates certainly has a degree of gravitas, but the real power of the Bill and Melinda Gates Foundation is its wealth. As of September 2010, the Foundation's endowment totaled US$36.4 billion (Bill and Melinda Gates Foundation n.d.). During 2009, it provided US$3 billion in grants in more than 100 countries. Since its inception, the Foundation has provided grants totaling US$23.91 billion in its focus areas. The global health program has received particular attention from the Gates Foundation, having received more than US$13 billion since 1994. In early 2010, the Gates Foundation announced a pledge, building on its global health legacy, of US$10 billion over 10 years for research and delivery systems for vaccines in developing countries (*Minneapolis Star-Tribune* 2010). In his annual letter for 2011, Bill Gates committed the Foundation and its resources to eradicating polio (Gates 2011).

The Gates Foundation has positioned itself as bringing business insights, technical know-how, and focused intensity to problems that go beyond what governments can address on their own. It has limited the areas in which it will work, and it can bring significant resources to address those issues. It can also be more nimble in changing course as need be since it lacks the large bureaucracy or established procedures of governments. At the same time, because the Foundation does not face the same pressures as governments, it can pledge money over the long term and sustain those commitments if it sees fit. "Foundations bring something unique when they work on behalf of the poor, who have no market power, or when they work in areas like health and education, where the market doesn't naturally work toward the right goals and where the innovation requires long-term investments" (Gates 2009: 16). Like the Clinton Foundation, the Gates Foundation seeks to use its philanthropy to correct market failures and make markets work to address social goods and needs. This role is increasingly important in the contemporary world, Gates argues, because the global economic recession has placed greater strain on national budgets. This may reduce the ability of traditional donor states to maintain their current levels of foreign aid. Into this gap, he notes, foundations like his can enter (Gates 2010: 15–17). The Gates Foundation has developed an informal responsibility divide with national governments. The Foundation tends to offer little support for health care infrastructure, since it sees that as a primary responsibility of government (Chen 2006: 663). Instead, it focuses its work on research and development of treatments for infectious diseases.

Clinton, Gates, and Global Health

Both the Clinton Foundation and the Gates Foundation have, in a relatively short period of time, become major players in setting the global health agenda. Their activities have helped to transform international research agendas, brought diverse stakeholders together, and directed the attention of governments and private companies toward neglected diseases.

The Clinton Foundation

The Clinton Foundation has focused its global health energies largely on HIV/AIDS through its Clinton HIV/AIDS Initiative (CHAI). CHAI's activities have focused largely on providing access to antiretroviral drugs in developing countries. Much like the initial decision to get involved with global health issues, CHAI's strategy and emphasis comes from personal connections. Clinton describes meeting, at the International AIDS Conference in 2002 in Spain, the prime minister of St Kitts and Nevis, who described his country's AIDS problems thus: "You know, we don't have a denial problem, we don't have a stigma problem. We have a money and organizational problem" (Rauch 2007: 66). As the Clinton Foundation began its work and looked into this problem, it discovered that it arose from the market itself. Pharmaceutical companies had adopted a "jewelry-store model" – one based on high margins and low volume. They priced their drugs high because they assumed there would be few buyers. This may have made sense from a business perspective, but it made no sense when trying to provide a social good. The Clinton Foundation's approach was to reorient the market toward a "grocery-store model" – low margin, high volume, and certain payment. In essence, CHAI would negotiate lower prices for a consortium of states, which would then place orders with the pharmaceutical manufacturers themselves. Instead of buying generic ARVs in bulk itself, the Clinton Foundation facilitated the opportunity for states to acquire these drugs at prices lower than those on the open market. In the process, there would be a larger market for the drugs, allowing pharmaceutical companies to profit from the higher volume sold – even if their margin on any individual order was lower. To make it easier for countries to make their purchases, CHAI works with UNITAID, the international drug purchasing facility created in 2006 by France, Brazil, Chile, Norway, and the United Kingdom to centralize ordering and ensure payment to the pharmaceutical companies (UNITAID 2007).

Why would generic pharmaceutical manufacturers participate in negotiations with the Clinton Foundation to increase access to ARVs in developing countries, let alone accept his proposed price ceilings? The international pharmaceutical industry's track record on expanding drug access to poor countries is less than stellar. Indeed, 't Hoen notes, "While the $406 billion-strong drug industry researches, develops, markets, and prices medicines for the industrialized world, there is no mechanism to make newer medicines affordable to developing countries" ('t Hoen 2001: 1). Furthermore, brand-name pharmaceutical companies showed no interest in negotiating with the Clinton Foundation (Rauch 2007: 68; see also Einhorn 2007).

Three potential answers emerge. First, the Clinton Foundation has negotiated with generic pharmaceutical manufacturers located in developing countries. It struck its first deal in 2003 with Ranbaxy Laboratories, Cipla, Matrix Laboratories, and Aspen Pharmacare Holdings – the first three being headquartered in India, and the last one in South Africa (Trotta 2003). By 2009, the foundation had reached agreements with six generic manufacturers, all of which have their headquarters in India or China. These manufacturers gained market access and reduced the uncertainty associated with producing generic versions of complicated pharmaceuticals like ARVs. Because of the high costs for reverse-engineering ARVs, generic manufacturers need a relatively stable and reliable market in order to justify the investment (Shadlen 2007: 570–1). Thus, there exists an economic motivation for these generic manufacturers to enter into negotiations with the Clinton Foundation. Second, the negotiations brought a sense of order to what had been a disorganized market filled with inefficiencies. When the Clinton Foundation started its work in the Bahamas in 2002, it discovered that the government was paying US$3,600 per year per person to provide ARVs with a list price of US$500. The steep price increase came from intermediaries between the generic manufacturers and the government (Rauch 2007: 66–7). Negotiating with the Clinton Foundation to eliminate these intermediaries allowed the generic manufacturers to increase their market share, expand their reach to additional countries, and reduce market inefficiencies that manufacturers could not eliminate on their own. This may also be preferable for generic drug manufacturers to more overt government involvement in the market (Shadlen 2007). Finally, the norms surrounding pharmaceutical access in developing countries have changed since the early 2000s. The market for ARVs has economic, political, and moral elements. Activists for greater ARV access in developing countries have successfully reframed the issue for national governments and drug manufacturers. Instead of their being a private good, these activists have repositioned ARVs as global merit goods – products that should be available to all regardless of ability to pay (Kapstein and Busby 2010: 75).[3] Such a change in perspective, combined with the economic incentives of a more stable market, alters the decisionmaking calculus for generic manufacturers. To not enter into negotiations with the Clinton Foundation was no longer merely an economic calculation; it also had moral and normative implications.

The Clinton Foundation's approach to expanding ARV access in developing countries proffers a unique model. The Foundation engages in third-party consultation and price negotiation with generic suppliers. It negotiates to establish price ceilings for generic ARVs and offers technical assistance to these manufacturers to find efficiencies and reduce the prices even further. The resulting prices should be affordable to developing countries while still offering the manufacturers a reasonable margin, and the manufacturers agree to offer generic ARVs at the negotiated price (or lower) to all members of CHAI's procurement consortium. To join this consortium, a state must sign a memorandum of understanding with CHAI, specifying monitoring and reporting requirements for the state government (Waning et al. 2009: 520). The Clinton Foundation facilitates the agreement between manufacturer and purchaser, but it does not do the purchasing itself or collect any monies for the drugs. Instead, it essentially acts as an intermediary.

CHAI's strategy of third-party consultation and negotiation differs from two other common approaches to reducing ARV prices. The first is pooled purchasing, used most prominently by the Global Fund to Fight AIDS, Tuberculosis, and Malaria. In this approach, the Global Fund brings together multiple purchasers to make one large purchase. Instead of negotiating a lower price, pooled purchasing operates on the assumption that higher volume will lead necessarily lead to lower prices (Waning et al. 2009: 520); and instead of simply facilitating the agreement, as the Clinton Foundation's strategy does, the Global Fund itself places the order for the pool. The second competing strategy is differential or tiered pricing, an approach embraced by a group of pharmaceutical manufacturers and international organizations through the Accelerating Access Initiative. This approach concentrates on branded, rather than generic, ARVs. Each manufacturer selects certain branded ARVs to be sold in low- and middle-income countries at a price lower than that charged in high-income countries. It is up to that manufacturer to determine which ARVs will be available under this strategy and which countries will be eligible for the lower-priced drugs on the basis of income and HIV prevalence levels (Waning et al. 2009: 520).

The Clinton Foundation trumpets the success of its more market-oriented approach. In October 2003, Clinton announced a price reduction of more than 50 percent for a leading three-drug AIDS cocktail (Rauch 2007: 70). Since then, the Foundation has achieved price reductions for more than 40 different ARV formulations from eight different suppliers. These negotiations have also reduced the costs for second-line AIDS drugs by more than 30 percent and for pediatric AIDS drugs by more than 90 percent. The cost reductions have provided 1.4 million people in at least 50 developing countries with access to ARVs – more than half of all people in developing countries that are on ARVs (William J. Clinton Foundation n.d. c). In many countries, this translates into making first-line ARVs available for only 50 cents a day (Farmer 2005b: 12).

Independent evaluation demonstrates the efficacy of the Clinton Foundation's approach. CHAI negotiated a statistically significantly lower price for 9 of 13 generic ARVs. These prices were between 6 and 36 percent lower. The other two strategies did not fare as well. Pooled purchasing led to a statistically significant lowering of price on only 2 of 24 ARVs. Branded ARVs available through differential pricing remained significantly more expensive than their generic equivalents. The price differences ranged from 23 to 498 percent (Waning et al. 2009: 525). In their assessment of the Clinton Foundation's strategy, Waning et al. say that it "shows promise." They caution, though, that the wide variation in price differentials gives some pause. The greatest discounts appear to exist in the first one to two years after negotiations with manufacturers conclude, with the discount decreasing after that. This tempers the authors' endorsement of third-party consultation and negotiation, but they note that the program appears to deliver the most substantial price reductions of the three (Waning et al. 2009: 525–6).

In addition to providing drug access, CHAI has also sought to increase access to HIV testing. Its negotiations have created significant cost reductions for 16 different HIV diagnostic tests from 12 different suppliers. It has also launched a number of country-specific programs, integrating HIV/AIDS care with other basic health care services, expanded health services in rural areas, and access to adequate nutrition (William J. Clinton Foundation n.d. c).

The Gates Foundation

The Gates Foundation has become one of the dominant funders for global health projects since its program began in 2000. Within two years, it had already donated US$400 million for AIDS projects. Observers credited the Gates Foundation's donation with creating a major ripple effect, increasing international funding for AIDS research. Peter Piot, the then-head of UNAIDS, argued that the Foundation's donations "sham[ed] many 'donor' governments" into contributing more (Cohen 2002: 2000). In 2005, the Foundation gave US$137.5 million for international AIDS-related projects. One year later, its outlays nearly doubled to US$257.9 million (Funders Concerned About AIDS 2007: 9–11). In 2008, the Gates Foundation's disbursements for international AIDS programs reached a peak of US$378 million. The following year, as the economy soured, its outlays declined to US$334 million – but this still totaled 57 percent of all private disbursements for international AIDS programs (Funders Concerned About AIDS 2010: 4). One of the more prominent projects receiving funding from the Gates Foundation is the African Comprehensive HIV/AIDS Partnership (ACHAP). Founded in 2000, ACHAP is a country-led public–private partnership between the Gates Foundation, the government of Botswana, and Merck Pharmaceuticals, with the goal of preventing HIV transmission and providing treatment for those already infected. In particular, it has focused energies on providing free access to ARVs to those in need in a country with one of the highest adult HIV infection rates in the world (Ramiah and Reich 2005: 545). ACHAP hopes to demonstrate that "progress [against AIDS] is possible, with the right level of political commitment, the right policies, and the right partners – including the private sector" (World Bank Institute 2006). The Foundation pledged US$56.5 million to implement the program.

While its work on AIDS may have received the most attention, the Gates Foundation's contributions have spanned a wide range of diseases. The Foundation contributed US$1.2 billion for malaria research and more than US$900 million for tuberculosis research between 2000 and 2008 (McNeil 2008). In the process, its actions encouraged other public and private donors to increase their tuberculosis-related donations, too (Chen 2006: 661).

Part of how the Gates Foundation has profoundly shaped the international health agenda comes through the creation of its Grand Challenges in Global Health (GCGH) Program. Announced in 2003, GCGH initially made US$200 million worth of grants available to researchers working on issues and diseases that had poor market incentives. Recipients had to work in research areas with a high degree of promise for saving and improving lives in developing countries (Gates 2003). These were the diseases that private industry paid too little attention to, since they saw little chance of recouping their investments or creating a large enough market. The Gates Foundation used its resources to reorient attention and overcome market failure for diseases that primarily afflicted the poor. The Foundation showed itself willing to invest in long-shot treatments and programs if they demonstrated a chance for a large payoff. It wanted researchers to focus on developing tools and treatments that would have long-term effects (McCarthy 2000: 154).

GCGH recipients receive a great deal of latitude, but they must make certain pledges to the Foundation in order to receive funding. First, they must identify specific milestones by which outside evaluators can assess their progress. Second, they must create a timeline for their work. Finally, they must pledge to make any pharmaceutical discoveries that emerge from their research affordable to people in developing countries (Chen 2006: 662). This program has led the Gates Foundation to become the largest donor for research on diseases in developing countries (McNeil 2008). It has also encouraged other public and private funders to get involved in research in developing-country diseases. It creates an assumption that there must be something good or important happening if the Gates Foundation is willing to provide funding (McCarthy 2000: 154). For instance, the United States' National Institutes of Health (NIH) increased their spending on global health issues by US$1 billion after the Gates Foundation announced GCGH at a time when most other NIH research programs saw their budgets remain flat. This contradicts the widely held assumption that funding will necessarily be a zero-sum game in which private funding will lead to a reduction in public funding (Matthews and Ho 2008: 409).

Despite the power of the Gates Foundation's endowment, it is important to put its global health spending into perspective. While it has become a large player, it is not necessarily the dominant one. In 2005, it distributed US$826.5 million via 283 grants for basic and clinical science research on infectious diseases. That same year, the Global Fund to Fight AIDS, Tuberculosis, and Malaria distributed US$1.05 billion for health services. The United States government spent US$3.5 billion on global health programs, distributing its monies to foreign governments, civil society organizations, and the private sector. The World Bank, though, spent the most on global health in 2005. It gave US$3.8 billion, mostly for disease prevention services (Sridhar and Batniji 2008: 1187–8). In 2007, the Bill and Melinda Gates Foundation contributed US$452.1 million for neglected disease research and development. This was 84 percent of all funds for neglected disease research and development from nongovernmental philanthropic sources. This is truly an impressive amount, but the United States government's spending on these same diseases dwarfs that figure – US$1.25 billion in 2007. Indeed, public funding for neglected disease research and development in 2007 totaled US$1.78 billion, while philanthropic sources contributed US$538.3 million and private and corporate interests contributed another US$231.8 million. The Gates Foundation's contribution is important, but it is less than half of what the United States NIH alone spend on these same issues (Moran et al. 2008: 34–42). These figures demonstrate that, while the Gates Foundation has come to play an increasingly important role in funding global health programs, national governments and international organizations still provide the bulk of global health funds.

Criticisms of the Clinton and Gates Foundations

The Clinton and Gates Foundations face four primary criticisms. First, critics charge that these foundations crowd out other voices and inappropriately claim credit for outcomes achieved by smaller, grassroots organizations. The

Clinton Foundation claims that its programs have allowed 1.4 million people to access ARVs, but others dispute this assertion. They argue that the Clinton Foundation "was flying with a tailwind" (Rauch 2007: 70). Activist groups had long been pressuring pharmaceutical companies and governments to make these drugs more affordable. Their efforts predated the Clinton Foundation's very existence, so it is disingenuous for the Foundation to take credit for increasing access. Any success the Foundation had came on the backs of the work done by these smaller, local organizations. Furthermore, by focusing so heavily on the numbers of people receiving ARVs, the Clinton Foundation fails to build the infrastructure necessary to make these programs sustainable and useful in the long term (Bate 2005).

Similarly, the Gates Foundation has faced accusations of operating as a veto player when it works with other organizations. The massive financial resources available to the Gates Foundation allow it to dominate other organization, pushing its priorities over others (Cooper 2008: 85). Pablo Eisenberg, a senior fellow at the Georgetown Public Policy Institute, describes the imbalance: "You may have foundations with assets larger than almost 70 percent of the world's nations making decisions about public policy and public priorities without any public discussion or political process" (Wadman 2007: 248). The priorities of the Gates Foundation, allege critics, may not necessarily align with those of local governments. Furthermore, these governments are in subservient positions because of their reliance on funds from the Foundation. That prevents them voicing objections or reorienting its work toward more broad-based and applicable programs. Instead, the Foundation creates a cartel mentality and discourages debate about appropriate treatments (Bate 2008).

The Gates Foundation's work on malaria has received much of this criticism. In 2008, Arata Kochi, the head of WHO's malaria program, wrote a memo to senior WHO officials, complaining about the Foundation's influence. He argued that the Foundation was stifling the diversity of views about the best ways to treat and combat malaria. Further, because the Foundation provided grants to so many malaria researchers, it was making it nearly impossible to find independent, impartial reviewers for project proposals. He alleged that the Foundation's grant-making process was far too opaque and internalized, which hindered necessary scientific conversations about research and treatment priorities for malaria. Instead of the Gates Foundation being a partner, Kochi saw it as trying to supersede WHO's policymaking function. One of Kochi's supporters described Gates Foundation-funded groups as "cowed into stomach-churning groupthink" (McNeil 2008). Kochi's memo, leaked to various newspapers, may have been "an imprudent career move," according to another supporter, "but Kochi was both courageous and correct to insist that global malaria policies would benefit from a more robust debate" (Bate 2008).

Similar criticisms emerged in 2011 with the Gates Foundation's emphasis on polio eradication. Richard Horton, the editor of the *Lancet*, blamed Bill Gates' promotion of polio eradication for distorting the Gates Foundation's global health priorities. Bioethicist Arthur Caplan called control, instead of the Gates Foundation's goal of eradication, "the best we can do," while Donald Henderson, who led the successful effort to eradicate smallpox, criticized polio eradication programs for spending so much money without achieving success (McNeil 2011).

Second, critics see conflicts of interest between the missions of these foundations and their funding sources. The Clinton Foundation has received donations from national governments and private businesses whose interests may be counter to universal ARV access (Bate 2005). Reports in the *Los Angeles Times* assert that the Gates Foundation invests its endowment in publicly traded corporations whose actions cause the very health problems that the Foundation seeks to alleviate. However, instead of trying to use its financial and moral clout to encourage those companies to change their practices and reduce their harmful and polluting actions, the Foundation very publicly rejects the idea of shareholder activism and establishes firm firewalls between its investment and philanthropy arms (Piller et al. 2007). Critics thus argue that support for and from potentially nefarious sources overshadows the potential good work. Investing in companies with poor environmental and health records and receiving donations from autocratic governments that deny adequate health care to their populations contradict the very messages that these foundations claim to promote.

In this same vein, critics allege that these charitable actions are merely a ruse designed to hide the failures of the current international economic system. Instead of fundamentally challenging the existing order, the work of the Clinton and Gates Foundations provides a cover for the deleterious effects of global neoliberal capitalism. Hindmarsh writes, "To overcome widespread disaffection with the new order's gross inequalities and labor relations, and to strengthen the institutions of capitalism, elite managerial ideals combined with corporate philanthropy" (Hindmarsh 2003: 12). The Clinton and Gates Foundations seek to mask the anger about and contradictions of globalization by creating philanthropies. Instead of changing the system, they seek to re-legitimate it.

Third, critics charge the Clinton and Gates Foundations with supporting inappropriate solutions and technologies. Their solutions ignore local needs and capabilities, and instead privilege predetermined favored approaches. The Clinton Foundation puts its resources into providing ARVs, but it does far too little to support the development of the infrastructure necessary to provide access to those drugs or promote prevention programs (Bate 2005). Without a robust health infrastructure, patients cannot get the follow-up care and monitoring that are so vital for preventing drug resistance. This also makes the distribution system far more fragile and entirely reliant upon external actors for its continued existence. The Gates Foundation's wealth comes from high technology, and the health solutions they pursue follow that same vein. It encourages the development of high-tech solutions and favors the development of new drugs over providing better access to currently existing useful medicines (McNeil 2008). By overemphasizing the new and the high-tech, it focuses too much on those approaches that might lead to greater financial rewards down the road.

Finally, critics disparage the lack of accountability measures within these foundations. They have disproportionate influence, yet the public has next to no opportunity to express its opinions or voice concerns about programs. This replaces a mass democratic voice with a top-down autocratic one. Organizations like the World Health Organization, the World Bank, and the Global Fund to Fight AIDS, Tuberculosis, and Malaria offer opportunities for both donors and recipients to voice their concerns and engage in a public dialogue about priorities and appropriate approaches. The Clinton and Gates Foundations, on the other hand, are not necessarily accountable to anyone. They rely upon the personal charisma of their leaders and returns from the stock market to retain their influence. "If Bill Gates' foundation can dole out more money to health care-related NGOs more quickly than the World Health Organization or the World Bank, who has more influence? . . . It also gives [Gates] considerable influence over the people who seek and later depend on [his] funding" (Rothkopf 2008: 84). Gates himself acknowledged that foundations like his lack the sort of democratic accountability measures that put pressure on governments and ensure that their policies are in line with the citizens that they represent (Gates 2003). Instead, these foundations assume the voice for those they claim to represent. To the critics, this hardly qualifies as representation. Rothkopf writes, "It is great to have Bono or the Gates Foundation or the Clinton Global Initiative speak for [the poor]. It would be better to give them the means to speak for themselves" (Rothkopf 2008: 307). Many of the other criticisms ultimately come down to questions of influence and accountability. Concerns about stifling debate and credit-claiming are, at their heart, concerns about whose voices are influencing the international health agenda and whether that influence is malignant.

By and large, the criticisms of the Clinton and Gates Foundations paint a picture of disconnected, unresponsive organizations that promote their own agenda over the needs of the people they purport to help. The criticisms express anxiety about private, unaccountable entities taking over the role of national governments, and about international organizations controlling the global health agenda and thus distorting that agenda to meet their own needs. These criticisms should certainly provide some pause to the international community, but, as the next section will demonstrate, they can also overstate dangers to the international system and gloss over the very real flaws in a state-centric approach to global health governance.

Benefits of Private Actors

Private actors have long played a role in providing health care and promoting access to health services. For example, the International Committee of the Red Cross, with its mission to alleviate human suffering without regard for status or politics, traces its lineage back to 1863, and it now possesses international legal standing to provide health services and investigate allegations of mistreatment. What's changed with the advent of the Gates and Clinton Foundations, though, is the scope and scale of these private philanthropic organizations in setting and contributing to the global health agenda. The Gates Foundation's massive financial resources and the Clinton Foundation's ready access to global policymakers increase the opportunities for private philanthropic organizations to play a significant role in contributing to meeting the international community's pressing health challenges.

First, private philanthropic actors increase the diversity of funding sources available to the international community for global health issues. Critics have long bemoaned the existence of "tied aid" – monies from donor states that require recipients to spend funds on specific services or products from the donor state. For example, food aid from the United States government must be purchased and packaged within the USA and US carriers must transport at least three-quarters of it (Oxfam America n.d.). Others have critiqued donor states for requiring recipient states to implement certain practices or policies that comport with the donor government's ideological stances but may not match the beliefs or needs of the recipients. The President's Emergency Plan for AIDS Relief (PEPFAR) came under sustained attack from activists and AIDS experts for originally mandating that aid recipients must spend at least one-third of AIDS prevention funds on abstinence-only programs and explicitly condemn commercial sex workers (Health GAP 2006). In both instances, recipient states, nongovernmental organizations, and international organizations find their hands tied by donor government policies. The resources made available by private philanthropic actors can allow recipient states to implement a greater diversity of programs. They can offer recipient governments significant levels of support that do not come with the stigma and strings that may be attached to official aid from some governments. They give recipient states greater choice in the types of programs they want to implement (Pipkin 1985: 385). This, of course, does not imply that private philanthropic aid comes without any strings attached, but the greater diversity of funding sources allows recipients to potentially implement a wider array of health programs and address more of their health concerns.

Second, private philanthropic actors can direct attention toward neglected aspects of the global health agenda. Bill Gates remarked in 2003, "Every year, $70 billion is spent on medical research and development, yet only 10 percent is devoted to diseases that cause 90 percent of the global health burden." He further highlighted the fact that the US Food and Drug Administration had approved 1,500 new drugs in the previous 25 years, but that fewer than 20 of those drugs addressed diseases that primarily afflict developing countries (Gates 2003). These health concerns receive less attention because they seemingly have little direct effect on donor states. Further, there exists little financial incentive for pharmaceutical companies to invest in this research because they see little commercial potential for these drugs. If the people who would most benefit from these drugs cannot afford to purchase them, then pharmaceutical companies will not use their resources to target those diseases (Matter and Keller 2008: 347–8). Private philanthropic actors can help fill this gap. They lack the commercial incentive of pharmaceutical companies, and their lack of a direct constituency may give them freer reign to invest resources in underexplored areas. The Gates Foundation provided more money than any other single organization in 2008 for research on malaria (Moran et al. 2008: 16–17), while the Clinton Foundation has taken a leading role in stabilizing and lowering the price of malaria treatments in developing countries (Drugs for Neglected Diseases Initiative 2008). Danzon argues that developing drugs for diseases that primarily afflict developing countries requires a combination of subsidization and differential pricing (Danzon 2007). She finds that private philanthropic organizations can play key roles in both of these areas through providing transparency and fostering public–private partnerships with governments. She specifically cites the actions of the Clinton Foundation as an exemplar for how a private philanthropic organization can help address a neglected issue in the global health agenda. In these ways, the Clinton and Gates Foundations seek to encourage other actors to get more involved in international health issues. Matthews and Ho cite the Gates Foundation's high-profile health activities as raising international health's profile within the US government and encouraging the federal government to devote more resources to these issues (Matthews and Ho 2008: 411–12).

Third, private philanthropic actors can spur innovation and offer unique tools for encouraging new approaches for advancing the global health agenda. Both the Gates and Clinton Foundations explicitly approach health issues with what they describe as an entrepreneurial approach. They employ methods commonly thought of as business tools, adapting them for global public goods for health. They want to encourage flexibility and results-oriented processes. They want to be nimble in ways that governments often are not. Bill Clinton talks about his vision of international health work and his Foundation's approach thus: "We wanted people who could operate efficiently in the nonprofit field in the same way they had in business" (Rauch 2007: 67). Ira Magaziner, one of the Clinton Foundation's first employees, described the Foundation's approach: "We did something that people would naturally do in a purely business context and apply it to the public goods market" (Rauch 2007: 68). The Clinton Foundation argues that many of the problems of pharmaceutical access in developing countries stem from disorganization in the market and the lack of effective delivery systems. Correct these problems by changing incentive structures, and you can increase access to life-saving drugs.

The Gates Foundation uses the Grand Challenges in Global Health Program described above to spur innovation. It encourages scientists and researchers to devote their energies to addressing neglected health concerns while also demonstrating to pharmaceutical companies that markets do exist for treating these diseases. "With greater encouragement and funding," advisors to GCGH wrote, "contemporary science and technology could remove some of the obstacles to more rapid progress against diseases that disproportionately affect the developing world" (Varmus et al. 2003: 398). The program provides a fiscal incentive to get involved with addressing gaps in the global health agenda. There is nothing that would inherently prevent a government from doing the same thing, but private philanthropic actors have so far shown themselves more able and willing to use these sorts of innovative techniques to get more people involved in global health issues.

Conclusion

The Clinton Foundation and the Bill and Melinda Gates Foundation demonstrate that private philanthropic actors, and private actors in general, can and do play a significant role in helping to shape the agendas for major international issues. The Gates and Clinton Foundations undoubtedly play a big role in the global health agenda, but they are largely filling the gaps left open within the international community. These foundations are not pushing other actors out; they are entering areas where state actors have largely failed to go. The foundations add another tool to the international community's arsenal for meeting its ethical obligation to provide health services to all. If states could provide the levels of funding or political will to bring public and private actors together, there would be no reason for these foundations to get involved. They also demonstrate that private actors hardly threaten to completely take over public actors. Instead of viewing the growing role of private actors as symptomatic of the decline of the state, it is more useful analytically to understand public and private actors as working in tandem. States show little interest in allowing their traditional roles to be completely usurped, and private actors appear unwilling to completely take over the traditional responsibilities, or uninterested in doing so. It is undoubtedly true that private actors are not subject to the approval of voters, but it is equally misleading to assume that they lack any accountability.

The emergence of private actors in international health, and international affairs in general, is not symptomatic of the complete privatization of public goods provision, nor does it signal to state governments that they need not fund these issues. Instead, the private actors operate in an additive manner, increasing the attention to these issues. They are not a panacea, but neither are they inimical to the larger goals of the global health governance system.

CHAPTER SIX

Civil Society Organizations

Rotary International, a service club with more than 1 million members worldwide, has taken the lead in the global polio eradication campaign. Its partnership with the World Health Organization has allowed the group to reach more than 2 billion children at risk of contracting the disease and raise more than US$900 million since 1986 (Rotary International 2010). Thanks largely to the efforts of the Carter Center, a non-profit organization founded by former US President Jimmy Carter, the number of cases of Guinea worm disease dropped from 3.5 million in 1986 to fewer than 4,000 in 2009. Such success may allow Guinea worm disease to be the first parasitic disease eradicated (Carter Center 2010). Transformate, a small Brazilian nongovernmental organization (NGO) based in Rio de Janiero, has led the way in promoting HIV/AIDS awareness in the city's sprawling *favelas* or slums on an annual budget of less than US$100,000. In 2005, the organization lost more than 70 percent of its annual funding when it refused to sign a pledge publicly declaring its opposition to prostitution required by the United States Agency for International Development (Pinheiro 2005).

In each of these three instances, civil society organizations have taken an active, and often leading, role in addressing global public health concerns. These organizations illustrate the diversity of civil society groups that have come to play prominent roles – from long-standing multinational voluntary organizations to local NGOs set up to address health needs in their home communities. These examples show that civil society groups can raise impressive amounts of money and make connections with top-level policymakers, but they also bear witness to the challenges that NGOs can face if their programs come into conflict with those of state governments.

Civil society organizations (CSOs) have assumed a more prominent place in global health governance since the early 1990s, but they fit somewhat uncomfortably into the existing structures. As non-state actors, they position themselves as above the political fray and able to adapt to changing circumstances quickly and efficiently. They have stronger connections to local communities than many governments possess, and they can inspire a level of trust and respect that state-based actors cannot. However, that same independence raises questions about their legitimacy and their ability to speak for the communities and groups they claim to represent. Some critics have charged that the rise of civil society organizations in global health governance has contributed to states shirking their obligations to provide basic services to their citizens.

This chapter explores the role that civil society organizations play in global health governance today. The first section defines civil society organizations and traces their emergence. The next section critically examines the benefits and criticisms of civil society organizations in addressing international health crises. Finally, the chapter will discuss the activities of two very different health-related civil society organizations – Oxfam and the Treatment Action Campaign (TAC) – to see how these groups operate on the ground.

Civil Society and Global Governance

Since the 1980s, international organizations of all different varieties have promoted the benefits and necessity of collaborating with civil society organizations. These groups occupy a "third place" between the government and the market, possessing a sense of independence that allows them to craft interventions that better respond to local needs. This description allows a large number of organizations to fit under the rubric of civil society. The World Bank's definition of CSOs reflects the diversity of organizations that may potentially qualify, describing them as:

> The wide array of non-governmental and not-for-profit organizations that have a presence in public life, expressing the interests and values of their members or others, based on ethical, cultural, political, scientific, or philanthropic considerations. CSOs therefore refer to a wide array of organizations: community groups, non-governmental organizations (NGOs), labor unions, indigenous groups, charitable organizations, faith-based organizations, professional associations, and foundations. (cited in Lee 2010: 1–2)

This wide-ranging definition covers both large international organizations with multimillion-dollar budgets and small local groups reliant entirely on volunteers. There exists no necessary template for organizational structure, finances, or constituency. What unites them is that they ostensibly represent some group and use that representation as the basis for providing some sort of service to the public. CSOs can pressure states into adopting policies that they might otherwise resist. CSOs' independent advocacy can compel states to take health-related actions. Davies locates this special power by noting that "they [CSOs] have often been the lone voice arguing for progressive change in there areas, where states have failed and WHO was unable to push these agendas forward" (Davies 2010: 49–50).

Since the 1980s, CSOs have become increasingly popular vehicles for delivering aid to developing states. A report published in December 1999 found that NGOs provided more aid to developing states than all United Nations agencies combined. The World Bank estimated the total dollar amount that year from NGOs to developing countries at more than US\$5 billion (Chaplowe and Engo-Tjega 2007: 257). This shift by international donors toward funneling aid through CSOs rather than official governmental channels reflected two important shifts within the international system. First, the predominance of neoliberal ideas in wealthy states and fears of corruption and cronyism within developing country governments discouraged donors from funneling development resources through donor states. Too often, according to this view, recipient states squandered aid, misappropriated funds, or committed outright theft. This fitted with the growing perception that developing countries would grow faster if they reduced the size and role of the government. Neoliberalism argued that nonessential functions, including the provision of many social services, should be the province of non-state actors. CSOs, operating outside the direct control of the state, rose to prominence as entities that would prevent corruption and theft by governments and take over nonessential functions from state bureaucracies.

Second, the concept of development itself shifted. Instead of focusing solely on economic growth, development should encompass a holistic sense of human well-being. Development is not charity, but a tool for empowering people. The beneficiaries of development therefore should take their rightful place as participants in the process. CSOs work within this vision of development because they are close to the people they represent. They provide an opportunity for people to express themselves to the powers that be, and their priorities reflect the needs of the local communities they serve (Chaplowe and Engo-Tjega 2007: 260–1). This latter role is especially useful in societies where political opposition is weak or absent. CSOs can provide an alternative venue for citizens to find their voice and play a role in articulating their needs (Jareg and Kaseje 1998: 821).

CSOs possess unique benefits and strengths that allow them to serve their communities, provide services, and implement a wide variety of interventions. First, CSOs are more nimble, transparent, and accountable than governments. Since they lack the opaque bureaucracies of state governments, it is easier to ensure that programs operate as they should. CSOs integrate their stakeholders into their operations, so the people who are being served have a stake in ensuring that programs operate smoothly. Furthermore, the organizations' relatively small size means that they can alter programs and adjust to changing conditions on the ground far more rapidly than a government can (Schurmann and Mahmud 2009: 537). Second, CSOs respond to democratic deficits at the domestic and global levels. They seek to create democratic foundations in those places where they are lacking by allowing the voices of the afflicted and affected to have a potential role in policymaking and service provision (Doyle and Patel 2008: 1931). The organizations operate along democratic lines, allowing poor and marginalized communities to have a voice (Muhumuza 2010: 5–6). Where people or groups cannot express their needs through governmental channels, they can use CSOs to get their concerns acknowledged and articulated.

Third, CSOs can keep an eye on the state, ensuring that it lives up to its obligations and working with it to create and maintain institutions. When a state violates the rights of its citizens, CSOs have a unique ability to document and call attention to such a crime. They rarely have the power to punish the state directly, but they can use their ability to name and shame the government for its violations (Rubenstein 2004: 847–8). They can get word of the violations to the press, mobilize their members to protest the government's actions, and encourage other states to put diplomatic pressure on the offender. In a more cooperative vein, CSOs can assist states with the creation and maintenance of new structures that will ensure that governments protect their citizens' rights. Instead of calling attention to past wrongs, CSOs can work toward creating affirmative structures that promote rights, including the right to health, in the long term (Rubenstein 2004: 850).

Fourth, CSOs can fill a void. When governments fail to provide necessary services, CSOs can step in. Muhumuza links the emergence of strong CSOs in Uganda to the failure of the government in the 1980s to provide services, especially in more rural and hard-to-reach parts of the country (Muhumuza 2010: 3). Likewise, CSOs can put competitive pressure on the state and serve as a model for governance reform efforts (Harman 2009a: 363).

Finally, CSOs can mobilize a unique set of resources and advantages to promote their interests. They have members and financial resources at their disposal. They also often possess useful, specialized knowledge in a particular area and connections with the public that can assist with building public support for initiatives and programs. CSOs frequently also have developed ties with policymakers (both domestic and international) and members of the media that allow them to have disproportionate levels of influence (Mays 2008: 652–3). CSOs have gotten savvier about how they deploy these resources since the 1970s, better at using the media, understanding the political processes, and building alliances with organizations that may help them to achieve their ultimate ends (Anderson 2000: 445–6).

Governments also realize particular and unique benefits from collaborating with CSOs. First, working with CSOs can provide an added layer of legitimacy for government projects. Because CSOs are considered more democratic and more geared toward broad public participation, their involvement can imbue a project with an air of respectability and acceptance among the general populace. Second, CSOs can provide valuable information. They often specialize in particular areas, and they therefore develop high levels of expertise. That expertise can be crucial for reducing uncertainty and understanding the dynamics of a particular need. Third, CSOs can defray the costs of implementing new programs. They may provide staffing, outreach, facilities, or other in-kind contributions that significantly reduce the outlays required of the government. Finally, collaborating with CSOs can reduce some of the uncertainty associated with health interventions. CSOs presumably have ties to the communities in which they work, and those ties should reduce the likelihood of ill-conceived interventions. Through the CSOs, then, governments seek a measure of order and stability for their programs (Mays 2008: 654).

CSOs in Global Health Governance

CSOs have a long, albeit complicated, relationship with the structures of global health governance. The Constitution of the World Health Organization (WHO), written in 1946 and entered into force in 1948, explicitly recognizes the potential contribution that NGOs can make in promoting international health. Article 18(h) permits the World Health Assembly, WHO's governing body, to invite NGOs to participate in its deliberations and contribute to its debates, though they do not receive voting rights. Similarly, Article 71 allows WHO to cooperate and consult with CSOs as appropriate (World Health Organization 1946). These two articles allow WHO – an organization with a wholly state-based membership – to make explicit outreach to and enter into partnerships with organizations that operate outside the formal control of state governments. However, Davies notes that the same constitutional articles that permit collaboration with CSOs place strict limits on the circumstances under which such cooperation can occur. She highlights the fact that Articles 18(h) and 71 state that partnerships with national NGOs may only occur "with the consent of the Government concerned." In other words, a government has the ability to block the participation of any NGO for any reason (Davies 2010: 49). Governments could thus exclude the voices of CSOs which oppose their policies or wish to call attention to their failings. Such ambiguous attitudes toward CSOs from WHO's earliest days reflect the debates and confusion over the appropriate role for nongovernmental entities in international health.

The emergence of CSOs confronts two of the most important geopolitical realities in global health governance. On the one hand, the growing complexity of international health issues makes the development of comprehensive, holistic management strategies all the more important. On the other hand, though, the proliferation of actors getting involved in international health concerns has led to a diffusion of political authority and increasing difficulty in coordinating action (Lee 2010: 4–5). In developing countries, CSOs have typically focused on delivering health services directly. They filled gaps where government health services were absent or inadequate, rapidly proliferating and taking on a new prominence since the 1980s (Lee 2010: 2). The emergence of HIV/AIDS drove much of the growth of CSOs. When governments proved themselves unable or unwilling to extend services to HIV-positive persons, CSOs came to the forefront of providing care. These efforts have tended to be local in nature, often going largely unknown outside the immediate community. Their relative obscurity masks the enormous size of their contribution. Rau reports that NGOs, not governments, have provided the bulk of the financial contributors for HIV/AIDS care and treatment in developing countries (Rau 2006: 285–6).

Various efforts have sought to bring a measure of order to the relationships between governments and CSOs. WHO created its Civil Society Initiative in 2001 to review the relationships, both official and informal, between WHO and various CSOs. It also sought to facilitate better dialogue and collaboration among partners. Over the course of the initiative, an internal WHO review identified 482 relationships between CSOs and WHO. Of those, 56 percent were officially formalized. The review process brought a measure of importance to the role of CSOs, but it largely fell by the wayside once WHO Director-General Gro Harlem Brundtland left office in 2003. In 2006, WHO Director-General Margaret Chan publicly identified building partnerships with CSOs as one of her top priorities, but the nature and form of that commitment have largely remained undefined (Lee 2010: 3–4).

The year 2001 also witnessed efforts to incorporate CSOs into the United Nations General Assembly Special Session on HIV/AIDS. Leaders of the Special Session billed it as an opportunity for NGOs to influence policy, craft resolutions, and take an active role in deliberations. Given the prominent role that CSOs played in addressing HIV/AIDS and in shaming governments into assuming a more active stance on the issue, such an opportunity for consultation seemed particularly important (Lieberman 2009: 79–80). The realities, unfortunately, fell short. One participant noted that the process tended to be dominated by Americans and US-based organizations – a far cry from the broad-based participation envisioned. Furthermore, the CSOs' deliberative processes were undermined by a lack of analysis and information. CSOs simply did not have access to the budgetary figures or other data that would have allowed them to put forward realistic proposals that could have significantly influenced governments. Instead of being an opportunity for legitimate dialogue,

> The meeting was as much a ritual as a forum for exchange of ideas. Decisions about policy and best practice are made by high-level experts and bureaucrats prior to a meeting, often in consultation with the important NGOs. Leaders of the global governance regime *perceive* that civil society organizations, particularly with roots in the global South, must be consulted if the regime is to govern with authority. (Lieberman 2009: 85; emphasis added)

Consultations with CSOs, in this view, gave the appearance of collaboration without actually engaging in any sort of genuine collaboration. They gave the regime an air of authority and legitimacy without ever significantly altering anything.

Despite the cynicism that greeted some of the WHO–CSO collaborative efforts in the early part of the twenty-first century, the international community has continued to pursue the creation of opportunities for both sides to work together in crafting the global health governance architecture and promoting international health. The architecture increasingly draws on the skills and expertise of CSOs to assist with the formulation and implementation of formal rules. While nongovernmental entities cannot replace the state, governments increasingly turn responsibilities over to CSOs (Lee 2010: 17). For instance, the revised International Health Regulations (IHR), adopted in 2005, directly draw on engaging with CSOs as vital elements in conducting infectious disease surveillance. In a significant change from previous iterations of the treaty, the IHR (2005) explicitly allow nongovernmental sources to report information about disease outbreaks to WHO. Instead of relying solely on state-run entities, the IHR (2005) create a "network of networks" that links government resources and CSOs to strengthen monitoring capacities. In this model, CSOs fill crucial gaps, particularly where states lack resources or may have an incentive to prevent the release of information about outbreaks (Lee 2010: 12–14).

CSOs have entered the realm of global health governance as voices for the voiceless. Because they are assumed to be more democratic, more connected to local communities, more efficient, and more adaptable to changing conditions, they have taken on a prominent role in directly providing health services and agitating for policy changes by governments. They can convince states to act counter to their narrow material interests through pressure, campaigns, and public shaming (Busby 2007: 248). CSOs portray themselves as outside the political systems, and therefore able to project images of progressive action and working to provide public goods without getting bogged down in the morass of political conflict (Berry and Gabay 2009: 342).

The most successful CSOs navigate through the opportunities afforded them by the government, the state's historical legacies, and the institutional framework to make their presence felt (Gomez 2006: 149–50). In Brazil, for example, CSOs played a crucial role in the creation of the country's fairly successful response to HIV/AIDS. Brazilian public health CSOs actively fought for democracy's restoration, explicitly tying the return of democracy to expanding access to health care for the poor and disenfranchised. This "pressure from below" compelled the government to put AIDS high on its agenda and address HIV as an integral part of building its democratic legitimacy (Lieberman 2009: 128). CSOs have also played vital roles in the polio eradication campaign. The efforts of Rotary International, working in conjunction with WHO, cut the number of polio cases from 350,000 in 1988 to roughly 1,600 in 2009. Rotary International has raised the funds and provided volunteers to vaccinate millions of people worldwide. Religious CSOs have also played significant roles in helping to reduce the spread of polio. In northern Nigeria, rumors spread that polio vaccines sterilized Muslim girls and were part of a plot against Muslims. Thanks to the involvement of Muslim religious leaders and organizations, it was possible to counter these claims and convince many objectors that it was in their interest to receive the vaccine and that it would not sterilize Muslim girls (Guth 2010; Kaufmann and Feldbaum 2009).

Despite this high promise, there exist significant limits on the ability of CSOs to provide services and effect meaningful changes within the international community. These limits constrain the independence of CSOs, restrict their authority, and undermine the democratic and participatory bona fides of these groups. Three limitations on CSO efficacy deserve particular attention. First, CSOs are assumed to be democratic and participatory, but these assumptions do not necessarily match reality. CSOs are not inherently egalitarian or member-driven, despite frequent rhetoric to the contrary. Chaplowe and Engo-Tjega remind us, "The participatory potential of African CSOs must not be romanticized . . . CSOs grapple with the same internal inequality and power relations that occur at any level of human organizations. CSOs should not be assumed to be fair and democratic" (Chaplowe and Engo-Tjega 2007: 262–3). CSOs exhibit a vast range of opportunities for members (and non-members) to have a voice and express their opinions. There is nothing about a small or local group that automatically dictates that it will provide multiple venues for meaningful dialogue and participation with that group's leadership structures. CSOs may not necessarily have established ties with the communities in which they work and thus may have little interest in facilitating participation by local residents. Mozambique in the late 1980s and 1990s saw waves of CSOs emerge as the state retreated from direct service provision. The large international NGOs attracted significant attention and funds, but they offered few venues for popular participation or democracy within their structures and encountered significant challenges in sustaining volunteer participation (Pfeiffer 2004: 360). Furthermore, there emerge serious questions about the representativeness and legitimacy of CSOs. No democratic procedures exist to designate one group or another the spokespeople for a group or a community (Doyle and Patel 2008: 1929). CSOs get access to funds from donors and contracts to provide services based in part on their claims of representativeness, but it is difficult to assess how well any CSO actually speaks for the group it claims to represent. No elections affirm the popular support a CSO has, and groups lack effective tools for withdrawing their support from CSOs that no longer enjoy popular confidence (Doyle and Patel 2008: 1932–3). There is thus an unrepresentative procedure to designate representative groups that may or may not actually be all that representative.

Second, CSOs' independence from outside groups may be questionable. CSOs need resources to function. Service provision and activism for better health services do not happen for free. Without some sort of revenue stream, a group's capabilities for participation decrease precipitously and the group becomes largely invisible to the very policymakers it wishes to influence (Schurmann and Mahmud 2009: 540–1). To get these resources, though, CSOs may find themselves beholden to outside interests and governments that have their own agendas. CSOs that provide health services and publicly disagree with the government may lose their access to funds. If those groups then turn to international funders, they tend to become dependent upon their donors and embrace a Western global agenda over more parochial local interests (Muhumuza 2010: 9). The need for continued funding from donors may discourage CSOs from working on longer-term structural issues. Donors want results, which induces a bias toward short-term, quantifiable measures at the expense of working on strengthening local health systems or ensuring access to health clinics. CSOs make the rational calculation to focus on the "low-hanging fruit" that increases the likelihood of continued funding (Doyle and Patel 2008: 1935). By the same token, international donors have demonstrated a reluctance to support any activities that may be construed as "activism." These donors aim to maintain an image of impartiality, staying out of domestic partisan politics, so they state that they will only fund service provision. Though some groups argue that activism and service provision are inseparable, international donors frequently disagree with CSOs that want to emphasize activism (Evensen and Stokke 2010: 161–2).

Finally, the increasing prominence of CSOs leads to increasing confusion over their identities. Many CSOs attempt to act as both *market* actors, by directly providing health services to their communities, and *social* actors, who are trying to represent nonmarket interests and give voice to the disenfranchised. These identities, though, are largely in opposition to each other (Berry and Gabay 2009: 344). CSOs have a difficult time operating both as service providers who have a stake in the system and as critics of that very system. If they act as contractors for the state, implementing programs and delivering services in areas where the government cannot or will not reach, then their dependence on the state for that contract weakens their ability to effectively challenge and chastise the state (Seckinelgin 2004: 298–9). CSOs are reluctant to bite the hand that feeds them by openly challenging the state structures upon which they depend, and CSO service providers frequently find it difficult to effectively serve as critics of the government or advocates for their own supporters (Schurmann and Mahmud 2009: 542).

A brief examination of two different types of CSOs – one a large international NGO working around the world (Oxfam International) and one a national NGO with a strong activist orientation that also engages in service provision for a single disease (Treatment Action Campaign, or TAC) – shows the opportunities and challenges for CSOs taking a more prominent role in global health governance.

Oxfam International

Oxfam International is a confederation of 14 national organizations working in more than 99 countries alongside more than 3,000 local organizations worldwide to combat poverty and injustice. Based in the United Kingdom,

Oxfam International traces its origins to 1942 with the creation of the Oxford Committee for Famine Relief. It originally focused on shipping food to starving families in occupied and blockaded Greece. In 1965, the organization renamed itself Oxfam to better reflect its expanding mission to combat the causes of famine, support long-term and sustainable economic development, and respond to humanitarian crises. Around the same time, Oxfam expanded beyond the United Kingdom to create affiliate organizations in Canada, the United States, and other countries. In 2010, official Oxfam organizations existed in Australia, Belgium, Canada, France, Germany, Hong Kong, Ireland, Mexico, the Netherlands, New Zealand, Quebec, Spain, the United Kingdom, and the United States; "observer" members of the confederation exist in India, Italy, and Japan. While each of the national affiliates maintains its own administrative offices, Oxfam International itself maintains its headquarters in Oxford; international advocacy offices in Washington, New York, Brussels, Geneva, and Brasilia; and an advocacy liaison office in Addis Ababa. For the 2007/8 biennium, Oxfam International spent US$771.75 million on direct program expenditures – an increase of approximately US$66 million over the 2006/7 biennium.

Historically, Oxfam International focused on providing assistance and relief to those afflicted by disasters. In 2000, the organization shifted its energies. Instead of responding to dire situations, it would concentrate on addressing the structural causes of poverty and injustice. This required the organization to redirect its attention to systemic analyses of global governance and understanding how those structures contributed to vulnerabilities and undermined people's abilities to realize their basic needs and rights (Aaronson and Zimmerman 2006: 999). Today, Oxfam International organizes its activities around a commitment to five broad-based areas of rights: the right to a sustainable livelihood, the right to basic social services, the right to life and security, the right to be heard, and the right to an identity. Within these rights, the organization prioritizes four key areas for action: economic justice, essential services, gender justice, and rights in crisis (Oxfam International 2007: 2–4). Health figures prominently in Oxfam International's work to provide essential services and ensure the rights to basic social services and to life and security. Oxfam works both as an advocate, trying to raise awareness and challenge national and international policies, and as a direct provider of health services itself.

In its advocacy work, Oxfam International has sought to call attention to inequities in access to health care services and vital pharmaceuticals, as well as the international trade and intellectual property rules that prevent those in poor countries from realizing their right to health. In February 2001, Oxfam partnered with a variety of other CSOs on the Cut the Cost Campaign to reduce prices and increase access for basic medicines in developing states.

This campaign operated on two levels. First, it sought to pressure pharmaceutical manufacturers to lower their prices in poor states and to refrain from taking aggressive actions to punish states for manufacturing their own generic versions of drugs or engaging in parallel importing. Second, the campaign encouraged WHO to invest in drug research itself and create a subsidy pool to lower drug costs in poor countries (Aaronson and Zimmerman 2006: 1013–14). The argument on this second level was essentially that trade- and market-based solutions to inequitable access to drugs would be unlikely to work. Instead, WHO needed to intervene to alter market incentives and conduct its own research as a global public good. As part of its efforts, Oxfam put notices on its website, chastising pharmaceutical companies like Pfizer for lobbying for stronger patent protections. It also encouraged letter-writing campaigns, had its activists interrupt corporate meetings, and sponsored a documentary on UK's Channel Four called *Dying for Drugs*. The public attention forced Pfizer and other pharmaceutical companies to sign the United Nations Global Compact, pledging to abide by ethical practices, and take more proactive measures to reduce barriers to drug access in the developing world in 2002 (Cuddeford Jones 2003: 23). GlaxoSmithKline went even further. In 2009, the pharmaceutical manufacturer announced that, in response to Oxfam's campaign, it would reduce the price of all of its drugs to the world's 52 poorest countries and invest 20 percent of its profits from sales in the least-developed countries in those states' health care infrastructures (Oxfam International 2009b: 9). While these steps did not end Oxfam's campaign, they demonstrated Oxfam's ability to rally public opinion and hold multinational institutions accountable for their actions.

As part of its Health and Education for All Campaign, Oxfam International has chastised the international community for under-providing health services, charging high health care fees in poor countries, and relying too heavily on the private market to deliver health care. Oxfam International challenges the notion that the private sector can better address health care needs in developing countries: private sector participation increases the costs associated with health care, provides little oversight or regulation of clinics, attracts minimal outside investment, offers lower-quality care, introduces additional inefficiency into the system, decreases access, and does not reduce corruption (Oxfam International 2009b: 2–5). This campaign involves an online petition, where signers pledge their willingness "to take action and to call for action from governments and institutions to ensure quality healthcare and education for all people" (Oxfam GB n.d.). The campaign also relies on celebrity advocates to raise public attention, encourage local involvement, and meet with policymakers.

When it comes to direct service provision, Oxfam generally partners with local organizations to establish health care clinics and ensure access to clean water and sanitation. One project, the Joint Oxfam HIV/AIDS Project (JOHAP), works in South Africa to ensure delivery of home-based services. Beyond that, though, it also incorporates a variety of efforts to foster economic development and provide a means of living for communities afflicted by HIV/AIDS (Oxfam International 2009a: 8). JOHAP and projects like it aim to address the structural factors that undermine access to health services. In addition to meeting short-term needs, these programs foster long-term projects and demonstrate the interconnectedness of health, justice, and economic development.

Oxfam International's efforts certainly reach a large number of people, but their methods and approach have attracted scrutiny from some critics. In particular, critics have challenged Oxfam for being too cozy with governments. Instead of representing the interests of the afflicted groups on whose behalf it claims to speak, Oxfam has prioritized maintaining access to governments and embraced and promoted their neoliberal ideologies. The exchange of personnel between the upper echelons of Oxfam International's management and board of directors and the British government under Tony Blair and Gordon Brown raised concerns (Quarmby 2005). Other groups have noted that, as these exchanges became more frequent during the Labour governments, Oxfam International's public messages and ideologies were far closer to the government's than those of other development-oriented CSOs. One senior official at a different development NGO chastised Oxfam for getting too close to the government and selling out fellow development organizations: "We have spent so much time hammering out agreed lines between the organizations, and then Oxfam just departs from the hymn sheet" (cited in Quarmby 2005). The close relationship makes Oxfam less effective in pressing the government to change its policies because it is seen as being too acquiescent.

Along these lines, Berry and Gabay argue that Oxfam International's approach pays far too little attention to conditions on the ground in the communities where it works. Instead, Oxfam promotes a universalized normative acceptance of the general outlines of neoliberal globalization – even though these are the very structural features that make it difficult for developing countries to achieve sustained development (Berry and Gaby 2009: 340). Instead of being a voice for genuine change, Oxfam becomes a tool for encouraging developing countries to accept the global political and economic system that is keeping them down.

These criticisms speak to the question of how well CSOs can be both insiders and outsiders. They also raise concerns about how responsive the large international NGOs in particular are to the communities they serve versus the access and donors they have in Western countries. Is it possible for large international CSOs to embrace and embody the ideals of democratic participation and collaboration with local communities? Oxfam International's critics suggest that talk of participation, democracy, and concern for local needs is largely rhetorical and does not actively affect policy decisions.

Treatment Action Campaign

The Treatment Action Campaign (TAC) draws explicitly on South Africa's struggle to abolish apartheid in order to press for greater attention to HIV/AIDS issues. TAC was founded on December 10, 1998 – International Human Rights Day – in Cape Town with a mission to build a racially diverse, grassroots movement to gain greater access to ARVs. The group's founders initially believed that their primary target would be the multinational pharmaceutical companies that produce ARVs. However, after the government refused to make ARVs available despite a Constitutional Court ruling compelling it to do so, the TAC began to focus its energies on changing government policies (Friedman and Mottiar 2005: 513–14).

Many TAC activists and volunteers derive inspiration from their backgrounds in the anti-apartheid movement and use that experience as their inspiration. Zackie Achmat, the group's founder and chairperson, cites Nelson Mandela, the former South African president and leader of the anti-apartheid movement, as his model. Mandela and the anti-apartheid movement expanded the frontier of freedom in South Africa, and Achmat sees TAC as continuing that work (Das 2004: 468). By its own admission, TAC draws heavily on the anti-apartheid movement, using similar language, symbols, and songs. Dwyer notes that TAC's activities are rooted within the tradition of resistance that developed during the apartheid era and that TAC finds similar uses for traditional songs, dances, and speeches to spread its message (Dwyer 2003: 77–9). To pressure the national government, the group also uses a wide variety of tactics, such as civil disobedience, mass protests, litigation, training future activists, and providing social services (Jones 2005: 436). Drawing on the legacy of the anti-apartheid movement also increases TAC's legitimacy and allows the group to counter accusations that it is unpatriotic or "un-African" (Robins 2004: 665).

With the government led by the African National Congress (ANC) sensitive to charges of rights abuses, TAC has brought legal cases charging violations in such venues as the Constitutional Court, Human Rights Commission, and Commission on Gender Equity. The cases have been key to TAC's tactics, as these draw specifically on the human rights guarantees embodied in the South African Constitution and Bill of Rights. These documents charge the government with specific positive obligations to uphold an array of individual rights, including those to equality, dignity, and access to health care (Fitzpatrick and Skye 2003: 675–7; Friedman and Mottiar 2005: 532–3). Moreover, the ANC and the government are relatively sensitive to charges of violating human rights (Friedman and Mottiar 2005: 532–3). Given the rhetoric and promises made by the ANC during the apartheid era, it wants to avoid being accused of the same thing it criticized the apartheid-era government for doing. Combining court cases and public actions creates a dynamism between the courtroom and civil society and furthers the group's mission of educating South Africans about their human rights in the context of AIDS (Jones 2005: 436).

AIDS activists in South Africa benefit from the country's expansive approach to human rights. Between the country's Constitution and Bill of Rights, South Africans enjoy perhaps the most generous guarantees of human rights in the world. This is not surprising, given the domestic and international context in which the Constitution and Bill of Rights were written. The Constitution was a repudiation of apartheid's denial of rights, while the international involvement in the anti-apartheid movement and the end of the Cold War opened up considerable political space. The Constitution and Bill of Rights charge the government with specific positive obligations to uphold the array of rights guaranteed to South Africa's citizens (Fitzpatrick and Skye 2003: 675–7). AIDS activists have recognized this reality and used it skillfully. Phillips writes, "Active involvement by [the courts and the South African Law Commission] in defense of individuals' rights again highlights that AIDS was the first epidemic in South Africa in which the rights of all infected citizens were vigorously asserted and upheld in public. It was the first epidemic to occur within a context of a burgeoning human rights culture" (Phillips 2004: 43).

TAC explicitly also draws on international human rights treaties to justify its positions. In a 2006 report to the African Peer Review Mechanism, TAC lambasted the government for failing to fully implement a comprehensive AIDS program that included access to antiretroviral drugs. "Government has a duty to respond appropriately to the HIV epidemic," the report's authors wrote (Treatment Action Campaign 2006: 6). As evidence, it singled out Article 25 of the Universal Declaration of Human Rights (on the right to an adequate standard of living for health and well-being), Article 16 of the African Charter of Human and Peoples' Rights (on the right to health and the government's responsibility to ensure it), the Rome Statute of the International Criminal Court (on crimes against humanity including the denial of medicine), and Section 27 of the South African Constitution (on the right to health care services and the government's responsibility to provide them) (Treatment Action Campaign 2006: 6–7). TAC uses these treaties, to which South Africa is a party, to shame the government and gain legitimacy for its own position.

AIDS activists in South Africa have portrayed access to anti-AIDS drugs as a human rights issue. Failure to provide these drugs, TAC argued, represented a failure by the government to positively uphold the rights of all South Africans to health care, dignity, and equality. When the government refused to provide ARVs to HIV-positive pregnant women, claiming that the drugs had too many side effects, TAC took the government to court for violating human rights – and won (Barnard 2002: 165–9). For many years, Achmat refused to take ARVs, even though his private insurance coverage would provide them, until all South Africans had access to these drugs. He stated,

"We also die because men have greater access to resources and power than women, because rich countries invest substantially more in war than public goods, and because many global corporations live outside the law of global human rights" (Achmat 2004). TAC and other groups have remained active on this issue, challenging the government's slow roll-out of a national ARV program and its failure to implement a coherent national strategy to fight the spread of AIDS.

As a service provider, TAC has concentrated on providing access to ARVs. Often, this occurs in partnership with other groups. Evensen and Stokke examine TAC's efforts in Lusikisiki, a rural area in the Eastern Cape of South Africa. This is one of the first large-scale rural HIV/AIDS treatment programs, and it exists as a partnership between TAC, Médecins Sans Frontières (MSF, known in English as Doctors Without Borders), and the South African Department of Health (SADOH) (Evensen and Stokke 2010: 151-2). Given the conflictual relationship between TAC and the South African government, this is a potentially fraught collaboration – but also one that draws on the respective strengths of each organization. TAC and MSF have worked together on prior projects, so they have an established relationship. TAC excels at mobilizing people and directing them toward service providers, so its history could help generate attention for the project and ensure that people take advantage of it. Further, as an activist organization, TAC could put pressure on SADOH to uphold its obligations and could call attention to any failures by the government to deliver sufficient quantities of ARVs. Because MSF holds contracts with SADOH for a wide range of service provision throughout the country, it did not feel that it could put those contracts at risk by publicly chastising the government (Evensen and Stokke 2010: 158-9).

This service provider relationship puts TAC in a somewhat awkward position. It traditionally engages in a "politics of engagement" by calling attention to and putting pressure on the government while also mobilizing the public on the basis of human rights. However, in entering into a relationship with the state to jointly provide services, it has made it difficult for itself to simultaneously oppose the government (Evensen and Stokke 2010: 160-1).

Conclusion

Civil society organizations have assumed a significant role in the global health governance system. They have called attention to failures by state governments to address health concerns, implemented their own health programs, and raised international awareness about health challenges. Because they exist independently of state governments, they position themselves above the political fray and are able to engage in actions that would be politically challenging. They can pressure governments to live up to their obligations to safeguard the human rights of their citizens by promoting good health. Conversely, many CSOs argue that human rights violations fuel ill health because they alienate people from support services and foster the structural violence that keeps marginalized groups disenfranchised. With their independence, though, CSOs position themselves as better able to respond to these needs and ensure people have access to care. They also argue that they are able to respond to changing situations quickly and efficiently.

It is, however, their very independence that raises questions about how representative and democratic they truly are. The organizations briefly profiled in this chapter show a small slice of the diversity that exists among health-oriented civil society organizations.

As CSOs play a greater role within global health governance, it becomes all the more imperative to find some way to coordinate the vast range of actors getting involved in the issue. Otherwise, the risk grows ever greater that global health governance will become increasingly scattershot and fail to address the entire range of international health concerns.

PART III

Key Issues

Key Issues

CHAPTER SEVEN

The Global Infectious Disease Surveillance Regime

Surveillance has long played a central role in the international community's response to cross-border health concerns. If states are to effectively mobilize to prevent the spread of infectious diseases, they need to know where those diseases are, how they are spreading, and who is getting infected. Early quarantine procedures offered a crude version of surveillance, and the International Sanitary Convention provided some measure of international public health surveillance on a small scale.

Since World War II ended, the international community's thinking about infectious disease has evolved significantly. With the massive changes to the international political and economic arenas in the war's aftermath, the previous international health governance institutions were not suited for the surveillance tasks that would face them in the remade world. Immediately after the war, the international community brought a measure of rationality and coherence to the global surveillance regime – but with a tight focus on a few specific infectious diseases. Over time, though, this approach proved inadequate and ushered in a wholesale revolution in the international community's conceptualization of and approach to infectious disease surveillance.

The changes in infectious disease surveillance mirror the evolving conceptions of global health within the international community. They also reflect the global health governance regime's move beyond its traditional state-centric model to embrace a more global perspective that involved a wider range of actors.

This chapter centers on the International Health Regulations. This treaty forms the basis of the international community's legal obligations to engage in infectious disease surveillance to this day, but it has undergone massive transformations since the end of World War II. The changes in the International Health Regulations reflect how the international community's thinking about who should conduct infectious disease surveillance and by what means have evolved over time. I begin by describing the creation of the International Sanitary Regulations, later renamed the International Health Regulations, in the early days of WHO. I then describe how and why the World Health Organization began to revise the International Health Regulations in the 1990s, and the resultant treaty. Finally, I describe the criticisms of the current version of the International Health Regulations and their benefits to the international community.

The International Sanitary Regulations and International Health Regulations

One of WHO's first orders of business after its creation was coordinating the hodgepodge of international sanitary conventions and treaties. Article 21(a) of the WHO Constitution specifically empowered the World Health Assembly (WHA), the annual meeting of all WHO member-states, to adopt regulations regarding "sanitary and quarantine requirements and other procedures designed to prevent the international spread of disease." Article 22 specified that any such regulations and requirements would be binding on WHO member-states unless they specifically opted out of them (World Health Organization 1946). Thus, WHO made it easier for the organization to adopt just one set of international legal rules to replace the panoply of conventions and ease the process of revising those regulations in the future (Fidler 2005: 332–3).

In 1951, the Fourth World Health Assembly adopted the International Sanitary Regulations (ISR), combining and replacing 12 existing international health conventions. On October 1, 1952, the ISR entered into effect (Jacobini 1952: 727). This established one set of international rules to guide infectious disease control measures, and it firmly entrenched WHO as the lead international organization on health-related matters. The revisions, it was hoped, would streamline international infectious disease control measures and clarify lines of responsibility (Fidler 2005: 333).

The ISR laid out five broad requirements for all member-states to follow. First, the Regulations identified six notifiable diseases: smallpox, cholera, yellow fever, typhus, relapsing fever, and plague. Second, governments were required to notify WHO of any human cases of the notifiable diseases within their territory, and subsequently to follow up with WHO when the area was free from infection. Third, countries had to implement hygiene measures at border crossings, ports, and airports to screen international cargo and personnel for notifiable diseases. Fourth, states could, at their discretion, require travelers to present health and vaccination certificates prior to entering their territory. Finally, the measures declared that the ISR were the maximum measures permissible under international law (Gostin 2004: 2624).

Revisions in 1969 renamed the ISR the International Health Regulations (IHR) and removed typhus and relapsing fever from the list of notifiable diseases. Later revisions amended the procedures for dealing with cholera (1973) and removed smallpox after the success of the global eradication campaign (1981). These changes were relatively minor, largely leaving intact the basic requirements to which all member-states were subject. The IHR

(1969) became the basis of international cooperation on controlling the spread of infectious diseases.

In the 1980s and 1990s, the IHR (1969) became the subject of controversy and acrimony. Critics called them anachronistic and irrelevant. The criticisms proceeded along five main lines. First, the IHR's disease-specific approach was increasingly viewed as too narrow. Most WHO-sponsored programs through the 1980s focused on technical solutions for discrete diseases (Walt 2001: 683). This approach spurred the development and promotion of techniques like spraying DDT to control malaria and developing vaccines to treat diseases like smallpox. As WHO's membership grew throughout the 1960s and 1970s thanks to decolonization, though, member-states increasingly called this strategy into question. Walt notes, "Health policies shifted from a technological, disease orientation to a more development, multisectoral primary health care approach in the late 1970s" (Walt 2001: 681). Governments and their citizens were less interested in protecting themselves from specific diseases and more interested in promoting their overall health in a holistic sense. They took seriously the Preamble of the WHO Constitution and its assertions that "health is a complete state of physical, mental, and social well-being and not merely the absence of disease or infirmity . . . the enjoyment of the highest attainable standard of health is one of the fundamental rights of every human being" (World Health Organization 1946). They rejected the previously dominant notion that health is separable from broader social and economic structures. Achieving health, therefore, was not simply about eliminating discrete diseases; it involved widespread economic, political, cultural, and social changes (Packard and Brown 1997: 183–4).

Second, developed states increasingly took less of an interest in the IHR and infectious disease control in general. Industrialized states had largely eliminated the IHR's notifiable diseases from their borders prior to 1969, and public health officials in some countries had declared the era of infectious disease to be over. Humanity has won the battle against microbes, they argued, so attention should focus on chronic disease like heart disease (Price-Smith 2001: 3–4). This decrease in interest from the industrialized states led to a concurrent decline in available funds and personnel. Fidler writes, "Neither WHO nor developing countries had the interest or incentives to replace or overhaul the engine" (Fidler 2005: 335). The states that could contribute the most to international infectious disease control efforts lacked the interest or desire to do so, and the countries that stood to benefit the most from such efforts lacked the resources to make it happen on their own.

Third, states were simply not complying with the IHR's requirements. Some states failed to report outbreaks to WHO in a timely manner, or they deliberately underreported the number of cases of a particular disease. Others failed to maintain the public hygiene measures required at ports of entry and exit. Governments also tried to require health certificates from travelers for non-notifiable diseases, particularly HIV/AIDS. These measures exceeded the maximum allowable requirements under the IHR, but states offered no scientific justification for introducing them (Gostin 2004: 2624). These failures to adhere to the basic tenets of the IHR sent a clear message to the international community that the Regulations were failing to meet their stated objectives.

The cause of these failures is multifaceted. In some instances, states lacked the resources and personnel necessary to conduct the required surveillance. In countries where even basic health services were largely absent, it is unsurprising that government officials would not prioritize the IHR's reporting and surveillance requirements. In many cases, spending more on disease surveillance resources came at the expense of spending less on primary health care resources (Morse 2007: 1072). States also feared the consequences of reporting human cases of cholera, smallpox, yellow fever, or plague. Failing to report an outbreak could lead to disapproval or even condemnation from WHO (Plotkin and Kimball 1997: 3). Acknowledging the presence of these feared diseases within its borders, though, could have a devastating effect on a country's economy and standing within the international community. Potentially compounding the situation, the IHR lacked any mechanism to prevent such overreaction by others (Abdullah 2007: 11–12). Proper surveillance could inadvertently cause sanctioning and ostracism. Velimirovic sympathized with a state's decision not to report outbreaks to WHO:

> This failure to report promptly need not be an arbitrary measure or a sign of misunderstanding the concept of surveillance; it is sometimes an unfortunate but necessary means of self-protection against irrational requirements imposed by other countries, which bring on the reporting country a severe penalty through loss in trade, tourism, etc. (Velimirovic 1976: 479–80)

No state wanted the stigma of being singled out within the international community as diseased or unable to handle its health problems. A cholera outbreak in Peru in 1991 cost the country an estimated US$700 million in lost trade and travel embargoes. A plague outbreak in Surat, India, three years later cost the country an estimated US$1.7 billion in lost trade and tourism revenues (Aginam 2002: 947). In both cases, the national governments of the afflicted states did their utmost to prevent information from getting out or downplayed the situation's severity – not out of malice, but out of fear of the consequences.

Fourth, the IHR relied on a completely passive surveillance system entirely dependent upon government sources. WHO had to wait for reports to trickle in from official sources within member-states. The IHR did not require, nor did they necessarily encourage, member-states to implement proactive surveillance measures that would allow for the timely notification of any human cases of the notifiable diseases. Article 3 of the International Health Regulations required the following of member-states:

Each health administration shall notify the [World Health] Organization by telegram or telex within twenty-four hours of its being informed that the first case of a disease subject to the Regulations, that is neither an imported case nor a transferred case, has occurred in its territory, and, within the subsequent twenty-four hours, notify the infected area. (World Health Organization 1983: 10)

This arrangement respected the sovereignty of the individual states, but it did little to encourage assertive actions to detect diseases. The IHR offered little semblance of structure to surveillance efforts. Who would or should report diseases to a state's health administration? Who within that health administration should transmit the information to WHO? Do rumors or reports from non-official sources count? The IHR are silent on all of these important questions. By not spelling out a framework for reporting, the Regulations allowed states to shirk their responsibilities and added to confusion. WHO, in this arrangement, is wholly dependent upon official government sources – the same government officials who, as noted above, may have a very real incentive *not* to report cases.

Finally, the IHR no longer reflected the health problems that afflicted the world. After the 1981 revisions, the IHR only covered three diseases: cholera, yellow fever, and plague. These diseases, while significant, were hardly the most pressing infectious disease concerns facing the international community. The IHR's narrow focus on three specific diseases undermined the Regulations' effectiveness. They instead became "a glorious monument and a self-serving ritual as much as a measure of protection, collective or individual" (Velimirovic 1976: 478). More importantly, the microbial world had changed since 1969. New diseases emerged, and previously contained diseases re-emerged with a vengeance. During the last quarter of the twentieth century, American public health officials identified at least 33 new pathogens that negatively affect human health (Price-Smith 2001: 3). The IHR were completely useless for addressing these diseases. If states attempted to use IHR measures to prevent the spread of these new diseases (such as requiring health certificates for travelers coming from infected regions), they would be found in violation of WHO rules and, by extension, international law. The Regulations proved far too inflexible to adapt to the changing realities of human health and disease around the world.

Revising the International Health Regulations

Frustration with the IHR led the World Health Assembly to pass WHA Resolution 48.7 in 1995. This resolution requested that the WHO Director-General undertake a massive revision of the IHR to make them more relevant and effective (Aginam 2002: 948). Passing this resolution, the World Health Assembly acknowledged that the IHR failed to accomplish their fundamental goals – providing maximum protection from the international spread of infectious diseases while causing minimal interference with global travel and commerce (Fidler 2003: 286).

Initial reform attempts sought to move from a disease-specific to a syndrome-specific reporting system. The 1998 Provisional IHR proposed notification of six acute syndromes: hemorrhagic fever; respiratory; diarrheal; jaundice; neurological; and others with a presumed infectious origin (Thuriaux 2003: 157). By emphasizing syndromes rather than specific diseases, WHO hoped that the Regulations would be more broadly applicable. WHO also hoped it would lead to more timely reporting of outbreaks; states need not wait until they had a specific diagnosis to make an official report to WHO. The revisions also proposed to only make outbreaks reportable if and when they constituted "an event of urgent international importance" (Thuriaux 2003: 157). States would only face a reporting obligation if the disease posed a significant threat of spreading internationally, had an unusually high fatality rate, represented a previously unrecognized condition, or threatened to require trade or travel restrictions. Under these revisions, though, the committee leading the rewriting process affirmed its continued belief that reports to WHO should only come from national governments (World Health Organization 1999).

While an improvement, these proposed revisions did not meet with widespread acceptance among WHO member-states. They objected that the reforms did not go far enough; they still relied too heavily on a passive surveillance system and focused on particular ailments. They presented the international community with some tinkering around the edges, not the restructuring called for in WHA Resolution 48.7.

Over the next five years, revising the IHR took a less prominent role on the international health agenda. The international community focused more on trade-related intellectual property rights and access to vital medicines, deflecting attention away from the IHR revisions. Initial hopes for completing the revisions by May 1998 got pushed back to May 1999 and later, until the World Health Assembly passed Resolution 56.23 in 2003 requiring that the revisions be completed in time for its 2005 meeting (Fidler 2004).

The outbreak of SARS in 2003 gave a new urgency to revising the IHR. Here was a previously unknown disease whose spread could be clearly and definitively linked with international travel, and the resulting trade and travel restrictions clearly cost the affected countries billions of dollars. Some states recognized the value and importance of sharing information, while others (most notably, China) refused to acknowledge the extent of SARS' spread within their borders. The SARS outbreak saw WHO clearly emerge as the central repository of information, analysis, and policy recommendations (Kamradt-Scott 2010: 2–4). It presented the world with "an opportunity to develop new governance structures between multiple actors as infectious diseases continue to interact with humans in the national, international, and global contexts" (Aginam 2005: 60). WHO received widespread praise for its handling of and response to the SARS outbreak (Fidler 2005: 354), but it took all of these actions outside of any specified international legal obligation. This disjuncture motivated the committee revising the IHR, encouraging them to present a document to the World Health Assembly quickly.

In January 2004, the first full draft of the revised IHR appeared.[4] Negotiations over the proposed revisions began in November 2004 and continued through May 2005. On May 14, 2005, the assembled delegates reached agreement on the proposed IHR and sent them to the World Health Assembly meeting in Geneva for its approval. On May 23, 2005, the World Health Assembly passed Resolution 58.3 and called upon states to ratify and implement the revised IHR (World Health Organization 2005d). Two years later, on June 15, 2007, the revised IHR formally entered into force as a legally binding agreement under international law.

The revised IHR, or IHR (2005), have the same basic purpose as previous versions – "to prevent, protect against, control and provide a public health response to the international spread of disease in ways that are commensurate with and restricted to public health risks, and which avoid unnecessary interference with international traffic and trade" (World Health Organization 2005a) – but they seek to achieve these goals in very different ways. Four key differences exist between the IHR (2005) and earlier versions, and these differences get to the heart of surveillance, human rights, and global health governance.

First, the scope of conditions that fall under the IHR's purview expanded tremendously. Previous versions focused on discrete diseases long associated with trade and travel. The IHR (2005) jettisoned that model. The new Regulations encompass an "all risks" approach (Fidler and Gostin 2006: 86–7). Instead of specifying particular diseases, the IHR (2005) require states to report "all events which may constitute a public health emergency of international concern within its territory" (Article 6). They further define a "public health emergency of international concern" as an "extraordinary event which . . . constitute[s] a public health risk to other States through the international spread of disease and . . . potentially require[s] a coordinated international response" (Article 1). This could include infectious diseases as well as radiological or chemical incidents. National governments must assess the severity of any such outbreak within 48 hours of initial detection and send a report to WHO within 24 hours of confirmation (Sturtevant et al. 2007: 118). This report should include case definitions, laboratory findings, morbidity and mortality incidents, risk factors, and initial public health responses.

Given the broadened scope of the IHR (2005), how can states assess whether a particular incident constitutes a "public health emergency of international concern"? Annex 2 of the IHR (2005) provides states with a decision making instrument (see figure 7.1). Human cases of smallpox, polio caused by wild-type poliovirus, SARS, and influenza of a new subtype are immediately

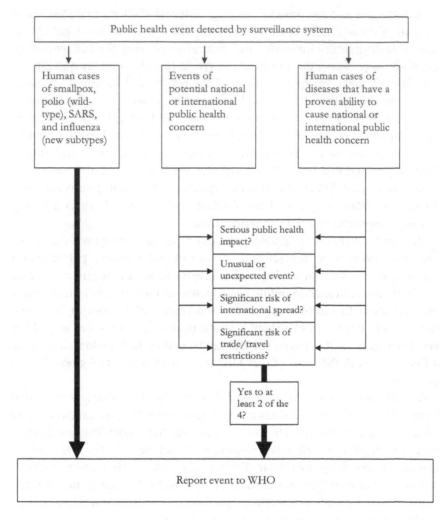

Figure 7.1 *Decisionmaking instrument for the IHR (2005), adapted from Annex 2*

reportable to WHO. Diseases that have historically demonstrated an ability to cause national and international concern (such as cholera, pneumonic plague, yellow fever, and viral hemorrhagic fevers) and other illnesses that could constitute an international public health concern (particularly unknown illnesses or those whose cause or source are unknown) are subject to four questions:

1. Is the public health impact of the event serious?
2. Is the event unusual or unexpected?
3. Is there a significant risk of the international spread of the disease?
4. Is there a significant risk of restrictions on international travel and/or trade?

If public health officials answer "yes" to at least two of the above four questions, then they must make a report to WHO.

Second, the IHR (2005) significantly change the surveillance structures at the national level. Each state must designate a National IHR Focal Point accessible at all times for communicating with WHO (Article 1). The National IHR Focal Point must take responsibility for sending communication required by the IHR (2005) to the appropriate contact at WHO. It must further collect and disseminate information from various sources within the state relevant for monitoring potential public health events of international importance (Article 4).

The national surveillance structures must also take a proactive role in monitoring the public health situation within their borders. Instead of waiting for reports, these Focal Points are responsible for "develop[ing], strengthen[ing], and maintain[ing] . . . the capacity to detect, assess, notify, and report events" (Article 5). A state's public health surveillance system must have the capability to find problems without waiting for other sources to pass the information along to it. This requires "establishing strong technical leadership during field responses, building local capacity for future epidemics, and ensuring respect for legal, human rights, and cultural sensitivities" (Sturtevant et al. 2007: 117). States must develop basic core surveillance capacities to detect unusual public health events, report vital epidemiological information to relevant authorities, and immediately implement control measures (Wilson et al. 2008: 216). The IHR (2005) do not specify the exact structure of the national surveillance systems, but they do tell states what those surveillance systems must produce. The IHR (2005) gave states until June 15, 2012, to assess their capacities and implement the required surveillance structures. By March 2008, nearly all WHO member-states had designated National IHR Focal Points.

These changes give far more guidance to states. Previously, the IHR left questions about surveillance relatively unspecified. With its focus on a few specific diseases, it encouraged passive surveillance systems. In order to adequately address the greatly expanded realm of potentially relevant public health events, the IHR (2005) require a far more proactive and expansive notion of surveillance.

Third, the IHR (2005) allow more actors to report public health emergencies to WHO. Under previous versions of the IHR, non-state sources could not report disease outbreaks. This exclusive reliance on official sources created a bottleneck in the reporting system. If a state government chose not to report an outbreak, there existed no alternative means by which WHO could learn about and act upon human cases of a notifiable disease. Earlier versions of the IHR also failed to make allowances for sub-state structures to bypass national officials and report cases directly to WHO.

Under the IHR (2005), WHO can "take into account reports from sources other than notifications or consultations" from official governmental sources

(Article 9). Upon receiving reports from these nongovernmental sources, WHO may request, and the member-state is obligated to provide, verification of the alleged public health event (Article 10). Article 11 obligates WHO to share any information it receives about public health events with the national government in whose territory the events allegedly are occurring, though it need not disclose to national authorities the source of the information. These non-official reports could come from other states, sub-national agencies, nongovernmental organizations, individuals, news reports, or Internet sources, and WHO is empowered to act upon these non-official reports as it sees fit (Mack 2006: 373). With these changes, the IHR (2005) transform disease surveillance into a collective responsibility.

The expansion of allowable reporting sources draws upon WHO's experience with the Global Outbreak Alert and Response Network (GOARN). GOARN is "a technical collaboration of existing institutions and networks who pool human and technical resources for the rapid identification, confirmation and response to outbreaks of international importance . . . [it] link[s] this expertise and skill to keep the international community constantly alert to the threat of outbreaks and ready to respond" (World Health Organization n.d. d). An earlier form of GOARN began in 1997, with its current version being unveiled in 2000. GOARN monitors local media reports, existing health networks, and other non-official sources in an attempt to learn of outbreaks at the earliest possible moment. It takes largely unstructured data and tries to "connect the dots" to find new outbreaks and new diseases (Sturtevant et al. 2007: 119). This means that it explicitly goes beyond the notifiable diseases listed in the IHR – and did so even before the IHR was rewritten and expanded (Fidler 2005: 347–8).

GOARN also represents a move away from a state-centric model of public health surveillance toward a more decentralized, electronically based approach. GOARN relies heavily on reports received through online sources and distributes information to its partners electronically instead of relying on more traditional means of diplomatic communication (Sturtevant et al. 2007: 119). GOARN quickly demonstrated its usefulness. WHO officials identified and investigated 538 outbreaks of international concern in 132 countries between January 1998 and March 2002 alone.

Finally, the IHR (2005), for the first time, acknowledge the role of human rights in addressing public health emergencies. Earlier versions of the IHR made no mention of human rights. This posed a problem, as responses to public health emergencies could potentially abrogate existing human rights standards. Gostin notes, "Infectious disease powers curtail individual freedoms, bodily integrity, and liberty. At the same time, public health activities can stigmatize, stereotype, or discriminate against individuals or groups" (Gostin 2004: 2626). Governments would introduce arbitrary trade and travel restrictions. Some would impose quarantine or isolation policies (Plotkin and Kimball 1997: 3–4). Though the earlier IHR specified that their policies were the maximum allowed under international law, states often chose to violate this provision knowing that WHO lacked the legal mechanisms to punish them for such transgressions (Calain 2007: 4).

Over the latter half of the twentieth century, public health officials came to recognize the importance of human rights in implementing effective disease control strategies. This growing acceptance of human rights as an integral part of a public health strategy led those rewriting the IHR to explicitly include human rights provisions in the new Regulations. Article 3 proclaims, "The implementation of these Regulations shall be with the full respect for the dignity, human rights, and fundamental freedoms of persons." Further, implementing the IHR should "be guided by the Charter of the United Nations and the Constitution of the World Health Organization" – both of which protect human rights and offer some guidance in doing so (Plotkin 2007: 843). States are not allowed to implement measures more intrusive or invasive than reasonable alternatives that would allow for the level of health protection desired (Articles 23, 31, and 43). States must also apply any and all health measures in a transparent and non-discriminatory manner (Article 42). Government officials need to obtain informed consent for searches of travelers (Articles 23 and 31), and they must endeavor to protect confidentiality (Article 45). Any public health measures to restrict civil or political rights must abide by the International Covenant on Civil and Political Rights (ICCPR). Under the ICCPR, the measure in question must respond to a pressing social need; pursue a legitimate aim; be proportionate to that aim; be no more restrictive than necessary; be implemented in a non-discriminatory manner; and treat the affected individuals with respect for the inherent dignity of human beings.

By making human rights a clear and important element of the document, the IHR (2005) attempt to avoid the punitive sanctions that would make people unwilling to report a disease outbreak. People can feel secure knowing that they will be treated with dignity and respect. The inclusion of human rights also signals to governments worldwide that their obligations to their citizens (as well as those temporarily within their borders) extend into all realms – including public health and infectious disease control.

Criticisms of the IHR (2005)

The IHR (2005) are not perfect. Critics allege that they overreach in some areas, underreach in others, and introduce unobtainable targets for many states. Three areas of criticism are of particular importance. First, the IHR (2005) may violate basic tenets of state sovereignty, forcing states to cede significant powers to WHO and giving the organization unprecedented reach into the domestic policy realm. The IHR (2005) require states to report events that *may* constitute an international public health problem. Mack points out, "Such intrusive duties on member states have never before appeared in the traditional law on infectious disease control" (Mack 2006: 371). These revised Regulations essentially give WHO direct influence over how public health data collection systems operate at the domestic level. It is true that the IHR (2005) do not specify the exact form of these surveillance structures. By mandating the results they should produce, though, the IHR (2005) introduce a new level of international involvement in domestic public health programs. A system that fails to produce the desired results violates the IHR (2005) and thus technically means that a state is in violation of international law.

While the IHR (2005) introduce substantially expanded reporting requirements, they do not come with financial resources to assist states with their implementation. Logistical difficulties exist for states that want to fulfill the IHR (2005)'s requirements. They require states to substantially upgrade their surveillance capabilities, yet many countries lack the resources to fund basic public health services. Noncompliance may thus be less a matter of intransigence and more one of resource absence. "Some nations are poor and cannot afford sophisticated public health systems, whereas others are failed states in the midst of civil strife, war, or other natural disaster" (Gostin 2004: 2626). Moves toward Internet-based surveillance reporting systems may offer some solution, but expanding Internet access in many developing countries is often prohibitively expensive and may not be a government priority (Sturtevant et al. 2007: 119).

Without resources to implement the reporting requirements, states may not be able to proactively screen for the wide range of conditions that could fall under the IHR (2005)'s purview. The IHR (2005) implicitly assume that states *already* have a relatively well-functioning public health infrastructure to which these additional surveillance systems can be attached. The Regulations also assume that the trained personnel needed to administer the programs are available (Mack 2006: 371). These assumptions are problematic. Further, the lack of explicit guidance for the development of their surveillance infrastructure could discourage political leaders from investing resources in the project. Passive surveillance systems, the same ones so disfavored by the IHR's reformers, may be all that some states can manage.

Second, while the expansion of the realm of notifiable infectious diseases is beneficial, it keeps the notion of global public health mired in an "absence of disease" framework. The IHR (2005) do not address the broader determinants of health or susceptibility to disease. The Regulations fail to acknowledge how structural violence conditions a person's vulnerability to infectious disease or access to treatment (Farmer 2005a). Indeed, they are silent on *health* itself as defined by the World Health Organization. Instead, the Regulations still focus their attention on diseases that may impede *international* travel and trade. The Regulations do not speak to domestic outbreaks, nor do they address the underlying socioeconomic issues that gave rise to the outbreak in the first place. This presents a curious outcome. The IHR (2005) reflect the international community's understanding of health, disease, and obligations

to one another. Calls for revising the IHR found their voice in countries recognizing the need for an expanded notion of health and disease. The final
treaty, though, continues to rely on a narrow notion of health as the absence
of disease and does nothing to support the underlying factors that support
health. This does little to advance the notion of health as a human right or
promote an interpretation of health as more than the absence of disease. It
does not move the international community toward the provision of *health*
as specified in the Constitution of the World Health Organization.

Third, the force of the human rights protections included in the IHR (2005)
leaves something to be desired. The Regulations do call upon member-states
to respect human rights, but they do so in a relatively passive manner. Only
two articles explicitly reference human rights. Article 3 calls upon states to
implement the IHR (2005) "with full respect for the dignity, human rights,
and fundamental freedoms of persons," and reminds them to implement the
Regulations in accordance with the Constitution of the World Health Organization (which calls "the enjoyment of the highest attainable standard of
health" a fundamental right) and the Charter of the United Nations (which
"reaffirm[s] faith in fundamental human rights").[5] Article 23 notes the importance of treating travelers who may be subject to search or investigation in
accordance with human rights. These two articles are certainly an improvement on previous versions of the IHR – the IHR (1969) contain no mention
of human rights, freedom, or dignity – but their mention of human rights
lacks much muscle behind it. There is little substance in the IHR (2005)
beyond informed consent prior to medical procedures or examinations. Plotkin's review of human rights in the IHR (2005) shows that the most explicit
human rights protections are reserved for travelers.[6]

Curiously, the IHR (2005) themselves fail to highlight or mention any
human rights treaties. This is especially odd in light of the trend during the
1990s and beyond toward greater acceptance of universal human rights and
increasing internalization of those norms (Donnelly 2006: 11–16). The Constitution of the World Health Organization and the Charter of the United
Nations acknowledge the importance of human rights, but they provide little
information about how to implement them – certainly far less than the
myriad of subsequent human rights treaties that have emerged since then.
The interaction between the IHR (2005) and existing international human
rights treaties remains largely unknown (Plotkin 2007: 844).

Benefits of the IHR (2005)

The IHR (2005), in many ways, offer the international community a dramatic
step forward in addressing the spread of infectious diseases and responding
to the health needs of the majority of the world. First, and perhaps most
importantly, the move toward focusing on disease threats to international
public health provides the IHR (2005) with both flexibility and adaptability.

While we may have a sense of the most important diseases today, recent history shows that we cannot predict which diseases will emerge or re-emerge in the coming years. Greater flexibility allows the international community to respond to these emerging situations, firm in the knowledge that all WHO member-states have already agreed to this expansive approach.

The IHR (2005) also ground WHO's responses to international infectious disease outbreaks firmly within international law. Outside of cholera, plague, and yellow fever, WHO found its responses to disease outbreaks hamstrung by its ambiguous legal status. Its response to SARS, while roundly celebrated, did not result from WHO's legal obligations or status. Instead, it happened more by accident. The organization lacked the ability to compel the Chinese government to share data and information about SARS because it had no legal right to do so. The IHR (2005) give WHO the legal rights to require states to provide needed information and cooperation. Similarly, GOARN has operated for nearly a decade in this murky netherworld of ambiguous legality. The Executive Director of Communicable Diseases for WHO claimed in 2002 that GOARN operated "within the framework" of the IHR (Heymann 2002: 179), but international legal scholars generally dismissed this position as wishful thinking (Fidler 2005: 348). Under the IHR (2005), GOARN clearly fits within a framework that allows it draw upon official and non-official sources for a wide range of potential health threats.

Second, the IHR (2005) recognize that non-state actors can provide valuable and reliable public health information. National government officials may lack the awareness of disease outbreaks, or they may have incentives for concealing that information. Nongovernmental organizations, local health clinics, local media sources, and individuals seeing changes in their communities may be better positioned to witness and understand that a problem is emerging. It can take time for information to trickle up to national health officials in the old passive surveillance systems. The more proactive, diffuse surveillance encapsulated in the IHR (2005) streamlines the process of getting necessary information to WHO in a timely manner.

Third, the IHR (2005) encourage states to engage in active surveillance. They should constantly be on the lookout for new outbreaks and new diseases. They need to implement structures that would allow them to quickly recognize problems. Passive surveillance provided states with a measure of plausible deniability; they did not report a particular outbreak because they did not know about it. With active surveillance and designated offices to gather information, communicate with WHO, and disseminate the reports received, governments are in a much better position to act.

Conclusion

Since World War II, the international health landscape has undergone significant changes. The World Health Organization has emerged, and the International Health Regulations form the international legal foundation for international health cooperation on infectious disease outbreaks. The treaty emerged out of concerns that "others" were going to infect Europe with specific, dangerous diseases and threaten the exchange of people and goods. It maintained a state-centric focus, but it failed to keep up with changes in the microbial world and the international community. In its most recent iteration, the IHR (2005) acknowledge a wider range of potential international infectious disease concerns and broadens the realm of relevant actors. They provide an important foundation for contemporary global responses to infectious disease outbreaks.

In the modern era, global health surveillance has moved from a reactive, state-based practice to one that incorporates a wide range of actors with a proactive approach. It also takes explicit account of human rights concerns. This makes the system better able to respond to outbreaks more quickly, but it is not a panacea. The IHR (2005) are a significant improvement for the surveillance regime, but they leave unanswered questions about the sufficiency of resources necessary to sustain such an approach.

CHAPTER EIGHT

Framing Health Security

Should global health governance systems react to infectious disease outbreaks as threats to national and international security? Starting in the mid-1990s, states and international organizations increasingly answered this question in the affirmative. National governments released policy statements and strategies that explicitly oriented their responses to infectious disease outbreaks as fundamental challenges to national and international security. These national-level discussions had a significant influence on the international community and the global health governance structures. In July 2000, the United Nations Security Council adopted Resolution 1308, specifically citing HIV/AIDS as "a risk to stability and security" if left unchecked (United Nations Security Council 2000). The following year, the United Nations General Assembly devoted a special session to the challenges HIV/AIDS posed to the international community, including its threats to national and international security. Conceptualizing these health threats as security problems has affected how global governance structures have responded to them and the sorts of interventions and coordinated responses planned.

While security may be a popular way of framing infectious disease outbreaks, that does not necessarily mean that it is an appropriate or useful response. A security frame brings with it certain responses and conceptualizations for the global health governance systems that may or may not be helpful. The best way to explore the usefulness of framing infectious disease outbreaks as a security threat is to use a case study.

This chapter uses the avian flu (H5N1) outbreak that began in 2003 as a vehicle for exploring the securitization of infectious disease outbreaks and their effects on global health governance systems. An avian flu epidemic could certainly pose a public health crisis. A more important question is whether an avian flu epidemic would pose a national and international security crisis that affected or influenced global health governance. Given the low number of deaths from avian flu at this point, the lack of confirmed or sustained human-to-human transmission, and the absence of human cases in the United States and other industrialized democracies, does it make sense to essentially securitize avian flu? Posing this question allows us to consider the tradeoffs that may accompany decisions to securitize infectious disease.

To flesh out this case study of H5N1, the chapter starts by discussing what we know about avian flu. It then discusses the concept of securitization and its use, particularly as it relates to public health. Finally, the chapter details why securitizing avian flu and other infectious diseases presents such strong negatives.

The Basics about Avian Flu

The most recent wave of avian flu officially began in December 2003 when two tigers and two leopards died at a Thai zoo after eating fresh chicken carcasses infected with H5N1. That same month, South Korean officials confirmed that highly pathogenic H5N1 had killed the birds on three poultry farms in the country (Food and Agriculture Organization 2006). By the end of the following month, Vietnam, Japan, Thailand, and Cambodia all reported H5N1 among wild birds. That same month, Vietnamese officials declared that H5N1 was responsible for respiratory failure deaths among humans, and Thailand confirmed its first two human cases of the disease.

Between December 2003 and December 2010, the World Health Organization tallied 509 laboratory-confirmed human cases of H5N1 in 15 countries (Azerbaijan, Bangladesh, Cambodia, China, Djibouti, Egypt, Indonesia, Iraq, Laos, Myanmar, Nigeria, Pakistan, Thailand, Turkey, and Vietnam). Of those cases, 303 (59.5 percent) proved fatal. The vast majority of cases occurred in Indonesia (170) and Vietnam (119). No new countries have reported human cases of H5N1 since 2008, when Bangladesh reported its first (and only) case. Four states – Bangladesh, Djibouti, Myanmar, and Nigeria – only had one confirmed instance of H5N1 each, while Azerbaijan, Iraq, Laos, Iraq, and Pakistan each had fewer than 10 cases over seven years (World Health Organization 2010a).

Policymakers in many different countries have turned avian flu, and other pandemic influenzas, into a security issue. The 2010 version of the United Kingdom's National Risk Register continued to describe pandemic influenza as having the highest relative impact of any potential civil emergencies. The Risk Register also ranked pandemic influenza high in terms of relative likelihood (United Kingdom Cabinet Office 2010: 5). The Register warned that such a pandemic could lower life expectancies, reduce economic output, cause social disruptions, and put essential services at risk (United Kingdom Cabinet Office 2010: 8). Officials in Canada, Mexico, and the United States devised the North American Plan for Avian and Pandemic Influenza in 2007 under the auspices of the Security and Prosperity Partnership in North America and its Security Agenda. The H5N1 outbreak inspired the need for this plan, as "the security and prosperity of the three countries are interdependent and complementary" (Security and Prosperity Partnership of North America 2007: 1–2). The plan envisioned the defense departments of the three states as taking active roles in limiting the spread of the disease and ensuring the maintenance of critical infrastructure (Security and Prosperity Partnership of North America 2007: 7–8). The United States developed its own National Strategy for Pandemic Influenza in 2006 and referenced pandemic diseases, including influenza, in its National Security Strategy.

Avian flu raises concerns among policymakers for three reasons. First, influenza vaccines offered little protection against an H5N1 outbreak until 2007. Even now, it is unclear how widely available the vaccine would be if a widespread outbreak were to occur. To understand why, consider how the influenza virus works. Each influenza virus has two surface proteins, hemagglutinin (HA) and neuraminidase (NA). These two surface proteins attack a cell by allowing the virus to attach to it, use it to reproduce, and then spread the virus to other cells in the body. Scientists have discovered 16 different HA proteins and 9 different NA proteins, generating over 140 different combinations. Not all combinations can cause illness in humans, and not all combinations will spread in any given year. This is what makes influenza vaccine production so difficult and of so much concern to officials when discussing avian flu. Any given flu vaccine will only offer protection against a limited number of influenza permutations, but it is impossible to know for certain which strains will spread during any given year. Public health officials around the world try to predict which strains will do so by looking at current trends and adjusting vaccines accordingly. Most years, this process works relatively well, and influenza vaccines protect most people against most flu strains. However, when different strains of the virus combine to form a new version, humans may have little immunity against this new subtype, and flu vaccines may not provide protection. If this happens, the conditions are ripe for a pandemic. If H5N1 were to spread through sustained human-to-human contact, such an antigenic shift would occur, and the population would have almost no protection. Given that common influenza vaccines would offer, at best, limited protection against H5N1 (and, since few people have had any exposure to H5N1, little natural immunity exists), many officials worry that sustained H5N1 transmission could run rampant, infecting millions and killing many.

Second, combined with the fears about lack of an effective prophylaxis, many officials suggest that the world is "overdue" for an international flu pandemic. This argument presumes that influenza pandemics occur with predictable regularity, and that it is now "time" for such a pandemic to occur. The world should have experienced a pandemic by now, so it is merely a matter of time before we have one.

While somewhat intuitive, this argument is extremely problematic. It is by no means clear how long this cycle lasts. Dr Anthony Fauci, the director of the National Institute of Allergy and Infectious Diseases, told the *New York Times* in 2005, "The last [flu pandemic] was in 1968, so it's 37 years. Just on the basis of evolution, of how things go, we're overdue" (Grady 2005). Others have suggested that the cycle is as short as 10 years or as long as 50. With no clear consensus, it is difficult to say how long the pandemic flu cycle lasts – or whether it even exists in the first place. For instance, the twentieth century witnessed three flu pandemics: 1918, 1957, and 1968. From this information, the cycle's length is entirely unclear. One commentator snarkily averred, "It was 39 years from the first pandemic to the second, but only 11 from the second to the third. Is that a pattern, or some white-jacketed yokel demonstrating his ability to do long division?" (Fumento 2005). Using a cyclical model for predicting an avian flu pandemic offers almost no real guidance for policymakers or the public.

Third, many officials continue to fear that avian flu is far more virulent and deadly than any previously known influenza strain. In a normal year, influenza kills approximately 1 percent of those infected. During the 1918 flu pandemic, the most lethal known, between 2 and 5 percent of those infected died from it. On the basis of the most current evidence from the World Health Organization, it seems over 60 percent of those infected with H5N1 die from the disease – a staggeringly high mortality rate. Laurie Garrett, one of the most prominent writers on global public health and a senior fellow at the Council on Foreign Relations, has called attention to the high death rate as cause for concern. Robert Webster of St Jude's Children Hospital cited a similar figure when writing in the *New England Journal of Medicine* in November 2006. Michael Osterholm, Director of the Center for Infectious Disease Research and Policy at the University of Minnesota and an advisor to the US government on pandemic influenza, emphasized the high mortality rate in a 2005 BBC interview (BBC 2005a). These figures, relied on by prominent public health officials in media interviews, encourage the perception among the public that an H5N1 pandemic could wipe out a large portion of the world's population. This figure is even more worrying when combined with predictions that upwards of one billion people worldwide could contract H5N1 during a pandemic outbreak.

Garrett, Webster, and Osterholm are technically correct; based on official statistics, it appears that H5N1 has a mortality rate of approximately 60 percent. That puts avian flu roughly on a par with the Ebola virus, which kills between 53 and 88 percent of its victims (Graber 2002). The sustained transmission of any disease with such a high level of lethality would (and should) give public officials a great deal of pause. However, that requires accurate figures that tell the complete story. The H5N1 figures omit some crucial information. Infections counted by the World Health Organization only include those confirmed with laboratory tests. In other words, the people who receive an official H5N1 diagnosis are those who are already likely to be the most ill. Given the expense and difficulty associated with testing for H5N1, few "mild" cases of the disease are likely to be found.

Though the veracity of these concerns is up for debate, questions about the current protections against H5N1, whether the world is "overdue" for an influenza pandemic, and the lethality of avian flu animate many policymakers. They argue that the world needs to be prepared against a coming influenza pandemic. The question is, what should the nature of that preparation be? Many policymakers at different governance levels answer that question by construing H5N1 as a threat to national and international security.

Securitizing Avian Flu and its Benefits

During much of the twentieth century, defining security was relatively straightforward: security concerns "the threat, use, and control of military force" (Walt 1991: 212). A security threat posed an existential physical threat to a state's continued survival, and combating such threats required military strength (if not outright superiority). Since the international arena was one where a Hobbesian anarchy reigned and a state could not rely on others to protect its interests, it must constantly be on guard. This does not necessarily mean that other problems, such as economic crises or natural disasters, posed no danger to states; rather, the traditional view of security emphasized the primacy of physical and military security. Without them, a state could not effectively function, so ensuring physical security was the state's top goal. This view dominated international relations throughout the Cold War. With two great powers diametrically opposed to one another and both possessing large military arsenals, ensuring physical security seemingly ranked as the most important consideration for all states.

With the Cold War's end, many criticized the traditional view of security as outdated for the new international situation. Ostergard (2002) called the old view overly Western-centric and unable to relate to the actual existential concerns of the vast majority of the population. Kolodziej (1992) argued that the traditional definition focused too much on *American national* security, and thus found itself analytically and geographically limited. Price-Smith (2001) and Homer-Dixon (1994) faulted traditional security studies for ignoring pandemic disease and environmental scarcity, respectively, as these both pose a far greater challenge to the lives of the vast majority of the population. The United Nations Development Programme (1994) sought to redefine security entirely, proposing the idea of human security with a focus on protecting people from chronic threats like poverty, hunger, and political repression and eliminating sudden, hurtful disruptions in the patterns of daily life. While these other definitions have gained some currency among various academic and government sectors, the traditional definition of security remains popular and relevant.

With growing debates over the nature of security, a growing number of scholars and policymakers have wondered about the ethical considerations of expanding or restricting its definition. Securitization theory, popularized by the Copenhagen School, can play a particularly important role here. Securitization theory focuses on *how* and *why* certain issues become security concerns in the first place. A wide range of non-military issues, like HIV/AIDS, environmental degradation, poverty, hunger, and global warming, could conceivably be security issues, but not all will successfully make it to the national security agenda. Securitization theory focuses on the performative nature of speech acts to understand which issues become securitized. Calling something a security issue or security threat constitutes a performative speech act, in which the words used to describe something themselves function as an activity. Describing a concern as a security issue gives it a special social quality for policymakers. The designation itself holds certain connotations and implies a certain sort of response. It also affects how other parties view the issue and its place on the political agenda. In essence, the act of securitizing an issue by calling it a security issue effectively forms an agreement among political actors. Waever notes that the security label "does not merely reflect whether a problem *is* a security problem, it is also a political choice" (1995: 65). Designating something as a security issue is thus a political tool to advance particular goals and aims.

The major implication of securitization theory is that there is not some sort of empirical criterion for determining which issues are security issues. Instead, the intersubjective understandings of a particular issue condition whether it holds a place on a nation's security agenda. It is less about any particular qualities of the issue itself, and more about how the issue is discussed, debated, and presented in public.

Securitization becomes a political choice on the part of the government. Securitizers choose, for some reason, to elevate a given issue into the realm of security. Buzan, Waever, and de Wilde themselves caution against securitizing non-military issues, arguing that it represents "a failure to deal with issues as normal politics" (Buzan et al. 1998: 29). Reaching for extraordinary powers signals a failure by existing political institutions to accommodate this new issue in a timely and beneficial manner.

Using these criteria, it can be seen that avian flu exhibits characteristics of a securitized issue. A wide variety of global health governance actors have taken some actions that have contributed to its securitization. The World Health Organization, for example, has taken the lead in collecting and disseminating information about human H5N1 outbreaks and best practices for countries to adopt. WHO's role largely focuses on knowledge, but elements of securitization have emerged. One document on basic facts on an influenza epidemic stresses that "widespread illness will occur," "large numbers of deaths will occur," and "economic and social disruption will be great" (World Health Organization 2005e). Securitization requires the securitizer to convince an audience that normal politics is insufficient for addressing a threat. The World Health Organization lacks the direct oversight of a population for whom it can effectively alter policies. However, it collects and distributes information – and member-states in turn integrate (or choose not to integrate) that information into their policy processes and contribute to the global efforts to securitize infectious disease outbreaks.

One element of the global health governance structures that has generally taken a direct interest in the securitization of infectious disease is the United States government. It can seek to securitize avian flu by trying to convince Americans (and others) that an avian flu epidemic would necessitate the suspension of normal politics. President Bush released his National Strategy for Pandemic Influenza on November 1, 2005, calling on Congress to allocate US$7.1 billion dollars to bolster (primarily domestic) responses and preparations for a pandemic. Announcing his program, President Bush made the potential existential threat posed by avian flu clear, remarking, "By putting in place and exercising pandemic emergency plans across the country, we can help our nation prepare for other dangers, such as a terrorist attack using chemical or biological weapons" (Bush 2005). This statement essentially equated a pandemic influenza outbreak with terrorism, shifting it into the realm of security. Paula Dobriansky, the Undersecretary of State for Democracy and Global Affairs at the time, noted in an address to a Washington, DC, think tank that an avian flu outbreak "could lead to civil unrest and instability." She argued, "If this [human-to-human H5N1 transmission] does begin to occur, in the worst-case scenario, it could kill millions of people, cripple economies, bring international trade to a standstill, and jeopardize political stability" (Dobriansky 2006). Her speech made clear that the United States government conceptualized its response to a potential avian influenza pandemic at least in part in national security terms. Perhaps most importantly, the Department of Homeland Security was to be the lead government agency to respond to a flu pandemic in the United States (Meeks 2005).

All of these political actors have spoken about the challenges avian flu potentially poses to the state, the international community, and the economy. If an avian flu pandemic occurs, and "the world is now closer to another influenza pandemic than at any time since 1968" (Palmore 2006: 115), the world economy stands to lose billions and the ability of governments at all levels to effectively provide services will be pushed to the limit.

What divides these various actors, and shows the incompleteness of the securitization of avian flu, concerns whether to enact emergency measures to counter the threat. The World Health Organization, whose response to a potential avian flu pandemic has relied far less on securitization, released a document in 2005 with recommended strategic actions for states to take to combat the threat of an avian flu pandemic. The recommendations emphasized strengthening a disease surveillance system, reducing opportunities for humans to contract the disease from birds, stockpiling antiviral drugs, fostering research on H5N1, and developing a vaccine (World Health Organization 2005c). None of these recommendations suggests extraordinary or emergency measures. The recommendations encourage states to strengthen their existing public health infrastructures, but they do not call on states to take any abnormal or unique actions. Instead, WHO has focused on sharing technical expertise among countries, facilitating information gathering, and coordinating research into new human cases and potential vaccines (World Health Organization 2006b).

This relatively non-securitized approach from WHO stands in stark contrast to the United States government's response. The US government shares WHO's concern for proper surveillance, stockpiling drugs, and limiting opportunities for humans to contract avian flu. However, the US government's response goes even further, in some cases calling explicitly for unique, emergency actions to combat H5N1 outbreaks. Prominent public health scientist and US government advisor Osterholm predicts that "The private and public sectors would have to develop emergency plans to sustain critical domestic supply chains and manufacturing and agricultural production and distribution" (Osterholm 2005: 32). Given this apocalyptic scenario, Osterholm paints a grim picture for the future of global health governance:

> The decision would likely be made to close most international and even some state or provincial borders . . . Border security would be made a priority, especially to protect potential supplies of pandemic-specific vaccines from nearby desperate countries. Military leaders would have to develop strategies to defend the country and also protect against domestic insurgency with armed forces that would likely be compromised by the disease. Even in unaffected countries, fear, panic, and chaos would spread as international media reported the daily advance of the disease around the world. (Osterholm 2005: 33)

Instead of bringing the world together and strengthening global health governance systems, Osterholm envisions global health governance efforts being destroyed due to the strain of responding to a transborder infectious disease outbreak.

This vision may seem fanciful and overly dramatic, but it is not far off from the United States government's official plans. In an October 2005 press conference in the White House Rose Garden, President Bush replied to a question about avian flu preparations by noting:

> The policy decisions for a President in dealing with an avian flu outbreak are difficult. One example: If we had an outbreak somewhere in the United States, do we not then quarantine that part of the country, and how do you then enforce a quarantine? When – it's one thing to shut down airplanes; it's another thing to prevent people from coming in to get exposed to the avian flu. And who best to be able to effect a quarantine? One option is the use of a military that's able to plan and move. (Bush 2005)

Pillar Three of the United States' National Strategy for Pandemic Influenza, Response and Containment, notes that responding to avian flu may include "us[ing] government authorities to limit non-essential movement of people, goods, and services into and out of an area where an outbreak occurs" and "determin[ing] the spectrum of infrastructure-sustainment activities that the US military and other government entities may be able to support during a pandemic" (Homeland Security Council 2006: 9). The government's plan potentially includes quarantine (either voluntary or forced) and a significant role for the military acting domestically in a wide array of areas.

The United States government's preparations for an avian flu pandemic clearly demonstrate its efforts to securitize the disease. Political leaders proclaim that an existential threat challenges the state and its institutions, and that in response, the government will need to adopt extraordinary measures to combat this threat. Those extraordinary measures are clearly designed to protect the United States from some outside threat. They focus few if any resources on foreign sources, and these measures seek to gather resources before anyone else can gather them.

The Costs of Securitizing Avian Flu

By moving avian flu higher up on the national agenda, securitization provides incentives for government policymakers to devote greater attention and resources to an issue that might otherwise be overlooked. With this greater attention, though, come some potential negative consequences. Two deserve greater attention here. First, securitizing avian flu encourages states to undertake inappropriate responses. Second, focusing such attention on avian flu diverts attention from more pressing public health concerns.

Inappropriate Responses

The framework of a security threat brings with it certain assumptions and ideas about how best to respond to a situation. Given its long association with the military, responding to a national security threat often implies a prominent role for a state's armed forces. Walt makes this connection explicit, stating that security studies "explores the conditions that make the use of force more likely, the ways that the use of force affects individuals, states, and societies, and the specific policies that states adopt in order to prepare for, prevent, or engage in war" (Walt 1991: 212). Security and military operations are essentially one and the same in the traditional view of security. While Walt would reject the integration of non-military threats like avian flu into the security paradigm, he does amply demonstrate what sort of policy baggage comes with that paradigm.

Worst-case-scenario thinking dominates pandemic influenza preparations. Some may argue that this is simply prudence; since no one can predict how a pandemic would unfold, it is better to be overprepared. However, there exists a fine line between adequate preparation and hysteria. While many media reports about avian flu include disclaimers, stating that the number of human cases so far has been low and no one can predict whether a pandemic will occur, many of these same reports play up the threat in a dramatic fashion. Extrapolating from the 1918 influenza pandemic, Osterholm suggests that 180 million to 360 million people could die worldwide (Osterholm 2005). David Nabarro, the United Nations official in charge of coordinating the international response to a pandemic, suggested that an avian flu pandemic could cause 5 million to 150 million deaths, though media reports largely focused on the higher figure (BBC 2005b). Nabarro was criticized for offering such a high figure, but he defended his actions on the ground that it was better to be prepared for any possibility. Dr Irwin Redlener of the National Center for Disaster Preparedness at Columbia University told an interviewer on ABC News that "we could have a billion people dying worldwide [in an avian flu pandemic]" (cited in Fumento 2005: 25).[7] That same channel began a news report about avian flu by declaring, "It could kill a billion people worldwide, make ghost towns out of major cities, and there is not enough medicine to fight it. It is called the avian flu" (cited in Fumento 2005: 25). The ABC network also produced and showed the made-for-TV movie *Fatal Contact: Bird Flu in America* in May 2006, which envisioned armed bandits roaming the country and up to 350 million people dying.[8] These high figures may preclude rational policymaking – especially in light of all the uncertainty that still surrounds avian flu. This same sort of worst-case scenario had dominated in 1976 amid fears of a swine flu pandemic. The result was a massive vaccination program that led to a number of cases of Guillian-Barré syndrome, high financial costs for the United States government (after it assumed all liability for vaccine manufacturers), and a generalized mistrust of the government's intentions (Krause 2006; Neustadt and Fineberg 1983; Sencer and Millar 2006).

Securitization also promotes short-term, us-versus-them thinking. Osterholm's prognostication envisions widespread looting and the need for roaming militias to ensure access to drug supplies as millions of people are dying. He speaks strongly about the need to protect our borders to keep people from coming to the United States to get *our* drugs. He focuses on protecting only Americans, even though disease epidemics respect no borders and will require some sort of coordinated international effort to effectively stop their transmission. Fidler points out, "Infectious disease measures historically have served as demarcations by which 'we' protect ourselves from the diseases of 'others'" (Fidler 1998: 9). The US framework for responding to a pandemic does not suggest that we are all in this together; instead, it suggests that "we" need to worry about "foreigners" who would infect us or bring the disease to our country.

What's more, the current securitized planning for an avian flu pandemic does little to promote the long-term strengthening of the public health infrastructure. Preparing the military to take a prominent role, encouraging people to stock up on antiviral drugs, and promoting vaccine research does not build the capacity necessary to fend off any epidemic. It is indeed true that we cannot predict when an infectious disease pandemic will occur, or even which disease will cause a pandemic. Given that reality, it makes little sense to develop a capacity that focuses almost exclusively on one disease. This short-term emphasis on avian flu does not prepare the public health system in the United States (or any other country, for that matter) to respond effectively to the myriad of public health needs of its populace.

Diverting Attention

In 2005, President Bush asked Congress for US$7 billion, and Congress allocated US$3.8 billion, to prepare for an avian flu pandemic. If the money allocated by Congress in 2005 were equally allocated for each confirmed case of avian flu anywhere in the world so far, that would equal over US$13 million per human case. This is for a disease which has not infected a single human being in the United States. Every single state in the United States has some sort of pandemic influenza response plan, committing resources and time to combat a disease that may not even affect the United States. Again, it is good to be vigilant and prepared for emergencies, but it is also important not to become hysterical or implement a response that is way out of line with the threat faced.

This singular focus on one disease and the possibility that it could at some point evolve to pose the threat of a worldwide epidemic essentially privileges avian flu over other health problems. The problem is not so much that a hierarchy of diseases exists; the problem is that this hierarchy places on top a disease that rarely affects humans. The international community is devoting billions of dollars to combat a disease that only has the potential to be an epidemic. Again, the problem is not with being prepared for a public health emergency; the problem is with preparing far out of proportion to the threat.

By devoting so much time, attention, and money to this one disease, we risk missing other diseases that could (and, in some cases, already do) cause far more damage to humans. Shiffman (2008) finds that a singular focus on HIV/AIDS has diverted foreign aid away from other diseases and from building health care infrastructures in developing countries. The problem threatens to replicate itself with avian flu. Since the preparations for a securitized avian flu tend to focus largely on the disease itself without building the infrastructure of the public health system, newly emerging problems could sneak up on us. Instead of trying to build public health capacity to make the system better able to identify and respond to an emerging disease pandemic, the securitized nature of avian flu focuses all of its energies on one disease to the potential exclusion of other problems. Instead of casting a wide net to search and prepare for emerging threats, securitizing avian flu leads to a focus on only one disease with laser-like precision to the exclusion of others.

Conclusion

Sustained human-to-human transmission of H5N1 could certainly pose a great threat to populations worldwide. If the outbreak were anywhere close to the scale of the 1918–19 influenza pandemic, the economic and human costs could be staggering. Given the uncertain nature of avian flu and its evolution, it makes some sense to prepare for a possible pandemic. However, if we are to effectively prepare for it, it should be along the lines of a public health crisis. Doing so would help strengthen public health infrastructures worldwide, allowing them to respond effectively and quickly to *any* sort of disease epidemic – not just avian flu.

Instead, the United States and other developed countries have conceptualized this possible pandemic as a threat to national and international security. By doing so, they have promoted inappropriate responses, reordered global health priorities, and widened the chasm between First and Third World states. Constructing an avian flu outbreak as an existential threat to the international community certainly moves the issue higher up the political agenda, but it comes with serious baggage and costs. This example highlights the tradeoffs associated with turning infectious diseases into security threats.

CHAPTER NINE

Access to Pharmaceuticals

Antiretroviral drugs (ARVs) are the main treatment used to fight HIV/AIDS. Since their discovery in the 1990s, they have extended the lives of millions of HIV-positive persons. Though they do not cure a person of HIV, they dramatically slow the virus' ability to replicate itself, thus significantly delaying the onset of AIDS-related complications. The treatment regimen can be complicated and difficult, as patients must be continually monitored to ensure the drugs' effectiveness and the drugs themselves can be hugely expensive, even when offered at substantial discounts.

Despite the expense and potential difficulty of administering ARV treatment, the international community has embraced universal access to antiretroviral drugs to a surprising degree. Lee and Piot argued, "In recent years an international consensus has emerged on the need to fight HIV/AIDS with a comprehensive response, including treatment, care, prevention, and impact mitigation" (World Health Organization 2005b: 5). This new concept, promoted most prominently by the 3 by 5 Initiative (to provide 3 million HIV-positive persons in the developing world with ARV access by the end of 2005), seeks to provide access to these drugs regardless of ability to pay or country of residence. Increased access to ARVs is also one of the United Nations' Millennium Development Goals, ensuring those infected with HIV in developing countries will have access to the same types of pharmaceuticals to treat HIV as those in developed countries regularly obtain. Even though these campaigns have fallen short of their ultimate goals, the International Treatment Preparedness Council enthused, "The movement for access to treatment is irreversible" (International Treatment Preparedness Coalition 2005: 5).

The number of people receiving ARVs has grown at a staggering rate. In 2001, only 240,000 people in low- and middle-income countries had access to ARVs. By 2005, the number had jumped fivefold to 1.3 million. In addition, 21 low- and middle-income countries offered ARVs to at least half of their citizens in need (UNAIDS 2006: 151). By the end of 2009, 5.2 million people in low- and middle-income countries needing access to ARVs received them – nearly 40 percent of the estimated 15 million in need (UNAIDS 2010a: 95). All regions of the world have seen dramatic increases in ARV availability, and national governments, donor states, international organizations, nongovernmental organizations, private philanthropic organizations, and multinational corporations have come together in a remarkable coalition to further expand ARV access to individuals without the ability to pay because they see it as the right thing to do.

Universal ARV access is perhaps the most ambitious global public health campaign undertaken since the successful quest to eradicate smallpox. Achieving this target will require international cooperation, vastly increased levels of financial assistance from developed countries, the active participation of international pharmaceutical companies, and rethinking and reapplying international intellectual property rights. Perhaps more importantly, this new program will require the international community to embrace a new way of thinking that places the right to health and health care above concerns about the ability to pay and the sovereign right of states to manage their national health programs. It draws on the expertise and resources of a vast array of global health actors, essentially requiring the global health governance regimes to reconceptualize how they deliver pharmaceuticals to those in need.

That said, the campaign's admirable ambition may fall prey to the costs associated with putting more people on ARVs – costs even harder to afford because of the global economic recession. Even with this impressive energy and normative commitment, the campaign to extend ARV access has encountered substantial limitations. People do not take a single dose of ARVs; once started on the treatment, they must continue it for the rest of their lives. Therefore, pledging to provide ARVs entails making a lifelong promise. Furthermore, success increases the number of people who require the drugs. This places strains on the ability of governments and aid agencies to continually increase their outlays for ARVs at a time when a global recession has severely strained public sector budgets. The cost pressures are stimulating debates over the relative merits of funding prevention over treatment programs.

The international movement to provide universal access to ARVs gives remarkable insight into a high-profile pharmaceutical campaign within the context of global health governance. With all the progress in creating medicines to treat human maladies, there exists a substantial gap in getting those drugs to people who need them. Many of those most in need are the least able to afford these pharmaceuticals. The campaign for universal ARV access illustrates the most high-profile concerted attempt by various elements of the global health governance regimes to get drugs into bodies. It also lends important insights into how the international community comes to embrace certain global health issues over others (Shiffman 2009).

This chapter begins by looking at the movement for universal ARV access in more detail, with particular emphases on the Millennium Development Goals and the 3 by 5 Initiative. The next section examines why universal ARV access was accepted by the international community when it was. After examining this success, though, the chapter details the very real limitations on maintaining and expanding this campaign.

Promoting and Internalizing Universal ARV Access

In September 2000, the United Nations hosted the Millennium Summit to consider the organization's role in the twenty-first century and how to realize the international community's collective responsibility to "uphold the principles of human dignity, equality, and equity at the global level" (United Nations 2000: 1). From this meeting, eight concrete goals emerged – the Millennium Development Goals (MDGs). The goals include eradicating extreme poverty and hunger; achieving universal primary education; promoting gender equality; reducing child mortality; improving maternal health; combating HIV/AIDS, malaria, and other diseases; ensuring environmental stability; and developing a global partnership for development (United Nations n.d.). Realizing these goals would promote human security and dramatically reduce global poverty. In all eight areas, all countries that signed the Millennium Declaration pledged their support for achieving the goals and providing the resources necessary to do so. Within each overarching goal, one to four subgoals with specific targets exist.

The delegates sought to distinguish the MDGs from previous UN declarations in two ways. First, each of these goals included quantifiable indicators that would demonstrate whether the target was met. Second, the MDGs established a specific timeframe for achieving the goals, calling on the world to meet all of them by 2015. Goal 6 – combating HIV/AIDS, malaria, and other diseases – explicitly recognized the need to improve access to pharmaceuticals like ARVs as a crucial component of promoting global health. Target 6.B calls on the international community to "achieve, by 2010, universal access to treatment for HIV/AIDS for all those who need it" (United Nations 2010: 45). ARV access in low- and middle-income countries was particularly low, with fewer than 400,000 people receiving treatment at the end of 2002. Coverage was particularly low in sub-Saharan Africa – the region with the highest need for ARVs, yet with the lowest rates of ARV access (World Health Organization et al. 2008: 19). Two additional Millennium Development Goals – Goal 4 on reducing child mortality and Goal 5 on improving maternal health – also addressed health issues and focused international attention on the importance of addressing health needs around the world.

Making expanded access to ARVs one of the Millennium Development Goals put the issue on the international agenda. That alone, though, did not spur a great deal of action. To get a serious commitment to providing universal ARV access, WHO, UNAIDS, and other global health governance institutions created a coordinated campaign: the 3 by 5 Initiative.

On September 22, 2003, Dr Lee Jong-wook, Director-General of the World Health Organization, Dr Peter Piot, Executive Director of UNAIDS, and

Richard Feachem, Executive Director of the Global Fund to Fight AIDS, Tuberculosis, and Malaria, announced a new initiative to combat the failure to deliver ARVs to people with HIV in developing countries. That year, UNAIDS estimated that 6 million HIV-positive people in the Third World required ARVs, but less than 8 percent actually received them. While 84 percent of those in need in Central and South America had access to ARVs, only 2 percent of those in Africa, the continent hardest hit by the AIDS epidemic, did (World Health Organization and UNAIDS 2003: 4–5). This new program aimed to correct that. It pledged to provide a sustainable and reliable supply of ARVs to 3 million people in the developing world, half the number who needed the drug, by the end of 2005. Though the leaders of this effort acknowledged that it was an extremely ambitious goal, they based their calculations on an article published in 2001 in *Science*. The article's authors cautioned that reaching this target would require optimal levels of both financing and technical capabilities. Still, they considered it doable (Schwartländer et al. 2001) – as did, apparently, WHO and UNAIDS. These organizations declared the lack of ARV access to be a global health emergency and an issue that urgently needed to be addressed.

The 3 by 5 Initiative did not create calls for universal ARV access by any means (see, for example, Farmer 1999 and Headley and Siplon 2006), but it focused them and gave them far greater prominence within the international community. Instead of being an amorphous call to help people with AIDS, this campaign framed its calls for action in relatively concrete terms of providing something tangible to individuals who could not otherwise acquire it as a human right. By declaring a health emergency, the 3 by 5 Initiative's promoters hoped to "propel action and upend 'business as usual' attitudes." This new program would "demand new commitment and a new way of working across the global health community" (World Health Organization and UNAIDS 2003: 6). To achieve this commitment, they situated the call within a framework of country ownership, human rights, and equity.

Not only would success require high-level political commitment, but the attendant financial outlays would also be quite high. When announcing the new program, WHO estimated that it would cost at least US$5.5 billion to achieve the target (World Health Organization and UNAIDS 2003: 24). The focus was not on the cost, though; it was on realizing human rights. The Initiative was seen as promoting the UN's human rights agenda in two ways. First, the Universal Declaration of Human Rights declares that all people have the right to the highest possible standard of health – a promise reaffirmed to explicitly include HIV/AIDS by the United Nations during its Special Session on HIV/AIDS in 2001. Second, the Initiative pledged to pay special attention to vulnerable groups who may have less access to treatment and prevention programs. By emphasizing equity, the Initiative sought to overcome economic barriers that had previously prevented most people in developing nations from being able to afford ARVs. It utilized the ideas of access to essential medicines and non-discrimination in the provision of care evident in the Alma-Ata Declaration. In their paper, Schwartländer et al. referenced the movement for realizing the right to health in Africa as emblematic of the international community's growing respect for this ideal (2001: 2436). The 3 by 5 Initiative's own materials were even more explicit. On its website, the Initiative proclaimed that its efforts were "a step towards the GOAL [*sic*] of making universal access of HIV/AIDS prevention and treatment accessible for all who need them *as a human right*" (World Health Organization n.d. a; emphasis added). From the earliest days, activists and organizations connected the drive for universal ARV access back to the earlier efforts to promote health as a human right.

Tactically, supporters of universal ARV access did not solely focus on states to realize this idea. Instead, they called on international organizations, non-governmental organizations, multinational corporations, and private philanthropic groups – in addition to national governments – to work together. They explicitly recognized this connection, noting, "'3 by 5' is a target that many organizations are working together to achieve, including national authorities, UN agencies, multilateral agencies, foundations, non-governmental, faith-based and community organizations, the private sector, labor unions and people living with HIV/AIDS. To succeed, full support and participation from all partners and governments are needed" (World Health Organization n.d. e). This shift moved the idea from being a collective public good whose realization depended solely on developed states to targeting individuals with diffuse responsibility for protecting the human rights of those in need.

These stunning accomplishments cannot diminish the fact that WHO and UNAIDS failed to meet their goals. They pledged to provide half of the people in developing countries who needed ARVs at the end of 2003 (a number that continued to grow over this two-year period), and they failed to do so. By the end of 2005, only 1.3 million people in developing states were receiving ARV treatment. Furthermore, the continued spread of HIV meant that even *more* people now required ARV therapy and did not have access to it. Critics lambasted the program for being overly optimistic, relying on unrealistic modeling, and failing to properly coordinate programs (*Economist* 2005). Others noted that national AIDS control programs often fell prey to petty turf battles and corruption, making them ineffective (International Treatment Preparedness Coalition 2005: 6–7).

Despite this seeming failure, most focused on the program's successes. In the span of two years, over 1 million people gained new access to life-prolonging drugs. Over 20 percent of those who needed ARVs in the developing world now had them – a significant improvement on the 7 percent who had them in 2003. Eighteen countries announced that they had met or exceeded their ARV treatment targets (World Health Organization and

UNAIDS 2006: 7). These are stunning accomplishments over an extraordinarily short period of time, even if they fell short of the original goal. The basic idea of universal ARV access continued to hold sway within the international community. State governments, international organizations, nongovernmental organizations, private philanthropic organizations, and multinational corporations have repeatedly reaffirmed their belief in the idea and pledged additional funds (though still short of what is necessary) toward its realization.

While expressing regret at the Initiative's inability to achieve its target, WHO and UNAIDS, in their final report, discussed ways to rectify the problems the Initiative faced in the future. Instead of remarking on the program's end, the report instead argued that it was just the beginning of ensuring universal ARV access for all. "The '3 by 5' target needs to be seen as an interim step toward the ultimate goal of universal access to antiretroviral therapy for those in need of care, as a human right, and within the context of a comprehensive response to HIV/AIDS" (World Health Organization and UNAIDS 2006: 49). The G8 nations, the very nations that provided the vast majority of funding for the programs that came under the 3 by 5 Initiative's umbrella, pledged in July 2005 to work toward universal access to ARVs worldwide by 2010. At the G8 summit in Gleneagles in July 2005, the leaders of the world's largest economies pledged at least an extra US$50 billion in aid annually, part of which would be specifically pledged for universal ARV access (Office of the Prime Minister 2005). Two months later, the United Nations passed a resolution calling on member-states to work toward this goal and to pledge the necessary resources (AVERT 2010b). In 2006, the UN High-Level Meeting on AIDS produced a resolution that stated in part

> [We commit] to pursue all necessary efforts to scale up nationally driven, sustainable and comprehensive responses to achieve broad multisectoral coverage for prevention, treatment, care and support, with full and active participation of people living with HIV, vulnerable groups, most affected communities, civil society and the private sector, towards the goal of universal access to comprehensive prevention programmes, treatment, care and support by 2010. (United Nations 2006)

African heads of state made a similar pledge in May 2006 at a summit in Abuja, Nigeria (Agence France-Presse 2006). The Clinton and Gates Foundations both have continued their efforts and have expanded them beyond their initial plans. Further, the momentum exhibited by the 3 by 5 Initiative encouraged UNAIDS to revise its treatment guidelines to encourage people to start taking ARV treatment sooner. This change added significantly more potential ARV patients and increased the costs associated with providing treatment, but the early successes of universal ARV access allowed UNAIDS to feel confident that the international community could meet the challenge.

Embracing and Expanding Universal ARV Access

The international community embraced the rhetoric of universal ARV access, tying it to the realization of individual human rights and a broadened conceptualization of governance. The United Nations' 2001 Declaration of Commitment on HIV/AIDS resolved that "access to medication in the context of pandemics such as HIV/AIDS is one of the fundamental elements to achieve progressively the full realization of the right of everyone to the enjoyment of the highest attainable standard of physical and mental health" (United Nations General Assembly 2001). Within months of the unveiling of the 3 by 5 Initiative, all 192 member-states of WHO publicly endorsed the program. They publicly pledged to aggressively work toward the realization of this goal and, in a broader sense, ensure that all those who needed ARVs could get them. The UN Economic and Social Commission for Asia and the Pacific passed a resolution that called on states in the region to scale up their public health programs specifically in response to the 3 by 5 Initiative (United Nations Economic and Social Commission for Asia and the Pacific 2004). In May 2005, over 120 delegates from around the world came together in Geneva to coordinate efforts to rapidly scale up efforts to expand access to ARVs across political, economic, and religious lines. The US President's Emergency Plan for AIDS Relief (PEPFAR), its primary AIDS programming effort, strongly emphasizes antiretroviral therapy (and its attendant infrastructure), considering it an integral part of its AIDS programs and the US' obligation as a leading member of international society (Office of the Global AIDS Coordinator n.d.). When announcing PEPFAR during his 2003 State of the Union address, US President George W. Bush noted,

> Because the AIDS diagnosis is considered a death sentence, many do not seek treatment. Almost all who do are turned away. A doctor in rural South Africa describes his frustration. He says, "We have no medicines. Many hospitals tell people, you've got AIDS, we can't help you. Go home and die." In an age of miraculous medicines, no person should have to hear those words. (Bush 2003)

This statement received a tremendous amount of applause. Making this proclamation during the President's most important speech of the year shows that the idea of universal ARV access was at least fomenting rhetorical changes. Four years later, when Bush called on Congress to reauthorize PEPFAR by providing US$30 billion over the next five years, he highlighted the normative and idealistic aspects of the program. Acknowledging the costs and the number of people affected by the program, he emphasized, "The statistics and dollar amounts I've cited in the fight against HIV/AIDS are significant. But the scale of this effort is not measured in numbers. This is really a story of the human spirit and the goodness of human hearts . . . Our citizens are offering comfort to millions who suffer, and restoring hope to those who feel forsaken" (Bush 2007).

Bush's statements about the moral rectitude of providing universal ARV access illustrate an important element of why the campaign took hold when it did. Policy commitments like universal ARV access represent hard cases for political science to explain, since they require states to undertake expensive actions that are not in their strict material interest. How can a campaign convince governments, international organizations, and private actors to make costly, multi-year commitments to people who have relatively little power? Busby (2010) demonstrates the importance of connecting the campaign with frames that resonate with the moral commitments of gatekeepers and government officials. In the case of universal ARV access, supporters framed their arguments as a moral imperative, imbuing it with Christian moral sentiments that appealed to the religious faith of political leaders in dominant states. Busby notes, "Most groups [supporting universal ARV access] emphasized the need to extend treatment and to confront AIDS as a matter of conscience . . . In fact, President Bush's own justification for PEPFAR was based on moral concerns rather than the security logic that had led the Clinton administration" (2010: 172). Framing universal ARV access as consistent with Christian morality helped overcome the objections that leading American policymakers had about increasing foreign assistance. The morality of the appeal and its action trumped the direct financial and material costs of the program.

Evidence also shows that recipient states internalized this new idea. Within months of its debut, 56 countries approached WHO, asking for assistance through the 3 by 5 Initiative (World Health Organization 2004: 9). These states sought to make the changes in their policies and infrastructure that would allow them to expand the ability of their citizens to access these drugs. The states publicly acknowledged that they did not have the resources to enact such a program, yet by approaching WHO, they also publicly acknowledged their desire to work with the international community to implement the norm's program. Further, nearly every country has created a Country Coordinating Mechanism (CCM) to receive funding from the Global Fund and coordinate AIDS activities. These CCMs explicitly incorporate representatives from the public and private sectors to promote the incorporation of all relevant voices (Global Fund to Fight AIDS, Tuberculosis, and Malaria 2008). These efforts show a willingness to adapt state structures in order to facilitate the provision of ARVs.

Private philanthropies and multinational corporations have also played a significant role in working toward universal ARV access precepts. The Clinton Foundation has focused its energies on transforming the economic incentives for pharmaceutical companies. Recognizing that these companies will not produce ARVs without an ability to make a profit, the Clinton Foundation has helped to aggregate demand for ARVs. It has sought to "transform the antiretroviral marketplace from a low-volume, high-margin market to a high-volume, low-margin market that serves millions of HIV/AIDS patients"

(William J. Clinton Foundation n.d. b). This strategy significantly reduces the price for ARVs while still allowing generic and branded pharmaceutical manufacturers to recoup their investment in developing ARVs. The Foundation has forcefully argued that it has not asked for charity, but rather sought to ensure supply at an affordable price in the face of a large demand (Rauch 2007). The Bill and Melinda Gates Foundation, the world's wealthiest philanthropic organization, collaborated with the government of Botswana and the pharmaceutical company Merck to create the African Comprehensive HIV/AIDS Partnership. This arrangement brings together the financial resources of the Gates Foundation, the manufacturing and distribution capabilities of Merck, and the infrastructure of Botswana to deliver ARVs to those in need (Bill and Melinda Gates Foundation 2006; Ramiah and Reich 2006). These two efforts demonstrate the significant role that non-state actors play in actualizing universal ARV access.

The efforts to ensure universal ARV access also led to some innovative funding mechanisms. UNITAID, an organization hosted by WHO, levies a small fee on the sale of airline tickets in 29 countries that have agreed to join the program. The revenues generated through this program are then given to other organizations and programs to purchase ARVs. UNITAID also structures its grants to recipients to provide long-term funding and cover all or nearly all of the costs of a particular program (Douste-Blazy and Altman 2010: 50). By linking the program to the purchase of airline tickets, UNITAID aims to create relatively stable, predictable, and long-term revenue streams. Its representatives argue that, even in the midst of the global economic recession and declines in resources available from governments and philanthropies, it is able to maintain consistent funding levels because airline ticket sales are only down 5 percent in participating countries. Thanks to careful budgeting and building a cushion into its yearly allocations, that decline has not had a detrimental effect on its operations (Douste-Blazy and Altman 2010: 51). Working with the Clinton Foundation, UNITAID has contributed to declining prices for first- and second-line ARVs and expanding pediatric ARV access (UNITAID 2010: 2).

It is indeed true that, even with the diversity of actors involved, international funding for universal ARV access has remained far below what is necessary. WHO and its partner organizations expressed gratitude for the support they received, but they repeatedly acknowledged that donations were coming in far below the level necessary to realize their goals. Six months before the Initiative formally ended, WHO announced "UNAIDS estimates that *at least an additional US$18 billion above what is currently pledged* is needed for global HIV/AIDS efforts over the next three years" (World Health Organization 2005b: 9; emphasis added). African governments pledged to increase their own budgetary outlays for health programs within their own borders. They promised to devote 15 percent of their national budgets to health (including HIV/AIDS programs) – but none of them met this target by the end of 2005 (International Treatment Preparedness Coalition 2005: 4). Funds from some donor states like the United States have, at times, come with conditions that have hampered their ability to be accessed in a timely and efficient manner.

Despite this reality, the commitment to realizing universal ARV access largely remains intact. Stephen Lewis, the UN's Special Envoy for HIV/AIDS in Africa, proclaimed in 2005,

> Mind you, I can even now hear the curmudgeonly bleats of the detractors, whining that we will fall short of the target of three million in treatment by the end of this year. Tell that to the million people who are now on treatment and who would otherwise be dead. The truth is that the 3 by 5 initiative – which, I predict, will be seen one day as one of the UN's finest hours – has unleashed an *irreversible momentum for treatment*. (United Nations News Service 2005; emphasis added)

No state declared that universal ARV access was undesirable or unworthy. Questions did arise as to how best to provide these medications to people in challenging environments and to ensure compliance with the drug regimen's requirements. Even these discussions, though, referred back to the notion of universal ARV access. The issue was not one of the *appropriateness* of universal ARV access; it was one of *delivery*. Activists managed to convince governments and the public that "it was morally wrong to allocate antiretroviral drugs solely on the basis of an individual's ability to pay" (Kapstein and Busby 2009: 2).

These actions do not mean that the debates over universal ARV access are over. The battles over funding levels alone demonstrate the continued discussion. Those debates, though, do not demonstrate a lack of faith in universal ARV access because they are largely over *how*, not *whether*, to work toward this goal.

Challenges to Universal ARV Access

Despite the rhetorical commitment to universal access to ARVs, actual outcomes have continued to lag behind expectations – and that occurred during a time of relative economic prosperity. With the global economic recession that began in 2008, budgets for health care and foreign aid face significant challenges to maintain current spending levels. The need for ARVs continues to grow, though, raising uncomfortable questions about the future viability of the pledge for universal access to ARVs.

Part of the problem facing the universal access campaign is that the definition of who should get ARVs has changed since the campaign itself began. Until 2010, WHO guidelines recommended that patients with a CD4 count below 200 should begin ARV treatment. In 2010, these recommendations changed. Under the new guidelines, patients should begin treatment if their CD4 count fell below 350. Research suggested that starting treatment earlier under the revised guidelines improves long-term health and is ultimately cost-effective. It also substantially increased the number of people in low- and middle-income countries that now required ARVs. Under the old guidelines, there were 10.1 million people in need in 2009. That number, though, jumped 45 percent to 14.6 million when adhering to the new guidelines (World Health Organization 2010d: 76). As a result, ARV access rates declined between 2008 (under the old guidelines) and 2009 (under the new guidelines) from 42 percent to 36 percent – even though 1.2 million more people started ARV treatment in 2009 (World Health Organization 2009: 4–5, 2010d: 76). While the change in treatment guidelines is ultimately beneficial to the health of HIV-positive persons and their communities as a whole, it also increases the financial and human resource burden on governments, international organizations, and donors.

Maintaining adequate financing for ARVs proves an even greater challenge. Universal ARV access is perhaps one of the clearest illustrations of making public health a global public good financed by the international community as a whole (Price-Smith 2009: 219). Even during the heyday of funding for ARV access programs, the amount of money fell far short of need. WHO found that donor governments made US$8.7 billion available for ARVs in 2008 – the highest amount on record. Despite this funding zenith, there still existed a gap of more than US$6 billion to reach all of those in need (World Health Organization 2009: 8). As the recession started and funding levels fluctuated in 2009, the international community made US$15.9 billion available for ARV treatment from all sources. This impressive figure was nearly US$10 billion short of the US$25 billion needed to achieve universal coverage (AVERT 2010b). PEPFAR, the largest single international funding source for HIV/AIDS programs, flatlined its funding for 2009–10 and decreased its budget specifically for ARVs by 17 percent (AVERT 2010b).

Complicating matters further, the promise of ARV treatment requires a lifelong commitment. It is morally impossible for a government to withdraw its pledge to provide funds for ARV treatment, despite the financial strain that may create (Over 2008: 18). People on ARVs need to take these drugs for the rest of their lives. Interrupting treatment allows the virus to mutate. When this happens, people living with HIV/AIDS need to take second-line ARVs, which are even more expensive. As people get access to ARVs and begin their treatment regimens, the number of people who must be supported in these programs continues to expand; not only must you treat the newly infected, but you must also continue to treat the burgeoning number who are already on treatment. Writing prior to the beginning of the global economic recession, Over found that the United States government would need to spend US$11.6 billion annually to meet the ARV access need by 2016. To do so, the government would need either to increase its total foreign assistance levels by 50 percent or to allocate half of all overseas development assistance to AIDS spending (Over 2008: 16–18).

Just as global economic growth in the early part of the 2000s facilitated expanded access to ARVs, so the global recession has seriously impeded maintenance of these programs. Kapstein and Busby ponder, "If the movement for access to treatment was mobilizing for the first time in 2009, in the midst of the worst global economic downturn in decades, would donor countries be as enthusiastic and as generous?" (Kapstein and Busby 2009: 29). The answer, they report sadly, is no. WHO reported that resource levels for ARVs were flat in 2009, after having increased significantly year over year in the past, because of increased financial strain (World Health Organization 2010d: 8). It warned, "Given the global economic crisis that started in 2008, providing HIV services free of charge may not be sustainable in some countries" (World Health Organization 2009: 124). The very cornerstone of universal access to ARVs – making the drugs available to people as a matter of human rights regardless of ability to pay – came into question because of depressed economic conditions. By 2009, 11 percent of governments surveyed reported that they were already seeing negative effects on their ARV programs because of reduced funding. An additional 31 percent of governments surveyed expected that they would face such problems in the near future (World Health Organization 2009: 124). The problem was particularly acute among countries whose ARV programs were highly dependent on foreign aid (AVERT 2010b).

The challenge is unlikely to disappear, as maintaining and increasing access to ARVs in the future will depend almost entirely on increased funds from foreign donors and higher public health expenditures by domestic governments. Lowering the price of ARVs below current levels is unlikely to expand access. Bendavid et al. found that, between 2003 and 2008, for every US$10 that the price of first-line ARV therapy dropped, access increased 0.19 percent. However, increasing foreign aid by US$1 per capita led to a 1 percent increase in coverage. Achieving universal access to ARVs would require foreign assistance at the level of US$64 per capita in low- and middle-income countries (Bendavid et al. 2010: 3–4). Additional price decreases are unlikely to expand ARV access in the future, these authors argue, because prices are already near their lowest sustainable levels. Instead, "further expansion will depend almost entirely on increasing expenditures from foreign donors or domestic sources" (Bendavid et al. 2010: 5). However, the recession is squeezing foreign aid budgets, and perceptions of success are perversely discouraging governments from seeing the need to continue to spend as much money on ARVs.

The costs of maintaining access for those currently receiving ARVs while adding more to the treatment rolls have raised questions about the long-term sustainability of treatment as a primary strategy for addressing HIV infection. The promotion of treatment programs has largely come at the expense of HIV prevention strategies, and prevention receives relatively little attention (Kapstein and Busby 2009: 12–13). Until 2008, PEPFAR required 55 percent of funds to go toward treatment. Of the monies available for prevention programs, one-third had to promote abstinence until marriage. Organizations receiving prevention funds were also required to sign a pledge explicitly condemning commercial sex work (Over 2008: 11–12). The abstinence requirement ended in 2008, but the law requires the Office of the Global AIDS Coordinator to submit a report to Congress if any country with a generalized epidemic spends "less than half of prevention funds [on] abstinence, delay of sexual debut, monogamy, fidelity, and partner reduction" (AVERT 2011). The anti-prostitution pledge remains in place, despite criticism from service providers that it limits their effectiveness and outreach. Prioritizing treatment over prevention, Over asserts, makes little financial sense – especially in times of economic downturn. He cites a study from Thailand that found that each US$1 spent on prevention programs saves US$43 in future treatment costs (Over 2008: 11). The emphasis on treatment distorts PEPFAR's priorities and makes it difficult to maintain its commitments. Over writes, "PEPFAR gratified those who benefited directly and immediately while creating massive problems for others to deal with in the future" (Over 2010). Given the ever-increasing costs associated with treatment programs, emphasizing prevention certainly makes sense. Such a shift in the near term, though, does little to help figure out how to deal with existing commitments to universal access to ARVs regardless of ability to pay.

Conclusion

The moves toward universal access to ARV therapy as embodied by the 3 by 5 Initiative represent a significant shift in global health governance – an attempt to provide access to life-prolonging drugs, without regard for ability to pay, premised on human rights grounds. States, intergovernmental organizations, and private actors continue to work toward universal ARV access despite the very high costs and the potentially negative consequences for Western pharmaceutical companies. These organizations engage in actions that may not be economically profitable to uphold this new notion.

That said, the effects of the global economic recession challenge the feasibility of universal ARV access. Government outlays for foreign health aid are not increasing, but the costs associated with universal ARV access continue to rise as more people acquire ARVs and need sustained access to the drugs for the rest of their lives. The expense has raised questions about the cost efficacy of treatment programs compared with prevention programs. These questions also demonstrate that, while human rights justifications have indeed come to play a significant role in underpinning global health governance efforts, economic considerations remain relevant and important.

Conclusion

Andy Spielman entered the Johns Hopkins School of Medicine in the 1960s, determined to study how insects transmit infectious diseases. Shortly after he enrolled, Lloyd Rozeboom, his advisor, took him out for a beer. Garrett relates their conversation at the bar:

> The downcast Rozeboom bought Spielman a pint and after a few quaffs said, "Look, I've got to get this off my chest . . . I should have never accepted you into graduate school. I should never have encouraged you to pursue medical entomology. It's a dead field. DDT is killing it . . . It's all over. There will be no career for you. By the time you've finished your thesis all the insect-borne disease problems will be solved." (Garrett 1994: 49–50)

Rozeboom's attitude was not unique in the mid-twentieth century. Smallpox was on its way to eradication, and many assumed that it would simply be a matter of time before other infectious diseases like polio and malaria followed suit. Indeed, in 1967, US Surgeon-General William H. Stewart reportedly told a meeting of state health officers at the White House that "it was time to close the book on infectious diseases and shift all national attention (and dollars) to what he termed 'the New Dimensions' of health: chronic diseases" (Garrett 1994: 33).

The hubris of the 1960s and 1970s lulled the international community into believing that health issues were largely inconsequential. Health problems were technical matters, merely requiring the appropriate application of proven techniques. The international community's main job was to ensure that information and best practices were shared, and a sense of optimism permeated international health discussions. Health was not a political issue in the classical sense, and thus did not require high levels of attention.

Today, health has assumed a prominent place on the international agenda. New infectious diseases have emerged, challenging the international community's ability to respond in a timely manner. Diseases largely thought to be under control re-emerged with a vengeance, forcing a re-evaluation of control strategies. Noncommunicable diseases are gaining more attention. The United Nations has debated whether ill health constitutes a threat to national and international security. States have largely embraced universal access to life-prolonging HIV drugs – a radical reconceptualization of access to pharmaceuticals. New intergovernmental organizations focused explicitly on health have emerged. Existing intergovernmental organizations have incorporated global health into their mandates. New funding structures have taken root. Civil society organizations and private philanthropic organizations have come to play significant roles in promoting and ensuring global health.

The global health governance regimes that exist today differ radically from those of the 1960s and 1970s, and they will no doubt continue evolving into the future. The architecture changes in response to changes in the environments – economic, political, international, and microbial. It is impossible to chart how global health governance will look in 30 years, as no one can predict the health challenges that will emerge or whether new organizations will come into existence. Think, for example, about the massive transformation in global health governance structures inspired by the emergence of HIV/AIDS. Here was a disease completely unknown before 1981, yet it has fundamentally altered the global health terrain, fostering the creation of new intergovernmental organizations, leading to new techniques for raising funds for international health concerns, reorienting the missions of existing organizations, and opening the realm of global health governance to non-state and private actors. The current economic downturn and the pressures it is placing on national budgets could potentially provide a similar shock to the global health governance system and lead to profound changes, but it is too early to know that, and moreover this is not the only event that could introduce such far-reaching changes.

Even though we cannot predict the future, examining the patterns and changes in the global health governance systems may provide worthwhile insights and give some clues about how any systemic changes might occur. It is instructive to understand and appreciate the sorts of changes that global health governance systems have undergone, as these trends may foreshadow future changes. In particular, let us call attention to three significant shifts in global health governance.

First, the move from *international* health governance to *global* health governance underscores the dramatic shifts in how we conceptualize responsibility for addressing cross-border health concerns. From the end of World War II until the 1980s, this was solely the province of states. The international organizations that took leading roles in addressing health concerns, like the World Health Organization, had membership rolls comprised entirely of national governments. While some private organizations got involved in cross-border health concerns, like the Rotary Foundation's work on polio eradication, the system was overwhelmingly oriented toward national governments and had few ways to effectively integrate non-state actors into the system. Since the 1980s, though, much of the explosion has come from new actors and new types of actors getting involved. It was not necessarily the case that private philanthropic organizations like the Gates Foundation or civil society groups like the Treatment Acton Campaign were explicitly barred from playing a role in cross-border health issues. Rather, the emergence of new health issues, particularly HIV/AIDS, demonstrated the limitations of a wholly state-centric system. It also demonstrated the necessity of reconceptualizing health issues more holistically as global rather than focusing entirely on the relationships between states inherent in the international conceptualization. By incorporating additional actors into the system, cross-border health concerns could draw on additional strengths and resources to find more optimal solutions. At the same time, though, more actors made it more difficult to coordinate activities and ensure relatively even coverage.

Second, the logic underlying global health governance has shifted over time, moving from one motivated largely by economics to one that also embraces human rights and security. Initially, starting with the International Sanitary Regulations, cross-border health cooperation derived entirely from its potential negative effects on international commerce. Governments came together to work on health issues only if those diseases threatened trade. Indeed, the International Sanitary Regulations explicitly stipulated that economic considerations drove the inclusion of specific illnesses on the list of notifiable conditions. Economic considerations did not disappear with the International Sanitary Regulations, though; cost concerns stymied many efforts to expand global health governance. Health for All by 2000, for example, fell victim to worries that its primary health care recommendations would cost too much. Furthermore, high cost severely limited access to antiretrovirals to combat HIV, making it highly unlikely that persons in developing countries could gain access to these life-prolonging drugs. Since the 1990s, though, global health governance has embraced more of a human rights-based logic to justify the expansion of its programs. Organizations like UNAIDS explicitly incorporate human rights into their programs and mandate partner states to recognize and protect the rights and dignity of those they assist. A variety of organizations and actors have taken action to ensure that people in developing countries could acquire life-prolonging drugs despite their inability to pay. Civil society organizations often frame their activities as necessary for ensuring the protection of the human rights of vulnerable populations. Governments have fundamentally reconceptualized their view of health, adopting a security framework to move health to a central position in their international security considerations. In the process, global health issues have assumed a far more prominent place on the political agendas of many states.

In many ways, these shifts have given a voice to many whose health concerns previously went unheard. It has allowed the international community to move closer to realizing the promise of the right to health embodied in the Constitution of the World Health Organization. The potential difficulties arise when these rationales come into conflict with each other. For example, the move toward a human rights-based logic for global health governance came largely during a time when the international community was relatively flush. The global economic downturn that began in 2008 could mean that states lack the resources to continue funding programs that recognize and celebrate health as a fundamental human right.

Finally, the international community has shown a willingness to expand the health issues it takes under its purview, but there remains a hierarchy of illnesses that drives global health interventions. Global health governance covers an increasingly broad array of illnesses – both communicable and noncommunicable – but there exists no real correlation between causes of death and resources devoted to causes of death. In 2004, WHO found that the top five causes of death worldwide were coronary heart disease (12.2 percent of all deaths that year), stroke and cerebrovascular illnesses (9.7 percent), lower respiratory infections (7.1 percent), chronic obstructive pulmonary disease (5.1 percent), and diarrheal diseases (3.7 percent) (World Health Organization 2011b). Shiffman demonstrates, though, that HIV/AIDS received 35.1 percent of all international health funding commitments in 2003 (Shiffman 2008: 97). Diseases conceptualized as threats to national and international security tend to get higher levels of funding, though those diseases do not necessarily cause the highest rates of death. Mickey Chopra, the chief of health at UNICEF, described the disjuncture in stark terms: "All the attention has gone to more glamorous diseases, but this basic thing [diarrheal diseases] has been left behind. It's a forgotten disease" (Dugger 2009). On the one hand, there exists no necessary relationship between the amount spent on a given disease or illness and its relative importance; one would expect AIDS to receive more resources than diarrheal diseases because it costs so much more to treat AIDS. On the other hand, though, if it truly costs so little to treat some of the infectious diseases that cause significant levels of mortality and morbidity in developing countries, the international community's uninterest or lack of will in addressing them raises questions about how and why the global health agenda prioritizes particular diseases the way that it does.

Moving Forward

Where should research on global health governance go from here? Three natural avenues for future research present themselves. First, how will the increased attention paid to noncommunicable diseases affect global health governance? Most global health governance structures focus their energies on infectious diseases, and this book concentrates the vast majority of its attention on those same illnesses. With 2011's United Nations High-Level Meeting on Noncommunicable Diseases, heart disease, stroke, cancer, and the like are moving to a more prominent place on the international health agenda. It is unclear, though, whether currently existent global health governance structures can provide the resources, direction, and political will that will allow the international community to address these conditions adequately. While four of the five leading causes of death worldwide are noncommunicable diseases, they generally do not inspire the same sense of urgency as infectious diseases. This may make it more difficult to generate sustained attention from policymakers worldwide.

Further, in some quarters, death from noncommunicable diseases is taken as evidence of progress. By this thinking, people dying of cancer or heart disease is a good thing, because it means that people are living long enough to die of chronic illnesses instead of infectious diseases. The same logic argues that the conditions giving rise to noncommunicable diseases come largely from modernization, economic progress, and the stresses of life common in wealthy states. Noncommunicable diseases come from increased pollution associated with manufacturing, diets high in meat and processed foods that require higher incomes, and the stresses and aggravations that come with life in advanced industrialized states (Cantor 2007: 18–19; Proctor 1996: 16–34). While this attitude may not dominate within major health organizations, it may hold sway among policymakers in some states and thus undermine efforts to convince countries to provide financial and human resources to address these problems.

Second, given the questions about the sustainability of current financial commitments for global health governance, it would be worthwhile to investigate the potential of various innovative funding mechanisms to maintain these programs. WHO Director-General Margaret Chan released a report in December 2010 that described the organization as overextended and unable to respond to emergencies with the speed and agility necessary. "The current financial crisis," she reported, "adds urgency to the need to address these problems" (World Health Organization 2010b: 1). Extrabudgetary funds for the World Health Organization provide it with additional resources, but the donor state gets to control exactly how and where those funds are used, which may or may not comport with WHO's priorities. The Global Fund to Fight AIDS, Tuberculosis, and Malaria presents a unique institutional structure, focusing entirely on funding proposals but not implementing programs itself. Its funding, though, is wholly dependent upon the good will of states, intergovernmental organizations, and private sources, and its pledges are consistently lower than the demonstrated need. UNITAID's model, levying a small tax on airline tickets, is one such new approach, but it so far is operational in only a few states and its approach could potentially run into problems in the face of a long-term economic recession. Private philanthropic organizations have taken an increasingly large role in funding global health programs, but the very agility and quick responsiveness that have made them useful within global health governance could also lead them away from health and into other areas of interest.

To reduce the funding uncertainties within global health governance, new mechanisms may be necessary. For example, would it be feasible to institute some sort of licensing agreement on international pharmaceutical patents that would provide some percentage of funds from drug sales to global health governance structures? This could be a way of adding additional levels of corporate social responsibility to international pharmaceutical companies while also maintaining a relatively stable line of funding. It may also be worthwhile to consider some sort of investment strategy or building an endowment for global health organizations distinct from their annual budgets. This could provide organizations with a bit of a financial cushion during economic downturns, but would also raise a host of issues around creating appropriate investment guidelines.

Prominent international economists have turned their attention toward finding new sustainable funding mechanisms for global health. Jeffrey Sachs, the American economist and former director of the United Nations' Millennium Project, proposed a Global Health Fund in 2010. Sachs' brainchild would expand the Global Fund to Fight AIDS, Tuberculosis, and Malaria to improve health services and tackle the wide range of infectious diseases that threaten human health. His fund would require US$12 billion per year to operate, an amount he described as "really very modest, representing around 0.033% (three cents per $100) of the donor countries' GNP. This is a tiny sum, which could be easily mobilized if donor countries were serious" (Sachs 2010). In 2011, 1,000 economists signed a joint letter to the finance ministers of G20 (Group of Twenty Finance Ministers and Central Bank Governors) countries, urging them to introduce a Tobin tax to benefit the world's poor. A Tobin tax, also called the Robin Hood tax, levies a charge on transactions in financial markets and uses the funds raised to benefit the poor. In their letter, the economists argued that a 0.05 percent tax on international currency trading could raise billions of dollars annually to improve global health, among other international development projects. Their proposal, they asserted, was both "technically feasible" and "morally right" (Stewart 2011). While neither proposal has come to fruition yet, they demonstrate that people are seriously considering how to generate higher levels of sustainable funding to benefit global health.

Finally, with the increasing emphasis on incorporating a diverse array of actors into global health governance, there exists a particular need to actually map out who is working on what projects in which countries. For all the discussion of coordination among actors, the potential for overemphasizing some places and some illnesses and underemphasizing others, and the need for public and private actors to collaborate, it is stunning that there exists no comprehensive directory of global health actors working on particular issues or in particular countries. Creating such a listing could present a myriad of benefits to both academics and policymakers. First, for positive collaborations and partnerships among different actors to occur, there must be better ways of knowing who is doing what where. This would move global health partnerships out of the realm of personal relationships and into something more formalized or transparent. Second, this directory could give greater empirical heft to arguments about whether certain diseases or countries get disproportionate levels of attention and resources. A comprehensive directory could facilitate analyses of resources and help determine the extent to which overlaps exist. Third, greater transparency through some sort of public directory could facilitate increased accountability. It could shine a spotlight on organizations and allow for greater investigation. It would also allow researchers and policymakers to assess how well existing global health governance structures respond to crises. Finally, creating and maintaining such a directory would provide early insights into changes within global health governance. Showing who does what where, it could bring emerging trends in global health governance to light sooner.

Health is one of the most dynamic realms of global governance today, and the system's evolution demonstrates the different ways in which the international community conceptualizes its responsibility for addressing cross-border health concerns. The global health governance system has gone from being almost entirely state-centric and focused on economic rationales to one that allows for a wide range of actors and incorporates human rights into its various operations. The current system is by no means perfect, but its history of change in response to new crises and changing circumstances suggests that continued change is inevitable.

Notes

1 The exact reason for extending the isolation period from 30 to 40 days remains unclear. One theory is that 30 days proved insufficient for preventing plague's spread, while a second sees the increase as paralleling significant biblical events. A third theory harkens back to the ancient Greek medical theory of "critical days," which held that infectious diseases will emerge within 40 days of exposure (Sehdev 2002: 1072).

2 Harman questions how unique the Global Fund truly is as an international organization dealing with the global AIDS pandemic. She argues that the systems established by the Global Fund to emphasize a multisectoral approach replicate ones previously created within the World Bank system (2010: 104–5). While the two systems have important commonalities, the Global Fund is unique in that it is an independent organization as opposed to being a program operating fully under the aegis of another international institution.

3 As described by Musgrave (1959), merit goods are commodities that should be available to persons on the basis of need rather than of ability to pay. There exists a market for these goods, but the market focuses on private costs and benefits without considering the external benefits, and so encourages under-production. Merit goods differ from public goods because they are potentially excludable and rivalrous. People without the ability to pay could be restricted from accessing the good, and one person's consumption of that good may decrease its overall accessibility. Public goods, on the other hand, would not be provided in a pure market system and are non-excludable and non-rivalrous in their consumption.

4 While various drafts and proposals circulated among WHO member-states after the 1998 Provisional IHR, the January 2004 Draft IHR was the first *complete* set of regulations for public distribution and comments.

5 Fidler expands upon this list, finding explicit human rights protections in Articles 23, 31, 32, 42, 43, and 45. Most of these, though, focus on requiring informed consent before medical examinations may occur. They also largely target travelers (Fidler 2005: 368).

6 Plotkin argues that there may be some ambiguity around the term "traveler" itself and how such status would be determined. He acknowledges, though, that his concerns may be more theoretical than practical in application (Plotkin 2007: 844).

7 Interestingly, Redlener criticized the Bush Administration's pandemic influenza plan for allowing too great a role for the military (CNN 2005).

8 Perhaps fortunately, the movie performed poorly and received only 5.3 million viewers. This put the show in distant fourth place during its time slot. For comparison, the top-rated show of the evening was *American Idol* with 28.1 million viewers.

Bibliography

Aaronson, Susan S. and Jamie M. Zimmerman (2006) "Fair trade? How Oxfam presented a systemic approach to poverty, development, human rights, and trade," *Human Rights Quarterly* 28(4), 998–1030.

Abbasi, Kamran (1999a) "The World Bank and world health: changing sides," *British Medical Journal* 318(7187), 865–9.

Abbasi, Kamran (1999b) "The World Bank and world health: under fire," *British Medical Journal* 318(7189), 1003–6.

Abdullah, Abdul Samad (2007) "International Health Regulations (2005)," *Regional Health Forum* 11(1), 10–16.

Achmat, Zackie (2004) "HIV/AIDS and human rights: a new South African struggle," 2004 John Foster Lecture, University College London (November 10). http://www.rothschildfostertrust.com/materials/lecture_achmat.pdf (accessed October 26, 2010).

Acuna, Hector R. (1977) "The Pan-American Health Organization: 75 years of international cooperation in public health," *Public Health Reports* 92(6), 537–44.

Agence France-Presse (2006) "African leaders pledge more access to AIDS, malaria treatment," (May 5). http://www.aegis.com/NEWS/AFP/2006/AF060510.html (accessed December 2, 2010).

Aginam, Obijiofor (2002) "International law and communicable diseases," *Bulletin of the World Health Organization* 80(12), 946–51.

Aginam, Obijiofor (2005) "Globalization of infectious disease, international law, and the World Health Organization: opportunities for synergy in global governance of epidemics," *New England Journal of International and Comparative Law* 11(1), 59–74.

Akande, Laolu (2003) "Victory over river blindness," *Africa Recovery* 17, 6.

Allen, Charles E. (1950) "World health and world politics," *International Organization* 4(1), 27–43.

Anand, Sudhir and Kara Hanson (1998) "DALYs: efficiency versus equity," *World Development* 26(2), 307–10.

Anderson, Ian (2000) "Northern NGO advocacy: perceptions, reality, and the challenge," *Development in Practice* 10(3&4), 445–52.

AVERT (2010a) "History of AIDS up to 1986." http://www.avert.org/aids-history-86.htm (accessed September 16, 2010).

AVERT (2010b) "Universal access to AIDS treatment: targets and challenges." http://www.avert.org.uk/aidstarget.htm (accessed December 2, 2010).

AVERT (2011) "President's Emergency Plan for AIDS Relief (PEPFAR)." http://www.avert.org/pepfar.htm (accessed September 27, 2011).

Awuonda, Moussa (1995) "Swedes support UNAIDS," *Lancet* 345(8964), 1563.

Barnard, David (2002) "In the High Court of South Africa, Case No. 4138/98: the global politics of access to low-cost AIDS drugs in poor countries," *Kennedy Institute of Ethics Journal* 12(2), 159–74.

Bartsch, Sonja (2007) "The Global Fund to Fight AIDS, Tuberculosis, and Malaria," in Hein, Wolfgang, Sonja Bartsch, and Lars Kohlmorgen (eds) *Global Health Governance and the Fight against HIV/AIDS*, New York: Palgrave Macmillan.

Bate, Roger (2005) "Slippery AIDS statistics: why loose HIV numbers create false hope and bad policy," *Health Policy Outlook* (May/June). http://www.aei.org/publications/pubID.22469/pub_detail.asp (accessed December 2, 2010).

Bate, Roger (2008) "Stifling dissent on malaria," *American* (December 8). http://www.american.com/archive/2008/december-12-08/stifling-dissent-on-malaria (accessed December 2, 2010).

Bate, Roger (2011) "Sweden, Germany suspend grants to Global Fund," *Enterprise Blog* (January 27). http://blog.american.com/?p=25795 (accessed February 14, 2011).

BBC (2005a) "Renewed warning over flu pandemic" (May 25). http://news.bbc.co.uk/2/hi/health/4579777.stm (accessed December 2, 2010).

BBC (2005b) "Bird flu 'could kill 150m people'" (September 30). http://news.bbc.co.uk/2/hi/asia-pacific/4292426.stm (accessed December 2, 2010).

BBC (2011) "Germany halts AIDS fund payment over corruption claims" (January 27). http://www.bbc.co.uk/news/world-europe-12294232 (accessed February 14, 2011).

Behrman, Greg (2004) *The Invisible People: How the US Has Slept through the Global AIDS Pandemic, the Greatest Humanitarian Catastrophe of Our Time*, New York: Free Press.

Benatar, Solomon R. and Renee C. Fox (2005) "Managing threats to global health: a call for American leadership," *Perspectives in Biology and Medicine* 48(3), 344–61.

Benatar, Solomon R., Abdallah S. Daar, and Peter A. Singer (2003) "Global health ethics: the rationale for mutual caring," *International Affairs* 79(1), 107–38.

Benatar, Solomon R., Stephen Gill, and Isabella Bakker (2009) "Making progress in global health: the need for new paradigms," *International Affairs* 85(2), 347–71.

Bendavid, Eran, Eric Leroux, Jay Bhattacharya, Nicole Smith, and Grant Miller (2010) "The relations of price of antiretroviral drugs and foreign assistance with coverage of HIV treatment in Africa: retrospective study," *British Medical Journal* 341, 1–6.

Berry, Craig and Clive Gabay (2009) "Transnational political action and 'global civil society' in practice: the case of Oxfam," *Global Networks* 9(3), 339–58.

Bill and Melinda Gates Foundation (n.d.) "Foundation fact sheet." http://www.gatesfoundation.org/about/Pages/foundation-fact-sheet.aspx (accessed December 2, 2010).

Bill and Melinda Gates Foundation (2006) "Working with Botswana to confront its devastating AIDS crisis." http://www.gatesfoundation.org/learning/Documents/ACHAP.pdf (accessed December 2, 2010).

Bloom, Barry R., David E. Bloom, Joel E. Cohen, and Jeffrey D. Sachs (1999) "Investing in the World Health Organization," *Science* 284(5416), 911.

Brown, E. Richard (1979) *Rockefeller Medicine Men: Medicine and Capitalism in America*, Berkeley: University of California Press.

Brown, Garrett Wallace (2009) "Multisectoralism, participation, and stakeholder effectiveness: increasing the role of nonstate actors in the Global Fund to Fight AIDS, Tuberculosis, and Malaria," *Global Governance* 15(2), 169–77.

Brown, Garrett Wallace (2010) "Safeguarding deliberative global governance: the case of the Global Fund to Fight AIDS, Tuberculosis, and Malaria," *Review of International Studies* 36(2), 511–30.

Busby, Joshua William (2007) "Bono made Jesse Helms cry: Jubilee 2000, debt relief, and moral action in international politics," *International Studies Quarterly* 51(2), 247–75.

Busby, Joshua W. (2010) *Moral Movements and Foreign Policy*, Cambridge: Cambridge University Press.

Bush, George W. (2003) "State of the Union Address," Washington, DC (January 28). http://www.c-span.org/executive/transcript.asp?cat=current_event&code= bush_admin&year=2003 (accessed December 2, 2010).

Bush, George W. (2005) "President outlines pandemic influenza preparations and response," Speech at National Institutes of Health, Bethesda, MA (November 1). http://merln.ndu.edu/archivepdf/hls/WH/20051101-1.pdf (accessed December 2, 2010).

Bush, George W. (2007) "President Bush announces five-year, $30 billion HIV/AIDS plan," Washington, DC (May 30). http://www.globalhealth.gov/news/news/ 060507.html (accessed December 2, 2010).

Buzan, Barry, Ole Waever, and Japp de Wilde (1998) *Security: A New Framework for Analysis*, Boulder: Lynne Rienner.

Calain, Philippe (2007) "Exploring the international arena of global public health surveillance," *Health Policy and Planning* 22(1), 2–12.

Cantor, David (2007) "Introduction: cancer control and prevention in the twentieth century," *Bulletin of the History of Medicine* 81(1), 1–38.

Carter Center (2010) "Countdown to zero: Carter Center Guinea Worm Eradication Program." http://www.cartercenter.org/health/guinea_worm/mini_site/ index.html (accessed October 26, 2010).

Chaplowe, Scott G. and Ruth Bamela Engo-Tjega (2007) "Civil society organizations and evaluation: lessons from Africa," *Evaluation* 13(2), 257–74.

Charles, John (1968) "Origins, history, and achievements of the World Health Organization," *British Medical Journal* 2(5600), 293–6.

Chen, Ingfei (2006) "Thinking big about global health," *Cell* 124(4), 661–3.

Cohen, Jon (2002) "Gates Foundation rearranges public health universe," *Science* 295(5562), 2000.

Collin, Jeff (2004) "Tobacco politics," *Development* 47(1), 91–6.

Collin, Jeff and Anna Gilmore (2002) "Corporate (anti)social (ir)responsibility: transnational tobacco companies and the attempted subversion of global health policy," *Global Social Policy* 2(3), 354–60.

Collin, Jeff, Kelley Lee, and Karen Bissell (2002) "The Framework Convention on Tobacco Control: the politics of global health governance," *Third World Quarterly* 23(2), 265–82.

Cooper, Andrew F. (2008) *Celebrity Diplomacy*, Boulder: Paradigm.

CNN (2005) "Bush military bird flu role slammed" (October 6). http://edition.cnn. com/2005/POLITICS/10/05/bush.reax (accessed January 16, 2007).

Cuddeford Jones, Morag (2003) "Pharma giants out of favor," *Brand Strategy* 173, 23.

Cueto, Marcos (2004) "The origins of primary health care and selective primary health care," *American Journal of Public Health* 94(11), 1864–7.

Danzon, Patricia M. (2007) "At what price?" *Nature* 449(7159), 176–9.

Das, Pam (2004) "Interview with Zackie Achmat – head of the Treatment Action Campaign," *Lancet Infectious Diseases* 4(7), 467–70.

Das, Pam and Udani Samarasekera (2008) "What next for UNAIDS?" *Lancet* 372(9656), 2099–102.

Davies, Sara E. (2010) *Global Politics of Health*, Cambridge: Polity.

Dees, J. Gregory (2007) "Taking social entrepreneurship seriously," *Society* 44(3), 24–31.

Dobriansky, Paula (2006) "Social, economic, and security implications of avian influenza," Speech at the Nixon Center, Washington, DC (June 26). http://www.nixoncenter.org/Program%20Briefs/DobrianskyRemarks6-26-06.pdf (accessed December 2, 2010).

Dodgson, Richard, Kelley Lee, and Nick Drager (2002) *Global Health Governance: A Conceptual Review*, CGCH Discussion Paper No. 1 (February). London: London School of Hygiene and Tropical Medicine and World Health Organization Department of Health and Development.

Donnelly, Jack (2006) *International Human Rights*, Boulder: Westview Press.

Douste-Blazy, Philippe and Daniel Altman (2010) *Power in Numbers: UNITAID, Innovative Financing, and the Quest for Massive Good*, New York: Public Affairs.

Doyle, Cathal and Preeti Patel (2008) "Civil society organizations and global health initiatives: problems of legitimacy," *Social Science and Medicine* 66(9), 1928–38.

Doyle, Joseph S. (2006) "An international public health crisis: can global institutions respond effectively to HIV/AIDS?" *Australian Journal of International Affairs* 60(3), 400–11.

Dressler, Carolyn and Stephen Marks (2006) "The emerging human right to tobacco control," *Human Rights Quarterly* 28(3), 599–651.

Drugs for Neglected Diseases Initiative (2008) "Sanofi-Aventis and DNDi welcome the Clinton Foundation announcement on ACTs and commit to providing fixed-dose combination 'ASAQ' at equally low prices" (July 21). http://en.sanofi-aventis.com/binaries/08-07-21_Fondation_Clinton_EN_tcm28-19822.pdf (accessed December 2, 2010).

Dubin, Martin David (1995) "The Health Organization of the League of Nations," in Weindling, Paul (ed.) *International Health Organizations and Movements, 1918–1939*, Cambridge: Cambridge University Press.

Dugger, Celia W. (2009) "As donors focus on AIDS, child illnesses languish," *New York Times* (October 29).

Dwyer, Peter (2003) "Dying to fight," *Transformation* 53(1), 76–80.

Economist (1995) "An unhealthy situation" (May 20), 80.

Economist (2005) "Spin doctors" (November 26), 103.

Einhorn, Bruce (2007) "India's Cipla: new prescription needed?" *Business Week* (September 17). http://www.businessweek.com/magazine/content/07_38/b4050422.htm (accessed December 2, 2010).

Evensen, Jane Vogt and Kristian Stokke (2010) "United against HIV/AIDS? Politics of local governance in HIV/AIDS treatment in Lusikisiki, South Africa," *Journal of Southern African Studies* 36(1), 151–67.

Farley, John (2004) *To Cast Out Disease: A History of the International Health Division of the Rockefeller Foundation (1913–1951)*, Oxford: Oxford University Press.

Farmer, Paul (1999) *Infections and Inequalities: The Modern Plagues*, Berkeley: University of California Press.

Farmer, Paul (2005a) *Pathologies of Power: Health, Human Rights, and the New War on the Poor*, Berkeley: University of California Press.

Farmer, Paul (2005b) "Global AIDS: new challenges for health and human rights," *Perspectives in Biology and Medicine* 48(1), 10–16.

Fee, Elizabeth and Theodore M. Brown (2002) "100 years of the Pan American Health Organization," *American Journal of Public Health* 92(12), 1888–9.

Fidler, David P. (1998) "Microbialpolitik: infectious diseases and international relations," *American University International Law Journal* 14(1), 1–53.

Fidler, David P. (1999) *International Law and Infectious Diseases*, Oxford: Clarendon Press.

Fidler, David P. (2003) "Emerging trends in international law concerning global infectious disease control," *Emerging Infectious Diseases* 9(3), 285–90.

Fidler, David P. (2004) "Revision of the World Health Organization's International Health Regulations," *ASIL Insights* (April). http://www.asil.org/insights/insigh132.htm (accessed December 2, 2010).

Fidler, David P. (2005) "From International Sanitary Conventions to global health security: the new International Health Regulations," *Chinese Journal of International Law* 4(2), 325–92.

Fidler, David P. (2008/9) "After the revolution: global health politics in a time of economic crisis and threatening future trends," *Global Health Governance* 2(2), 1–21.

Fidler, David P. (2010) *The Challenges of Global Health Governance*, Council on Foreign Relations Working Paper (May). New York: Council on Foreign Relations.

Fidler, David P. and Lawrence O. Gostin (2006) "The new International Health Regulations: an historic development for international law and public health," *Journal of Medicine, Law, and Ethics* 34(1), 85–94.

Fitzpatrick, Joan and Ron C. Skye (2003) "Republic of South Africa v. Grootboom, Case No. CCT 11/00.2000(11) BCLR 1169 and Minister of Health v. Treatment Action Campaign, Case No. CCT 8/02," *American Journal of International Law* 97(3), 669–80.

Food and Agriculture Organization (2006) "Cats and avian influenza." http://www.fao.org/avianflu/conferences/rome_avian/documents/Cats%20and%20Avian%20Influenza.pdf (accessed December 2, 2010).

Frati, P. (2000) "Quarantine, trade and health policies in Ragusa-Dubrovnik until the age of George Armmenius-Baglivi," *Medicina nei Secoli* 12(1), 103–27.

Friedman, Steven and Shauna Mottiar (2005) "A rewarding engagement? The Treatment Action Campaign and the politics of HIV/AIDS," *Politics and Society* 33(4), 511–65.

Fumento, Michael (2005) "Fuss and feathers: pandemic panic over the avian flu," *Weekly Standard* (November 21), 24–30.

Funders Concerned About AIDS (2007) *US Philanthropic Commitments for HIV/AIDS: 2005 and 2006*, New York: Funders Concerned About AIDS.

Funders Concerned About AIDS (2010) *US Philanthropic Support to Address HIV/AIDS in 2009*, New York: Funders Concerned About AIDS.

Garrett, Laurie (1994) *The Coming Plague: Newly Emerging Diseases in a World Out of Balance*, New York: Penguin.

Garrett, Laurie (2007) "The challenge of global health," *Foreign Affairs* 86(1), 14–38.

Gates, Bill (2003) "Humane research," *Wall Street Journal* (January 26).

Gates, Bill (2009) *2009 Annual Letter from Bill Gates*. http://www.gatesfoundation.org/annual-letter/Documents/2009-bill-gates-annual-letter.pdf (accessed December 2, 2010).

Gates, Bill (2010) *2010 Annual Letter from Bill Gates*. http://www.gatesfoundation.org/annual-letter/2010/Documents/2010-bill-gates-annual-letter.pdf (accessed December 2, 2010).

Gates, Bill (2011) *2011 Annual Letter from Bill Gates*. http://www.gatesfoundation.org/annual-letter/2011/Documents/2011-annual-letter.pdf (accessed February 9, 2011).

Gensini, Gian Franco, Magdi H. Yacoub, and Andrea A. Conti (2004) "The concept of quarantine in history: from plague to SARS," *Journal of Infection* 49(4), 257–61.

Global Fund to Fight AIDS, Tuberculosis, and Malaria (2008) "Country Coordinating Mechanism model: governance and civil society participation." http://www.theglobalfund.org/documents/ccm/CCMOnePageBrief_GovernanceAndCSPartn_2008_10_en.pdf (accessed September 14, 2010).

Global Fund to Fight AIDS, Tuberculosis, and Malaria (2010a) "About the Global Fund." http://www.theglobalfund.org/en/about/?lang=en (accessed September 10, 2010).

Global Fund to Fight AIDS, Tuberculosis, and Malaria (2010b) "Grant portfolio." http://portfolio.theglobalfund.org/?lang=en (accessed September 9, 2010).

Godlee, Fiona (1994a) "WHO in retreat: is it losing its influence?" *British Medical Journal* 309 (6967), 1491–5.

Godlee, Fiona (1994b) "The World Health Organization: WHO in crisis," *British Medical Journal* 309(6966), 1424–8.

Gomez, Eduardo J. (2006) "Learning from the past: statebuilding and the politics of AIDS policy reform in Brazil," *Whitehead Journal of Diplomacy and International Relations* 7(1), 143–64.

Goodman, Neville M. (1971) *International Health Organizations and Their Work*, London: Churchill Livingstone.

Gostin, Lawrence O. (2004) "International infectious disease law: revision of the World Health Organization's International Health Regulations," *Journal of the American Medical Association* 290(21), 2623–7.

Gostin, Lawrence O. and Emily A. Mok (2009) "Grand challenges in global health governance," *British Medical Bulletin* 90(1), 7–18.

Graber, Mark (2002) "Bioterrorism update: viral hemorrhagic fever," *Emergency Medicine* 34(5), 44.

Grady, Denise (2005) "Danger of flu pandemic is clear, if not present," *New York Times* (October 9).

Guth, Robert A. (2010) "Gates rethinks his war on polio," *Wall Street Journal* (23 April). http://online.wsj.com (accessed October 14, 2010).

Hall, John J. and Richard Taylor (2003) "Health for All beyond 2000: the demise of the Alma-Ata Declaration and primary health care in developing countries," *Medical Journal of Australia* 178(1), 17–20.

Hammonds, Rachel and Gorik Ooms (2004) "World Bank policies and the obligation of its members to respect, protect, and fulfill the right to health," *Health and Human Rights* 8(1), 26–60.

Harman, Sophie (2009a) "Fighting HIV and AIDS: reconfiguring the state?" *Review of African Political Economy* 36(121), 353–67.

Harman, Sophie (2009b) "The World Bank and health," in Kay, Adrian and Owain David Williams (eds) *Global Health Governance: Crisis, Institutions, and Political Economy*, New York: Palgrave Macmillan.

Harman, Sophie (2010) *The World Bank and HIV/AIDS: Setting a Global Agenda*, London: Routledge.

Headley, Jamila and Patricia Siplon (2006) "Roadblocks on the road to treatment: lessons from Barbados and Brazil," *Perspectives on Politics* 4(4), 655–61.

Health GAP (2006) "President's Emergency Plan for AIDS Relief." http://www.healthgap.org/camp/pepfar.html (accessed December 2, 2010).

Heymann, David L. (2002) "The microbial threat in fragile times: balancing known and unknown risks," *Bulletin of the World Health Organization* 80(3), 179.

Hindmarsh, Richard (2003) "Genetic modification and the doubly green revolution," *Forum* 40(6), 9–19.

Holden, Chris and Kelley Lee (2009) "Corporate power and social policy: the political economy of the transnational tobacco companies," *Global Social Policy* 9(3), 328–54.

Homeland Security Council (2006) *National Strategy for Pandemic Influenza*, Washington, DC: Homeland Security Council.

Homer-Dixon, Thomas (1994) "Environmental scarcities and violent conflict: evidence from cases," *International Security* 19(1), 5–40.

Howard-Jones, Norman (1975) *The Scientific Background of the International Sanitary Conferences, 1851–1938*, Geneva: World Health Organization.

Howard-Jones, Norman (1978) *International Public Health Between the Two World Wars: The Organizational Problems*, Geneva: World Health Organization.

Howard-Jones, Norman (1981) *The Pan-American Health Organization: Origins and Evolution*, Geneva: World Health Organization.

Independent Evaluation Group of the World Bank (2007) "Evaluation of the World Bank's assistance for health, nutrition, and population." http://www.oecd.org/dataoecd/52/11/39598722.pdf (accessed July 21, 2010).

International Treatment Preparedness Coalition (2005) *Missing the Target: A Report of HIV/AIDS Treatment Access from the Frontlines*, Bangkok: International Treatment Preparedness Coalition.

Jacobini, H. B. (1952) "The new International Sanitary Regulations," *American Journal of International Law* 46(4), 727–8.

Jareg, Pal and Dan C. O. Kaseje (1998) "Growth of civil society in developing countries: implications for health," *Lancet* 351(9105), 819–22.

Johnson, Toni (2009) "The World Health Organization," *Council on Foreign Relations Backgrounder*, http://www.cfr.org/publication/20003/world_health_organization.html (accessed December 2, 2010).

Jones, Peris S. (2005) "'A test of governance': rights-based struggles and the politics of HIV/AIDS policy in South Africa," *Political Geography* 24(4), 419–47.

Kaiser Family Foundation (2009) "The US and the Global Fund to Fight AIDS, Tuberculosis, and Malaria." http://www.kff.org/globalhealth/upload/8003.pdf (accessed August 28, 2010).

Kamradt-Scott, Adam (2010) "The evolving WHO: implications for global health security," *Global Public Health* (September 24), 1–10.

Kapstein, Ethan B. and Josh Busby (2009) "Making markets for merit goods: the political economy of antiretrovirals," CGD Working Paper 179. Washington, DC: Center for Global Development. http://www.cgdev.org/content/publications/detail/1422655 (accessed December 7, 2010).

Kapstein, Ethan B. and Joshua W. Busby (2010) "Making markets for merit goods," *Global Policy* 1(1), 75–90.

Kates, Jennifer, J. Stephen Morrison, and Eric Lief (2006) "Global health funding: a glass half full?" *Lancet* 368(9531), 187–8.

Kates, Jennifer, Kim Boortz, Eric Lief, Carlos Avila, and Benjamin Gobet (2010) *Financing the Response to HIV/AIDS in Low- and Middle-Income Countries: International Assistance from the G8, European Commission, and Other Donor Governments in 2009*, Henry J. Kaiser Family Foundation and UNAIDS. http://www.kff.org/hivaids/upload/7347-06.pdf (accessed November 30, 2010).

Kaufmann, Judith and Harley Feldbaum (2009) "Diplomacy and the polio immunization boycott in northern Nigeria," *Health Affairs* 28(4), 1091–101.

Knight, Lindsay (2008) *UNAIDS: The First Ten Years, 1996–2006*, Geneva: UNAIDS.

Kolodziej, Edward (1992) "Renaissance in security studies? Caveat lector!" *International Studies Quarterly* 36(4), 421–38.

Krause, Richard (2006) "The swine flu episode and the fog of epidemics," *Emerging Infectious Diseases* 12(1), 40–3.

Lancet (1927) "The Rockefeller Foundation," *Lancet* 209(5392), 40.

Lee, Kelley (2009) *The World Health Organization (WHO)*, London: Routledge.

Lee, Kelley (2010) "Civil society organizations and the functions of global health governance: what role within intergovernmental organizations?" *Global Health Governance* 3(2), 1–20. http://www.ghgj.org/Lee_CSOs.pdf (accessed October 28, 2010).

Lee, Kelley and Jeff Collin (2005) *Global Health and Change*, Maidenhead: Open University Press.

Levine, Ruth (2006) "Open letter to the incoming director general of the World Health Organization," *British Medical Journal* 333(7576), 1015–17.

Lieberman, Evan S. (2009) *Boundaries of Contagion: How Ethnic Politics Have Shaped Government Responses to AIDS*, Princeton: Princeton University Press.

Liese, Bernard H., John Wilson, Bruce Benton, and Douglas Marr (1991) *The Onchocerciasis Control Program in West Africa: A Long-Term Commitment to Success*, Policy, Research, and External Affairs Working Paper No. WPS 740. Washington, DC: World Bank.

Lisk, Franklyn (2010) *Global Institutions and the HIV/AIDS Epidemic: Responding to an International Crisis*, London: Routledge.

Mack, Eric (2006) "The World Health Organization's new International Health Regulations: incursion on state sovereignty and ill-fated response to global health issues," *Chicago Journal of International Law* 7(1), 365–77.

Magnussen, Lesley, John Ehiri, and Pauline Jolly (2004) "Comprehensive versus selective primary health care: lessons for global health policy," *Health Affairs* 23(3), 167–76.

Mallaby, Sebastian (2004) *The World's Banker: A Story of Failed States, Financial Crises, and the Wealth and Poverty of Nations*, New York: Penguin.

Mamudu, Hadii M., Ross Hammond, and Stanton Glantz (2008) "Tobacco industry attempts to counter the World Bank report *Curbing the Epidemic* and obstruct the WHO Framework Convention on Tobacco Control," *Social Science and Medicine* 67(11), 1690–9.

Matter, Alex and Thomas H. Keller (2008) "Impact of non-profit organizations on drug discovery: opportunities, gaps, and solutions," *Drug Discovery Today* 13(7–8), 347–52.

Matthews, Kirstin R. W. and Vivian Ho (2008) "The grand impact of the Gates Foundation," *EMBO Reports* 9(5), 409–12.

Mays, N. (2008) "Interest groups and civil society in public health policy," in Heggenhougen, Kris (ed.) *International Encyclopedia of Public Health*, Amsterdam: Elsevier.

McCarthy, Michael (2000) "A conversation with the leaders of the Gates Foundation's Global Health Program: Gordon Perkin and William Foege," *Lancet* 356(9224), 153–5.

McCarthy, Michael (2002) "A brief history of the World Health Organization," *Lancet* 360(9340), 1111–12.

McColl, Karen (2008) "Europe told to deliver more aid for health," *Lancet* 37(9630), 2072–3.

McCoy, David, Sudeep Chand, and Devi Sridhar (2009) "Global health funding: how much, where it comes from, and where it goes," *Health Policy and Planning* 24(6), 407–17.

McFadden, David F. (1995) *International Cooperation and Pandemic Disease: Regimes and the Role of Epistemic Communities in Combating Cholera, Smallpox, and AIDS*, PhD dissertation, Claremont Graduate University.

McInnes, Colin and Simon Rushton (2010) "HIV, AIDS, and security: where are we now?" *International Affairs* 86(1), 225–45.

McLean, Bethany (2006) "The power of philanthropy," *Fortune* (September 7). http://money.cnn.com/magazines/fortune/fortune_archive/2006/09/18/8386185/index.htm (accessed December 2, 2010).

McNeil, Donald G., Jr. (2008) "Gates Foundation influence criticized," *New York Times* (February 16).

McNeil, Donald G., Jr. (2011) "Gates calls for final push to eradicate polio," *New York Times* (January 31).

McNeill, William H. (1998) *Plagues and Peoples*, Garden City, NY: Anchor Books.

Meeks, Brock N. (2005) "Homeland Security to be lead in flu crisis," *MSNBC News* (October 11). http://www.msnbc.msn.com/id/9654456 (accessed December 2, 2010).

Ministry of Foreign Affairs of Japan (2000) *G8 Communiqué Okinawa 2000* (July 23). http: //www.mofa.go.jp/policy/economy/summit/2000/communique. html (accessed September 9, 2010).

Minneapolis Star-Tribune (2010) "Gates says foundation will give $10 billion to research, deliver vaccines for world's poor" (January 29). http://www.startribune. com/business/83017812.html?elr=KArksLckD8EQDUoaEyqyP4O:DW3ckUiD3 aPc:_Yyc:aUUI (accessed January 29, 2010).

Moran, Mary, Javier Guzman, Anne-Laure Ropars, Alina McDonald, Tanja Sturm, Nicole Jameson, Lindsey Wu, Sam Ryan, and Brenda Omune (2008) *Neglected Disease Research and Development: How Much Are We Really Spending?* Sydney: George Institute for International Health.

Morrison, J. Stephen and Todd Summers (2003) "United to fight HIV/AIDS?" *Washington Quarterly* 26(4), 177–93.

Morse, Stephen S. (2007) "Global infectious disease surveillance and health intelligence," *Health Affairs* 26(4), 1069–77.

Muhumuza, William (2010) "State–civil society partnership in poverty reduction in Uganda," *Eastern Africa Social Science Research Review* 26(1), 1–21.

Muiu, Mueni wa (2002) "Globalization and hegemony: which way Africa?" *Journal of African Policy Studies* 8(1), 61–93.

Murphy, Craig N. (2001) "Political consequences of the new inequality," *International Studies Quarterly* 45(3), 347–56.

Musgrave, Richard A. (1959) *The Theory of Public Finance*, New York: McGraw-Hill.

Neustadt, Richard and Harvey Fineberg (1983) *The Epidemic That Never Was: Policy-Making and the Swine Flu Scare*, New York: Vintage Books.

Nuruzzaman, Mohammad (2007) "The World Bank, health policy reforms, and the poor," *Journal of Contemporary Asia* 37(1), 59–72.

Office of the Global AIDS Coordinator (n.d.) "About PEPFAR." http://www.pepfar. gov/about/index.htm (accessed December 14, 2011).

Office of the Prime Minister (2005) "Gleneagles 2005: chairman's summary" http://www.number-10.gov.uk/output/Page7883.asp (accessed December 2, 2010).

O'Neill, Onora (2002) "Public health or clinical ethics: thinking beyond borders," *Ethics and International Affairs* 16(2), 35–45.

Organisation for Economic Co-operation and Development (2010) "Donors' mixed aid performance for 2010 sparks concern" (February 17). http://www.oecd.org/ document/20/0,3343,en_21571361_44315115_44617556_1_1_1_1,00.html (accessed November 30, 2010).

Organization of African Unity (2001) *Abuja Declaration on HIV/AIDS, Tuberculosis, and Other Related Infectious Diseases* (April 24–7). http: //www.un.org/ga/aids/pdf/ abuja_declaration.pdf (accessed September 9, 2010).

Ostergard, Robert L., Jr. (2002) "Politics in the hot zone: AIDS and national security in Africa," *Third World Quarterly* 23(2), 333–50.

Osterholm, Michael (2005) "Preparing for the next pandemic," *Foreign Affairs* 84(4), 24–37.

Over, Mead (2008) "Prevention failure: the ballooning entitlement burden of US global AIDS treatment spending and what to do about it," CGD Working Paper 144. Washington, DC: Center for Global Development. http://www.cgdev.org/ content/publications/detail/15973 (accessed December 7, 2010).

Over, Mead (2010) "What Bush got wrong on AIDS," *Global Health Policy Blog* (December 1). http://blogs.cgdev.org/globalhealth/2010/12/what-bush-got-wrong-on-aids.php (accessed December 21, 2010).

Oxfam America (n.d.) *The Tied Aid "Round Trip."* http://www.oxfamamerica.org/files/aidnow-tiedaidroundtrip.pdf (accessed December 2, 2010).

Oxfam GB (n.d.) "Sign the '6 Million More' pledge." http://www.oxfam.org.uk/get_involved/campaign/actions/health_edu.html (accessed November 4, 2010).

Oxfam International (2007) *Oxfam International Annual Report 2007*, Oxford: Oxfam International.

Oxfam International (2009a) *Oxfam International Annual Report 2008/2009*, Oxford: Oxfam International.

Oxfam International (2009b) *Blind Optimism: Challenging the Myths about Private Health Care in Poor Countries*, Oxfam Briefing Paper No. 125. Oxford: Oxfam International. http://www.oxfam.org.uk/resources/policy/health/downloads/bp125_blind_optimism_private_health_care.pdf (accessed November 4, 2010).

Packard, Randall M. and Peter J. Brown (1997) "Rethinking health, development, and malaria: historicizing a cultural model in international health," *Medical Anthropology* 17(3), 181–94.

Palmore, Julian (2006) "A clear and present danger to international security: highly pathogenic avian influenza," *Defense and Security Analysis* 22(2), 111–21.

Pfeiffer, James (2004) "Civil society, NGOs, and the Holy Spirit in Mozambique," *Human Organization* 63(3), 359–72.

Phillips, Howard (2004) "HIV/AIDS in the context of South Africa's epidemic history," in Kauffmann, Kyle D. and David L. Lindauer (eds) *AIDS and South Africa: The Social Expression of a Pandemic*, Houndsmill: Palgrave Macmillan.

Piller, Charles, Edmund Sanders, and Robyn Dixon (2007) "Dark cloud over good works of Gates Foundation," *Los Angeles Times* (January 7). http://articles.latimes.com/2007/jan/07/nation/na-gatesx07 (accessed December 2, 2010).

Pinheiro, Gabriela (2005) "Small NGOs in the wake of Brazil's response to the 'anti-prostitution pledge.'" http://www.globalhealth.org/reports/report.php3?id=225 (accessed October 26, 2010).

Piot, Peter (2000) "Global AIDS epidemic: time to turn the tide," *Science* 288(5474), 2176–8.

Pipkin, Augusta (1985) "Innovations in philanthropy: towards a new ideology for international giving," *Fletcher Forum* 9(2), 383–400.

Plotkin, Bruce Jay (2007) "Human rights and other provisions in the revised International Health Regulations (2005)," *Public Health* 121(11), 840–5.

Plotkin, Bruce Jay and Ann Marie Kimball (1997) "Designing an international policy and legal framework for the control of emerging infectious diseases: first steps," *Emerging Infectious Diseases* 3(1), 1–9.

Poku, Nana (2002) "The Global AIDS Fund: context and opportunity," *Third World Quarterly* 23(2), 283–98.

Price-Smith, Andrew T. (2001) *The Health of Nations: Infectious Disease, Environmental Change, and Their Effects on National Security and Development*, Cambridge, MA: MIT Press.

Price-Smith, Andrew T. (2009) *Contagion and Chaos: Disease, Ecology, and National Security in the Era of Globalization*, Cambridge, MA: MIT Press.

Proctor, Robert N. (1996) *Cancer Wars: How Politics Shapes What We Know and Don't Know about Cancer*, New York: Basic Books.

Quarmby, Katherine (2005) "Why Oxfam is failing Africa," *New Statesman* (May 30). http://www.newstatesman.com/200505300004 (accessed November 4, 2010).

Ramiah, Ilavenil and Michael R. Reich (2005) "Public–private partnerships and antiretroviral drugs for HIV/AIDS: lessons from Botswana," *Health Affairs* 24(2), 545–51.

Ramiah, Ilavenil and Michael R. Reich (2006) "Building effective public–private partnerships: experiences and lessons from the African Comprehensive HIV/AIDS Partnership (ACHAP)," *Social Science and Medicine* 63(2), 397–408.

Rau, Bill (2006) "The politics of civil society in confronting HIV/AIDS," *International Affairs* 82(2), 285–95.

Rauch, Jonathan (2007) " 'This is not charity,' " *Atlantic* (October), 64–76.

Ravishankar, Nirmala, Paul Gubbins, Rebecca J. Cooley, Katherine Leach-Kemon, Catherine M. Michaud, Dean T. Jamison, and Christopher J. L. Murray (2009) "Financing of global health: tracking development assistance for health from 1990 to 2007," *Lancet* 373(9681), 2113–24.

Robins, Steven L. (2004) " 'Long live Zackie, long live': AIDS activism, science, and citizenship after apartheid," *Journal of Southern African Studies* 30(3), 651–72.

Roemer, Ruth, Allyn Taylor, and Jean Lariviere (2005) "Origins of the WHO Framework Convention on Tobacco Control," *American Journal of Public Health* 95(6), 936–8.

Rosenberg, Charles (1987) *The Cholera Years: The United States in 1832, 1849, and 1866*, Chicago: University of Chicago Press.

Rotary International (2010) "End polio." http://www.rotary.org/en/EndPolio/Pages/learn.aspx (accessed October 26, 2010).

Rothkopf, David (2008) *Superclass: The Global Power Elite and the World They Are Making*, New York: Farrar, Straus, and Giroux.

Rowden, Rick (2009) *The Deadly Ideas of Neoliberalism: How the IMF Has Undermined Public Health and the Fight Against AIDS*, London: Zed Books.

Rubenstein, Leonard S. (2004) "How international human rights organizations can advance economic, social, and cultural rights: a response to Kenneth Roth," *Human Rights Quarterly* 26(4), 845–65.

Ruger, Jennifer Prah (2004) "Ethics of the social determinants of health," *Lancet* 364(9439), 1092–7.

Ruger, Jennifer Prah (2005) "The changing role of the World Bank in public health," *American Journal of Public Health* 95(1), 60–70.

Ruger, Jennifer Prah and Derek Yach (2005) "Global functions at the World Health Organization: WHO must reassert its role in integrating, coordinating, and advancing the worldwide agenda on health," *British Medical Journal* 330(7500), 1099–100.

Sachs, Jeffrey D. (2010) "Funding a Global Health Fund," *Guardian* (March 25). http://www.guardian.co.uk/commentisfree/2010/mar/25/global-health-fund-funding-tb-aids (accessed September 27, 2011).

Schurmann, Anna T. and Simeen Mahmud (2009) "Civil society, health, and social exclusion in Bangladesh," *Journal of Health, Population, and Nutrition* 27(4), 536–44.

Schwartländer, B., J. Stover, N. Walker, L. Bollinger, J. P. Gutierrez, W. McGreevey, M. Opuni, S. Forsythe, L. Kumaranayake, C. Watts, and S. Bertozzi (2001) "Resource needs for AIDS," *Science* 292(5526), 2434–6.

Seckinelgin, Hakan (2004) "Who can help people with HIV/AIDS in Africa? Governance of HIV/AIDS and civil society," *Voluntas: International Journal of Voluntary and Nonprofit Organizations* 15(3), 287–304.

Seckinelgin, Hakan (2009) "Global social policy and international organizations linking social exclusion to durable inequality," *Global Social Policy* 9(2), 205–27.

Security and Prosperity Partnership of North America (2007) *North American Plan for Avian and Pandemic Influenza*, Washington, DC: SPPNA. http://www.spp-psp. gc.ca/eic/site/spp-psp.nsf/vwapj/pandemic-influenza.pdf/$FILE/pandemic-influenza.pdf (accessed September 30, 2011).

Sehdev, Paul S. (2002) "The origin of quarantine," *Clinical Infectious Diseases* 35(9), 1071–2.

Sencer, David J. and J. Donald Millar (2006) "Reflections on the 1976 swine flu vaccination program," *Emerging Infectious Diseases* 12(1), 29–33.

Shadlen, Kenneth C. (2007) "The political economy of AIDS treatment: intellectual property and the transformation of generic supply," *International Studies Quarterly* 51(3), 559–81.

Shaplen, Robert (1964) *Toward the Well-Being of Mankind: Fifty Years of the Rockefeller Foundation*, Garden City, NY: Doubleday.

Sharp, Walter R. (1947) "The new World Health Organization," *American Journal of International Law* 41(3), 509–30.

Shiffman, Jeremy (2008) "Has donor prioritization of HIV/AIDS displaced aid for other health issues?" *Health Policy and Planning* 23(2), 95–100.

Shiffman, Jeremy (2009) "A social explanation for the rise and fall of global health issues," *Bulletin of the World Health Organization* 87(8), 608–13.

Shimkin, Michael B. (1946) "The World Health Organization," *Science* 104(2700), 281–3.

Siddiqi, Javed (1995) *World Health and World Politics: The World Health Organization and the UN*, Columbia: University of South Carolina Press.

Sridhar, Devi (2007) "Economic ideology and politics in the World Bank: defining hunger," *New Political Economy* 12(4), 499–516.

Sridhar, Devi (2010a) "Seven challenges in international development assistance for health and ways forward," *Journal of Law, Medicine, and Ethics* 38(3), 459–69.

Sridhar, Devi (2010b) "Why no one talks about non-communicable diseases," *UN Chronicle* (July). http://www.un.org/wcm/content/site/chronicle/cache/bypass/ home/archive/issues2010/achieving_global_health/whynoonetalksaboutnonco mmunicablediseases?ctnscroll_articleContainerList=1_0&ctnlistpagination_ articleContainerList=true (accessed November 30, 2010).

Sridhar, Devi and Rajaic Batniji (2008) "Misfinancing global health: a case for transparency in disbursements and decision making," *Lancet* 372(9644), 1185–91.

Sridhar, Devi, Sanjeev Khagram, and Tikki Pand (2008/9) "Are existing governance structures equipped to deal with today's global health challenges? Toward systematic coherence in scaling up," *Global Health Governance* 2(2), 1–25.

Stewart, Heather (2011) "World economists urge G20 ministers to accept Robin Hood tax," *Guardian* (April 13). http://www.guardian.co.uk/business/2011/apr/13/world-economists-robin-hood-tax?intcmp=239 (accessed September 27, 2011).

Studlar, Donley T. (2006) "Tobacco control policy instruments in a shrinking world: how much policy learning?" *International Journal of Public Administration* 29(4&6), 367–96.

Sturtevant, Jessica L., Aranka Anema, and John S. Brownstein (2007) "The new International Health Regulations: considerations for global public health surveillance," *Disaster Medicine and Public Health Preparedness* 1(2), 117–21.

't Hoen, Ellen (2001) "Pills and pocketbooks: equity pricing of essential medicines in developing countries," Presentation for WHO/WTO Workshop on Differential Pricing and Financing of Essential Drugs, Hosbjor, Norway (April 8–11). http://www.wto.int/english/tratop_e/TRIPS_e/hosbjor_presentations_e/15thoen_e.pdf (accessed December 2, 2010).

't Hoen, Ellen (2002) "Public health and international law: TRIPs, pharmaceutical patents, and access to essential medicines: a long way from Seattle to Doha," *Chicago Journal of International Law* 3(1), 27–46.

Tesh, Sylvia Noble (1987) *Hidden Arguments: Political Ideology and Disease Prevention Policy*, New Brunswick, NJ: Rutgers University Press.

Thuriaux, M. C. (2003) "Revision of the International Health Regulations," *Journal of Travel Medicine* 5(3), 157.

Treatment Action Campaign (2006) "The HIV campaign: a discussion of the response of the South African government," Submission to African Peer Review Mechanism (February). http://www.tac.org.za/Documents/AfricanPeerReview MechanismReportFinal-20060217.pdf (accessed October 26, 2010).

Trotta, Liz (2003) "Clinton crafts low-cost AIDS drug pact," *Washington Times* (October 24), A3.

Ugalde, Antonio and Jeffrey T. Jackson (1995) "The World Bank and international health policy: a critical review," *Journal of International Development* 7(3), 525–41.

UNAIDS (n.d.) "Full matrix of the division of labor." http: //www.unaids.org/Resources/UNAIDS/images/Cosponsor/FullMatrix.gif (accessed September 16, 2010).

UNAIDS (2006) *2006 Report on the Global AIDS Epidemic*, Geneva: UNAIDS.

UNAIDS (2009) *UNAIDS Second Independent Evaluation 2002–2008 Final Report*, Geneva: UNAIDS.

UNAIDS (2010a) *2010 Report on the Global AIDS Epidemic*, Geneva: UNAIDS.

UNAIDS (2010b) *UNAIDS Governance Handbook*, Geneva: UNAIDS.

UNITAID (2007) "UNITAID mission." http://www.unitaid.eu/index.php/en/UNITAID-Mission.html (accessed December 2, 2010).

UNITAID (2010) "UNITAID facts." http://www.unitaid.eu/images/Factsheets/EN_UNITAID_facts_Aug2010.pdf (accessed December 21, 2010).

United Kingdom Cabinet Office (2010) *National Risk Register of Civil Emergencies, 2010 Edition*, London: Stationery Office. http://www.cabinetoffice.gov.uk/sites/default/files/resources/nationalriskregister-2010.pdf (accessed September 30, 2011).

United Nations (n.d.) "United Nations Millennium Development Goals." http://www.un.org/millenniumgoals/index.shtml (accessed February 10, 2011).

United Nations (2000) "United Nations Millennium Declaration," General Assembly, 55th Session. A/RES/55/2 (September 18).

United Nations (2006) "Draft political declaration: 2006 high-level meeting on AIDS (31 May–2 June, New York)." http://www.un.org/ga/aidsmeeting2006/declaration.htm (accessed December 2, 2010).

United Nations (2010) *The Millennium Development Goals Report 2010*, New York: United Nations.

United Nations Economic and Social Commission for Asia and the Pacific (2004) "Regional call for action to enhance capacity-building in public health," Resolution 60/2, Bangkok, Thailand (April 28). http://www.unescap.org/esid/hds/officialdocs/60session/60-2.pdf (accessed December 2, 2010).

United Nations General Assembly (2001) *Declaration of Commitment on HIV/AIDS*, A/RES/S-26/2 (June 27). http://www.un.org/ga/aids/docs/aress262.pdf (accessed December 9, 2010).

United Nations News Service (2005) "UN goal of treating 3 million HIV/AIDS victims by 2005 unlikely to be met" (June 29). http://www.un.org/apps/news/story.asp?NewsID=14807&Cr=hiv&Cr1=aids (accessed December 2, 2010).

United Nations Security Council (2000) *Resolution 1308 (2000)*, S/RES/1308 (2000) (July 17). http://daccess-ods.un.org/TMP/4292117.35725403.html (accessed December 9, 2010).

Usher, Ann Danaiya (2010) "Defrauding of the Global Fund gives Sweden cold feet," *Lancet* 376(9753), 1631.

Varmus, H., R. Klausner, E. Zerhouni, T. Acharaya, A. S. Daar, and P. A. Singer (2003) "Grand challenges in global health," *Science* 302(5644), 398–9.

Vaughan, J. Patrick, Sigrun Mogedal, Stein-Erik Kruse, Kelley Lee, Gill Walt, and Koen de Wilde (1996) "Financing the World Health Organization: global importance of extrabudgetary funds," *Health Policy* 35(3), 229–45.

Vaughan, Patrick, Gill Walt, and Anne Mills (1985) "Can ministries of health support primary health care? Some suggestions for structural reorganization and planning," *Public Administration and Development* 5(1), 1–12.

Velimirovic, Boris (1976) "Do we still need international health regulations?" *Journal of Infectious Diseases* 133(4), 478–82.

Wadman, Meredith (2007) "Biomedical philanthropy: state of the donation," *Nature* 447(7142), 248–50.

Waever, Ole (1995) "Securitization and desecuritization," in Lipschutz, Ronnie (ed.) *On Security*, New York: Columbia University Press.

Walsh, Julia A. and Kenneth S. Warren (1979) "Selective primary health care: an interim strategy for disease control in developing countries," *New England Journal of Medicine* 301(18), 967–74.

Walt, Gill (1993) "WHO under stress: implications for health policy," *Health Policy* 24(2), 125–44.

Walt, Gill (2001) "Global cooperation in international public health," in Merson, Michael H., Robert E. Black, and Anne J. Mills (eds) *International Public Health: Diseases, Programs, Systems, and Policies*, Sudbury, MA: Jones and Bartlett.

Walt, Stephen (1991) "The renaissance of security studies," *International Studies Quarterly* 35(2), 211–39.

Waning, Brenda, Warren Kaplan, Alexis C. King, Danielle A. Lawrence, Hubert G. Luefkens, and Matthew P. Fox (2009) "Global strategies to reduce the price of antiretroviral medicines: evidence from transactional databases," *Bulletin of the World Health Organization* 87(7), 520–8.

Warner, Kenneth E. (2008) "The Framework Convention on Tobacco Control: opportunities and issues," *Salud Publica de Mexico* 50 (Suppl. 3), S283–S291.

Washington Post (1997) "Good riddance" (May 3).

Wegman, M. E. (1977) "A salute to the Pan American Health Organization," *Bulletin of the Pan American Health Organization* 11(4), 296–302.

Weindling, Paul (1993) "Public health and political stabilization: the Rockefeller Foundation in Central and Eastern Europe between the two world wars," *Minerva* 31(3), 253–67.

Weindling, Paul (1997) "Philanthropy and world health: the Rockefeller Foundation and the Health Organization of the League of Nations," *Minerva* 35(3), 269–81.

Werner, David and David Sanders (1997) *Questioning the Solution: The Politics of Primary Health Care and Child Survival*, Palo Alto: HealthWrights.

William J. Clinton Foundation (n.d. a) "About the Clinton Foundation." http://clintonfoundation.org/about-the-clinton-foundation (accessed December 2, 2010).

William J. Clinton Foundation (n.d. b) "HIV/AIDS Initiative: drug access." http://www.clintonfoundation.org/what-we-do/clinton-health-access-initiative/information-center-resources (accessed December 2, 2010).

William J. Clinton Foundation (n.d. c) "What we've accomplished." http://clintonfoundation.org/what-we-do/clinton-hiv-aids-initiative/what-we-ve-accomplished (accessed December 2, 2010).

William J. Clinton Foundation (2009) *Independent Accountants' Report and Financial Statements*. http://clintonfoundation.org/files/reports_cf/cf_audited_financials_2008-2009.pdf (accessed February 9, 2011).

Wilson, Kumanan, Christopher McDougall, David P. Fidler, and Harvey Lazar (2008) "Strategies for implementing the new International Health Regulations in federal countries," *Bulletin of the World Health Organization* 86(3), 215–20.

Winslow, C.-E. A. (1951) "International cooperation in the service of health," *Annals of the American Academy of Political and Social Sciences* 273, 192–200.

World Bank (n.d. a) "World Bank Group historical chronology: 1944–1949." http://web.worldbank.org/WBSITE/EXTERNAL/EXTABOUTUS/EXTARCHIVES/0,,contentMDK:20035657~menuPK:56307~pagePK:36726~piPK:437378~theSitePK:29506,00.html (accessed July 14, 2010).

World Bank (n.d. b) "World Bank historical chronology: 1960–1969." http://web.worldbank.org/WBSITE/EXTERNAL/EXTABOUTUS/EXTARCHIVES/0,,contentMDK:20035660~menuPK:56316~pagePK:36726~piPK:437378~theSitePK:29506,00.html (accessed July 14, 2010).

World Bank (n.d. c) "World Bank historical chronology: 1970–1979." http://web.worldbank.org/WBSITE/EXTERNAL/EXTABOUTUS/EXTARCHIVES/0,,contentMDK:20035661~menuPK:56317~pagePK:36726~piPK:437378~theSitePK:29506,00.html (accessed July 14, 2010).

World Bank (1993) *1993 World Development Report: Investing in Health*, New York: Oxford University Press.

World Bank (2007) *Healthy Development: The World Bank Strategy for Health, Nutrition, and Population Results*, Washington, DC: World Bank.

World Bank Institute (2006) *ACHAP: The African Comprehensive HIV/AIDS Partnership.* http://www.businessactionforafrica.org/documents/CaseStudiesMerckandCo.pdf (accessed December 2, 2010).

World Health Organization (n.d. a) "The 3 by 5 Initiative." http://www.who.int/3by5/en (accessed December 2, 2010).

World Health Organization (n.d. b) "Archives of the Office International d'Hygiène Publique (OIHP)." http://www.who.int/archives/fonds_collections/bytitle/fonds_1/en/index.html (accessed November 30, 2010).

World Health Organization (n.d. c) "The Executive Board." http://www.who.int/governance/eb/en/index.html (accessed December 2, 2010).

World Health Organization (n.d. d) "Global Outbreak Alert and Response Network." http://www.who.int/csr/outbreaknetwork/en (accessed December 2, 2010).

World Health Organization (n.d. e) "Partnerships: working together for '3 × 5.'" http://www.who.int/3by5/partners/en (accessed December 2, 2010).

World Health Organization (n.d. f) "Program budget 2008–2009," http://apps.who.int/gb/ebwha/pdf_files/AMTSP-PPB/a-mtsp_4en.pdf (accessed December 2, 2010).

World Health Organization (n.d. g) "Structural Adjustment Programs." http://www.who.int/trade/glossary/story084/en/index.html (accessed July 14, 2010).

World Health Organization (1946) *Constitution of the World Health Organization.* http://www.who.int/governance/eb/who_constitution_en.pdf (accessed December 2, 2010).

World Health Organization (1978) "Declaration of Alma-Ata." http://www.paho.org/English/DD/PIN/alma-ata_declaration.htm (accessed December 2, 2010).

World Health Organization (1983) *International Health Regulations (1969), Third Annotated Edition*, Geneva: World Health Organization.

World Health Organization (1999) "Revisions and updating of the International Health Regulations: progress report," Fifty-Second World Health Assembly, Provisional Agenda Item 13, A/52/9 (April 1). http://apps.who.int/gb/archive/pdf_files/WHA52/ew9.pdf (accessed December 2, 2010).

World Health Organization (2004) *3 By 5 Progress Report, December 2003 through June 2004*, Geneva: World Health Organization.

World Health Organization (2005a) "Frequently asked questions about the International Health Regulations (2005)." http://www.who.int/ihr/about/FAQ2009.pdf (accessed December 2, 2010).

World Health Organization (2005b) *Progress on Global Access to HIV Antiretroviral Therapy: an Update on "3 × 5," June 2005*, Geneva: World Health Organization.

World Health Organization (2005c) *Responding to the Avian Influenza Pandemic Threat: Recommended Strategic Actions*, Geneva: World Health Organization.

World Health Organization (2005d) "Revision of the International Health Regulations (2005)," Fifty-Eighth World Health Assembly, Geneva, Switzerland, document WHA 58.3. http://www.who.int/gb/ebwha/pdf_files/WHA58/A58_4-en.pdf (accessed December 2, 2010).

World Health Organization (2005e) "Ten things you need to know about pandemic influenza." http://www.who.int/csr/disease/influenza/pandemic10things/en (accessed December 2, 2010).

World Health Organization (2006a) "Fifty-Ninth World Health Assembly." http:// www.who.int/mediacentre/events/2006/wha59/en/index.html (accessed December 2, 2010).

World Health Organization (2006b) *WHO Activities in Avian Influenza and Pandemic Influenza Preparedness, January–May 2006*, Geneva: World Health Organization.

World Health Organization (2009) *Toward Universal Access: Scaling Up Priority HIV/ AIDS Interventions in the Health Sector: Progress Report 2009*, Geneva: World Health Organization.

World Health Organization (2010a) "Cumulative number of confirmed human cases of avian influenza A/(H5N1) reported to WHO." http://www.who.int/csr/ disease/avian_influenza/country/cases_table_2010_12_08/en/index.html (accessed December 9, 2010).

World Health Organization (2010b) "The future of financing for WHO: Report by the Director-General," EB 128/21 (December 15). http://apps.who.int/gb/ebwha/ pdf_files/EB128/B128_21-en.pdf (accessed April 11, 2011).

World Health Organization (2010c) "Sixty-Third World Health Assembly." http:// www.who.int/mediacentre/events/2010/wha63/en/index.html (accessed December 2, 2010).

World Health Organization (2010d) *Toward Universal Access: Scaling Up Priority HIV/ AIDS Interventions in the Health Sector: Progress Report 2010*, Geneva: World Health Organization.

World Health Organization (2011a) "Metrics: Disability-Adjusted Life Year (DALY)." http://www.who.int/healthinfo/global_burden_disease/metrics_daly/en/ (accessed December 9, 2011).

World Health Organization (2011b) "The top 10 causes of death." http://www.who. int/mediacentre/factsheets/fs310/en/index.html (accessed March 29, 2011).

World Health Organization and UNAIDS (2003) *Treating 3 Million by 2005: Making It Happen*, Geneva: World Health Organization.

World Health Organization and UNAIDS (2006) *Progress on Global Access to HIV Antiretroviral Therapy: a Report on "3 × 5" and Beyond*, Geneva: World Health Organization.

World Health Organization, UNAIDS, and UNICEF (2008) *Towards Universal Access: Scaling Up Priority HIV/AIDS Interventions in the Health Sector: Progress Report 2008*, Geneva: World Health Organization.

Yach, Derek and Douglas Bettcher (2000) "Globalization of tobacco industry influence and new global responses," *Tobacco Control* 9(2), 206–16.

Zacher, Mark W. and Tania J. Keefe (2008) *The Politics of Global Health Governance: United by Contagion*, New York: Palgrave Macmillan.

Index